D1090599

WEEKNIGHT BAKING

Recipes to Fit Your Schedule

MICHELLE LOPEZ

SIMON & SCHUSTER

New York   London   Toronto   Sydney   New Delhi

Simon & Schuster
1230 Avenue of the Americas
New York, NY 10020

Copyright © 2019 by Michelle Lopez

All rights reserved, including the right to reproduce this book or portions thereof in any form whatsoever. For information, address Simon & Schuster Subsidiary Rights Department, 1230 Avenue of the Americas, New York, NY 10020.

First Simon & Schuster hardcover edition October 2019

SIMON & SCHUSTER and colophon are registered trademarks of Simon & Schuster, Inc.

For information about special discounts for bulk purchases, please contact Simon & Schuster Special Sales at 1-866-506-1949 or business@simonandschuster.com.

The Simon & Schuster Speakers Bureau can bring authors to your live event. For more information or to book an event, contact the Simon & Schuster Speakers Bureau at 1-866-248-3049 or visit our website at www.simonspeakers.com.

Interior design by Suet Yee Chong
Interior icons by Sze Wa Cheung
Interior photography by Michelle Lopez

Manufactured in China

10   9   8   7   6   5   4   3   2   1

Library of Congress Cataloging-in-Publication Data has been applied for.

ISBN 978-1-5011-8987-6
ISBN 978-1-5011-8988-3 (ebook)

CONTENTS

Introduction   *1*

Ingredients   7

Substitutions   15

Tools   27

Techniques   37

Recipes: Before You Start   47

LOAF CAKES   52

CAKES   72

FROSTINGS   96

DROP COOKIES   110

ROLL-OUT COOKIES   130

BROWNIES, BLONDIES, AND LAYER BARS   148

TARTS   174

PIES   190

MUFFINS AND SCONES   220

BRUNCH TREATS   238

ALTERNATIVE DIETS   254

DOLLOPS, DRIZZLES, FILLINGS, AND SPRINKLES   272

Resources   *287*
Acknowledgments   *289*
Index   *293*
Conversion Charts   *297*

INTRODUCTION

WHAT IS WEEKNIGHT BAKING?

Weeknight Baking is a cookbook with recipes for baked goods, desserts, and sweets that do at least one of these things:

Come together quickly . . .

Most recipes in this book have an Active Time—the time in which you are actively following recipe instructions like prepping and chopping ingredients, mixing batters and doughs, or decorating cakes and cookies—no longer than 30 minutes, and usually much less than that.

. . . Or come together quickly over a few nights.

That being said, there are desserts like cakes and pies that you really just can't make in 30 minutes! For more time-intensive recipes, I've split up the steps over the course of a few days so you're only actively working for 30 minutes or less each day. You'll still end up with a dessert that's as delicious as one that required you to spend all day in the kitchen baking.

Use ingredients you have in a well-stocked baker's pantry . . .

Most of the recipes in this book—with the exception of a handful that take advantage of fresh seasonal ingredients, or those meant for specific dietary restrictions—use ingredients every baker should already have in the pantry or fridge. I'll teach you which ingredients are worth always having on hand so you'll always be ready for spontaneous weeknight baking projects.

. . . Or can be easily substituted with other similar ingredients.

But I also know we've all found ourselves in a pinch, either running low on ingredients or forgetting to put an item on our shopping list. I'll show you which ingredients you can substitute for others to avoid a last-minute rush to the grocery store.

Store well for baking, decorating, assembling, or serving in the future . . .

Many of the recipes in this book will produce doughs, batters, frostings, and even whole cakes and pies that keep well in the refrigerator or freezer. You can have a fresh-baked treat in your hand in 15 minutes or less, all thanks to the batch of cookie dough in your freezer or the bowl of muffin batter in your fridge.

. . . Or are made with parts that do.

Breaking up a recipe into different parts that all store well helps you manage your time in the kitchen. You can decide when to start and finish every baking project.

My hope is that when you flip through this book, you'll find these time-saving qualities in classic, accessible recipes to match your cravings—like chocolate chip cookies, fudge brownies, and banana bread. Because it's usually the simple stuff I crave most on a weeknight, and I suspect that's the case for you, too.

Along the way, you'll also find lots of advice on baking methods and techniques to help you become a more efficient baker. But these tips wouldn't exist without the years I spent balancing my traditional nine-to-five job with my popular baking blog, *Hummingbird High*—so let's rewind.

MY DOUBLE LIFE

Several years ago, on a cold and blustery November evening, I had an idea that would change my life forever. It was Sunday night and I had just moved to Denver, Colorado, where I had accepted a new job as a financial analyst at a prestigious consulting firm. I was supposed to be pulling together some reports that my boss wanted the following morning. But instead of working through the necessary spreadsheets, I was dreaming about cupcakes.

I first started baking cupcakes during my sophomore year in college as a way to procrastinate from schoolwork. In the kitchen, with the smells of browning butter and caramelizing sugar wafting from the oven door, it was easy to forget about homework and other looming deadlines. I'd invite my friends and classmates to enjoy the baked goods. We would sit around the table, with a cupcake in one hand and a can of cheap beer in the other, gossiping and venting about minor dramas. It was then that I realized that baking made me happy: it was a way for me to bring all my friends together quickly (since none of them ever turned down a fresh cupcake), and it allowed us all to escape, however briefly, from the stresses of our lives.

A few years after I graduated, I found myself in the kitchen again. At that point, I had no idea what I wanted to do with my life; only that, at the end of the work day, I wanted to bake. I didn't like my job that much—my workplace was the kind of high-stress, super-competitive environment that inspires books like *Liar's Poker* and movies like *The Wolf of Wall Street*. Although baking helped me unwind, I felt lost and lonely. I wished I could have an honest conversation with the friends I'd left behind to ask them for advice on how and when to change career paths. I remembered us all back in our tiny dorm kitchen, passing a bottle of cheap wine around and snacking on cupcakes I had made earlier that day, offering moral support and good vibes.

It was this memory that inspired me to start my baking blog, *Hummingbird High*. I began with a project that gave my blog its name: chronicling my adventures baking all the recipes in *The Hummingbird Bakery Cookbook*, my favorite cookbook at the time, and adapting those recipes to work in Denver's unforgiving high-altitude environment. Soon, I graduated to writing recipes of my own. Recipe ideas would hit me while I was running financial reports; I would furtively scribble them down in quick emails to myself. Later, I would spend my evenings developing and testing those ideas, photographing the results for my friends and family to see on *Hummingbird High*. Even after long hours at the office, I still had the energy to stay up late in the kitchen.

In that period of uncertainty, *Hummingbird High* brought me joy. At first, it was a way to distract myself from the misery of my day job, and it was an easy way to keep in touch with the faraway friends I missed so much. But as my baking adventures and projects grew more ambitious, strangers from different states and even different *countries* began to follow along. Readers would give me advice on troubleshooting notoriously finicky baked goods, and leave comments and photos to show me they'd tried my recipes at home. It was heartwarming and inspirational. I worked harder than ever to improve my recipes, along with my photography and writing skills.

Working on *Hummingbird High* in those early days taught me I had skills beyond the quantitative and analytical ones I used in my finance job. It gave me the confidence to seek out a new opportunity that would allow for even more creativity. After six months, I decided to quit my day job and start a new career from scratch. I moved back to my college town of Portland, Oregon, for an internship at an up-and-coming tech start-up. Although I was much happier and eventually worked my way up from a lowly intern role to become a systems manager, I still found myself in the kitchen every spare moment I had. It turns out that I didn't need homework or a boring job to bake; I loved it enough on its own. Not only did it continue to bring me joy, but it now brought many others joy, too: my old friends and new coworkers who reaped the benefits of my experiments, and the readers of *Hummingbird High* who baked my recipes. It felt like I was bringing everybody back together in my tiny dorm kitchen to share cupcakes once more.

WHY I WEEKNIGHT BAKE

These days, when I talk about my blog, the first question people often ask is: "But how do you have time to bake so much?" Because for several years, I did what many thought was impossible—I ran my baking blog while maintaining a full-time job, first in finance as an analyst, and then in tech as an engineer.

The truth was, I didn't *have* the time. My jobs in both finance and tech required me to be at the office at least forty hours a week, if not more. There were weekends, sure, but that was competing with the limited time I had to spend with friends and family. And on top of that, there was my commute to the office, trips to the gym, errands, chores, and so on. All these commitments and obligations left me with *at most* an hour every evening to bake for *Hummingbird High*.

So I found myself managing my time as best as I could. I began by reading the recipes I wanted to tackle, trying to figure out where I could split up the steps within the recipe. I specialized in this sort of time management in my day job—often, I was given months-long engineering projects that I would break down into two-week chunks for my team to work through. I applied those same skills in the kitchen: my goal was to break down a recipe into parts that I could tackle in the limited amount of time I had. A cake recipe that would ordinarily take two consecutive hours to make would be spread out over a few days—30 minutes on the first day to bake the cakes, 10 minutes on the second day to make the frosting, another 30 minutes on the final day to put it all together and decorate it.

At first, this didn't always work. Sometimes, a cake I'd baked on the first night would deflate and grow stale by the second night. To troubleshoot these issues, I read culinary textbooks about the chemical reactions behind the different steps of baking, figuring out how to combine different techniques to create shortcuts. Through research and trial and error, I started to figure out what *really* worked. I also spent far too much money on a variety of different kitchen tools in an attempt to discover which ones actually helped save time in the kitchen. Over the years, slowly but surely, I built myself a set of reliable recipes, a battery of time-saving techniques, and a collection of useful kitchen equipment.

The funny thing is, on *Hummingbird High*, with the exception of a cheery baker's note now and again, I never candidly discussed what it was like to bake all the time while balancing a nine-to-five. My recipes were presented with beautiful pictures, but often without mention of my time constraints and struggles. That can happen on the internet and social media, where we choose to present only the best parts of ourselves; I felt both implicit and explicit pressure to maintain an illusion of paradise in my kitchen. Blogs are where everything is perfect, where everybody has all the time in the world to spend as they wish. But I know that's not true—and that's why I wrote this book! We're all doing the best we can with what we have. And I'm going to help you bake any night of the week that works for you.

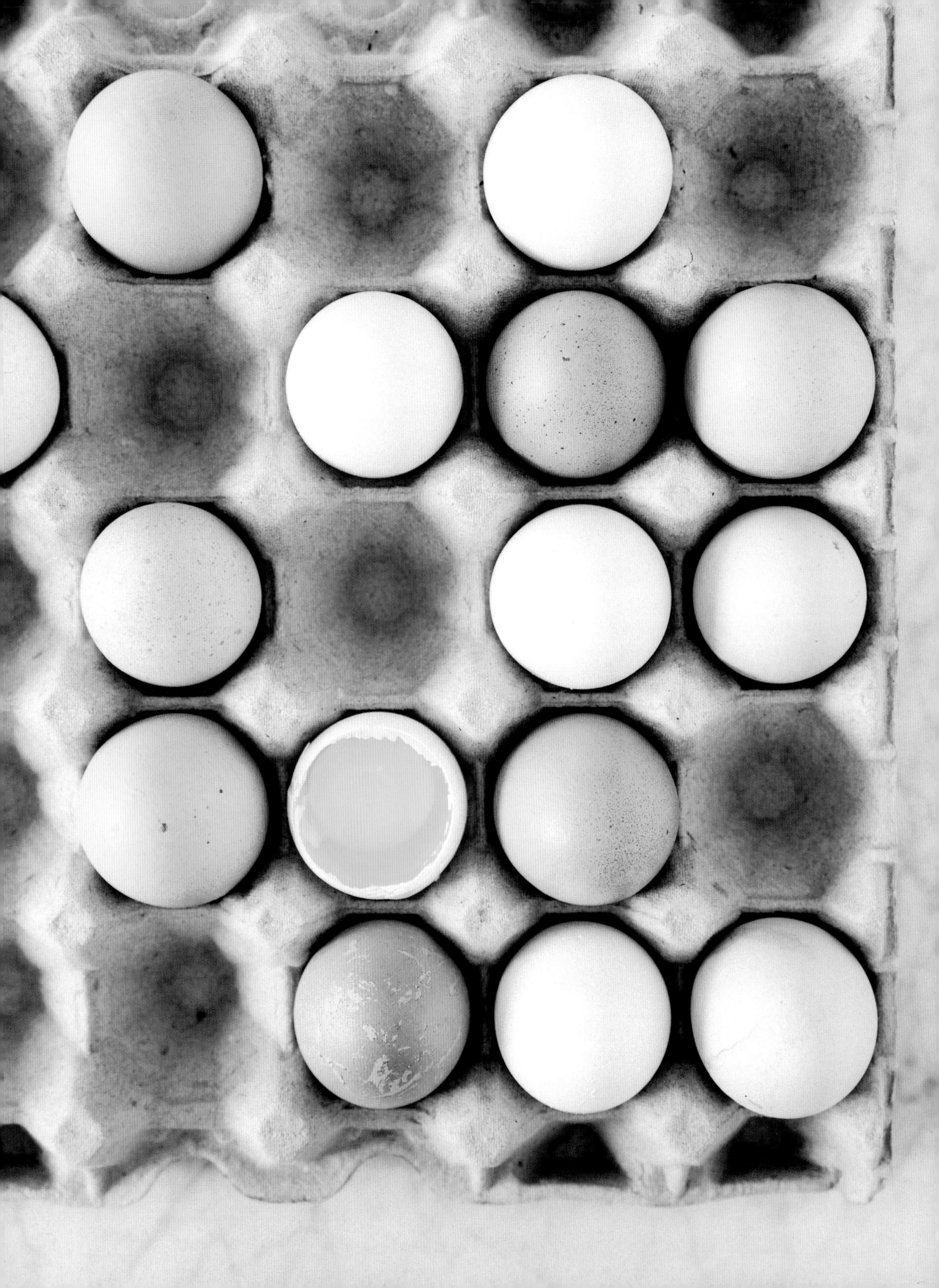

THE WEEKNIGHT BAKER'S INGREDIENTS

The most important part of becoming a Weeknight Baker is setting yourself up for success, and that starts with making sure you have all the ingredients you need. I've definitely been guilty of getting a third of the way through a recipe only to realize I'm missing a necessary ingredient. It's the *worst*.

There's only one solution: keep a well-stocked pantry. These are the staples I always have on hand to ensure that I'll be ready for any spontaneous weeknight baking projects. The best part? Many are shelf-stable and will keep for extended periods of time if stored properly. With these ingredients in your pantry and fridge, you'll be able to make 90 percent of the recipes in this book without an extra trip to the grocery store.

FLOURS

In the grocery store, you'll likely find an aisle of more flour varieties than you would have thought existed: all-purpose, bread, cake, pastry, and many more. These varieties are defined by their protein percentages. Flours with a higher protein percentage (such as bread flour) are used for recipes that result in baked goods with hearty crumbs like bread and pizza, whereas flours with a lower protein percentage (like cake flour and pastry flour) are used to make baked goods with light and tender crumbs. The best way to store flour is to pour it from the bag into a container with an airtight seal; this will prevent it from clumping, drying out, and losing its flavor quickly. I like to use a container with a large opening so I can easily scoop out what I need without making a huge mess.

all-purpose flour
All-purpose flour is the baker's true workhorse. In a pinch, all-purpose flour works in almost every recipe because its protein level falls directly in the middle of cake and bread flour. I used Bob's Red Mill Unbleached White All-Purpose Flour when developing recipes for this book, but you can use any brand you prefer.

cake flour

Cake flour has a lower protein content than all-purpose; it also tends to be more finely ground, with a silky texture that feels similar to confectioners' sugar. I used Bob's Red Mill Unbleached Enriched Super-Fine Cake Flour when developing recipes for this book, but you can use any brand you prefer—some bakers are very loyal to bleached cake flour, which you can read more about on page 22.

SUGARS

granulated sugar

When people say the word *sugar*, they're usually referring to granulated sugar, which is the white sugar we all know and love. I tested the recipes in this book with a range of brands, from the big names like Domino and C&H to the generic brands you can buy at the supermarket. It all came out tasty. The only advice I have is to **choose a non-organic, non-raw sugar variety**—organic and raw sugars are coarser, leading to longer creaming, mixing, and dissolving times in recipes (for a deep dive on this issue, check out page 24). Granulated sugar keeps well in its bag, but it's best to pour it into an airtight container to maintain freshness.

brown sugar

Brown sugar usually comes in two varieties—light and dark. I prefer dark because I love the complex flavor it can add to baked goods, but you can often swap out one for the other with no problem. Just be sure to store brown sugar properly, since it has a tendency to dry out and clump over long periods of time—unlike granulated sugar, it's important to keep brown sugar in an airtight container. Place one or two marshmallows in the container; the brown sugar will draw moisture out of the marshmallows, keeping the sugar soft and moist.

confectioners' sugar

Confectioners' sugar, also known as powdered sugar, icing sugar, or 10x, is granulated sugar that's processed into a fine powder with a texture similar to flour or cocoa powder. Confectioners' sugar is often used in recipes like whipped cream and frostings to produce light and silky textures. Even though it's technically the same stuff as granulated sugar, it's important to keep both on hand—you can't substitute one for the other without changing the overall texture, outcome, and even flavor of your baked goods. Although confectioners' sugar will keep well in its bag, I like to pour it into an airtight container with a big opening. The big opening will help prevent messes when measuring out quantities for recipes.

DAIRY AND OTHER FATS

butter

It's worth spending the money to get real butter—not margarine, and definitely not "butter spread." For a deeper dive on all the different types of butter and what you can and can't substitute, check out page 15. My favorite butter is Vermont Creamery Unsalted Cultured Butter; not only do I genuinely believe that it's the best butter available, it's also a European-style butter, which means it has a higher butterfat content and results in a richer flavor. For a more readily available option, I usually turn to Land O'Lakes unsalted butter, which is more budget-friendly and still very good.

Although unsalted butter can be kept at room temperature for up to 2 days, I recommend storing it in the refrigerator, where it will keep for up to 1 month. You can further extend its shelf-life by freezing it for up to 6 months: place each butter stick (still wrapped) in a heavy-duty zip-top bag to prevent the butter from absorbing any odors or flavors in the freezer. To thaw frozen butter, move it to the fridge the night before using it in any recipe.

eggs

All the recipes in this cookbook use large eggs. One large egg is equivalent to about 3 tablespoons (2 tablespoons for the whites, and 1 tablespoon for the yolk) or 1.5 ounces of liquid. I don't have any recommendations for which brand of eggs to buy, since I trade my friend Greg baked goods for fresh eggs from the chicken coop he keeps in his backyard (I live in Portland, what can I say?). But I do have a tip: there are a handful of recipes in this book that call for only egg yolks or only egg whites. You can save the rest of the egg in an airtight container in the refrigerator to use in another baking recipe or in your everyday cooking. Egg whites generally keep longer than egg yolks because of their high water content, so plan accordingly: yolks will keep for up to 3 days, while whites will keep for up to 1 week.

oils

A handful of cake, cookie, and bar recipes in this book call for oil. In these recipes, I exclusively use canola oil, which has a neutral taste that doesn't impart any flavor. Any generic brand in the supermarket will do, and you can substitute any other neutral-flavored oil like grapeseed or vegetable (learn more on page 20). For vegan goods, I switch to more flavorful oils like olive oil and coconut oil, both of which give the baked goods extra earthy and/or tropical flavors. I love Whole Foods' 365 extra-virgin olive oil and Trader Joe's organic virgin coconut oil, both of which are well priced and have subtle flavors that don't overwhelm baked goods. Store oils in their container in a cool, dark cupboard away from the oven or stovetop; exposure to heat and light will cause oils to go rancid faster.

milk and cream

Make sure to get the full-fat versions of both—low- and nonfat milks will lead to less flavorful baked goods. Any brand you like will work in the recipes in this book. Use cow's milk unless specifically stated otherwise since alternative milks like coconut and nut milks will work differently in recipes. Store cartons of milk and cream toward the back of the refrigerator. Keeping them in the door compartments will cause them to spoil faster (since that's the warmest and draftiest part of the refrigerator).

buttermilk

Traditionally, buttermilk is made from the sour liquid left over after cream has been churned into butter. These days, buttermilk is made by dairy processing plants injecting cultured enzymes into low-fat milk. The final product of both methods is more acidic than regular milk, giving baked goods a wonderful, tangy flavor. I'm partial to Darigold's Bulgarian-Style Buttermilk, but any brand should do the trick. Unlike milk and cream, buttermilk is a naturally low-fat product; the reduced- and low-fat cultured versions will work just fine in the recipes in this book. Similar to milk and cream, store it toward the back of the fridge, where it's coldest.

I know it can be hard to justify the fridge space for buttermilk, especially since it's almost exclusively used for baking and is not as shelf-stable as other ingredients in this chapter. But hear me out: For many years, especially when I was living in small apartments with fridges that could fit only a few days' worth of groceries at a time, I avoided buying buttermilk. Instead, I used a powdered buttermilk substitute, or sometimes even made my own with milk and vinegar (it can be done!). While these substitutions worked, none of my bakes ever tasted as good as they did when I made them with actual buttermilk. With the real stuff, my baked goods were infinitely more flavorful, all without any extra effort beyond having a carton of buttermilk in the fridge. It's worth it, I promise.

sour cream and crème fraîche

A ton of recipes in this book call for either sour cream or crème fraîche. I suggest picking one and always having it on hand, especially since you can use them interchangeably in any of the recipes in this book (along with yogurt—learn more on page 20). The main difference between the two ingredients is their acidity level; crème fraîche is the least acidic, and will yield a baked good with a subtle tangy flavor, whereas using sour cream will result in a tarter flavor. As with milk and cream, always opt for the full-fat versions. Although I don't have any brand loyalty when it comes to sour cream, I always look for Vermont Creamery's crème fraîche, which I love for both its consistency and flavor. Like all dairy products, store both toward the back of the fridge, where it's coldest.

LEAVENERS

baking powder and baking soda

Any brand of baking powder or baking soda will work in the recipes for this book. I like to use a double-acting baking powder that is aluminum-free. Aluminum in leaveners has a tendency to turn batters and doughs a bluish green if they're not baked immediately and can leave a weird metallic taste in the dessert. Store baking powder and baking soda in airtight containers in a cool, dry pantry cupboard. Some people store an open box of baking soda in the fridge to absorb odors, but if you do, I don't recommend using it for baking (unless you want those bad flavors and smells in your baked goods, too).

cream of tartar

Cream of tartar is an acidic by-product of fermenting grapes into wine; in baking, it's primarily used for stabilizing meringues and whipped cream. Although not many recipes in this book call for it, it's worth keeping around, because it lasts forever and when you need it, you *really* need it. Store cream of tartar in a cool, dry place, and always give it a quick look and a sniff before using it—it should be white in color with no major clumps, and it should smell mildly acidic. If it's discolored and clumpy, it's time for a new bottle.

yeast

There are three main types of yeast: fresh, active dry, and instant (also known as RapidRise or "quick-rise"). Because fresh yeast is extremely perishable, I prefer to stick with either active dry or instant yeast, both of which you can use interchangeably in the recipes in this book (with some caveats—learn more on page 22). I like to buy both in bottles as opposed to individual packets; a bottle makes it easier to measure out the exact quantity needed for a recipe. Store the bottle in the freezer, where it will keep for up to 1 year.

FLAVORS

vanilla extract, beans, and powder

Vanilla is crucial in almost every baked good. Think of it as dessert MSG: it gives butter and sugar more nuance, and it makes chocolate taste more intense and flavorful. Similar to butter, it's worth sourcing high-quality vanilla; cheaper vanilla extracts have a sharp alcohol taste. I highly recommend Nielsen-Massey's vanilla extracts—their extracts are very flavorful. Store vanilla extract in a cool, dark place, away from any heat sources. Light and heat will cause the extract to weaken in flavor.

Occasionally, I'll ask you to use a vanilla bean or vanilla bean powder (which is made by processing vanilla bean pods into a fine powder and can save you an additional step in a recipe). Check out Resources on page 287 for more information on how to find these ingredients.

kosher salt

I like kosher salt for its larger crystals, which make it difficult to confuse with granulated sugar (like I once did when I was rushing through a recipe—yikes!). However, not all kosher salts are created equal—some have smaller granules than others, which will result in a saltier-tasting baked good (learn more on page 25). For consistency, I recommend sticking to one brand: Diamond Crystal kosher salt, which is budget-friendly and readily available in most grocery stores. Diamond Crystal is one of the few 100% pure salts in the grocery store; other brands have additives that impart unexpected flavors to baked goods, and can affect the outcomes of certain recipes. Kosher salt is fine to keep in its box, but I always transfer mine to an airtight container with a large opening since I find it easier to scoop out the quantities needed for recipes that way. Just be sure to not store salt in metal containers—the salt can leach elements from the metal, potentially contaminating the salt.

chocolate

If there's one thing I want you to take away from this chapter, it's this: don't skimp on chocolate. Most grocery store brands—even the ones that offer products specifically made for baking— contain all sorts of additives like paraffin wax and palm oil that compromise the flavor and texture. I've stopped using chocolate chips in 90 percent of my recipes, and my baked goods have tasted so much better as a result. I rely on Guittard chocolate discs and Valrhona fèves (a fancy pastry school term for a flat, bean-shaped disc of chocolate), both of which are expensive but 100 percent worth it since they contain almost none of those additives. If you're on a budget, opt for Trader Joe's Pound Plus or Ghirardelli chocolate bars.

Chocolate can be stored, either in its original form or chopped and ready to use in any recipe, in a cool, dark spot in the pantry for up to 1 year. If storing long-term, tightly wrap any opened bars in a layer of plastic wrap and then aluminum foil, and store any unused fèves, discs, or chopped chocolate in an airtight container. Keep it away from light and heat sources to prevent the chocolate from melting and blooming.

cocoa powder

Cocoa powder comes in three major varieties: sweetened, natural unsweetened, and Dutch-processed. You can learn more about the differences between the three varieties on page 18, but I always recommend having both unsweetened and Dutch-processed on hand. Store the cocoa powder in its original packaging (which should be an opaque bag or carton), in a cool, dark spot in the pantry away from light and heat sources. Stored properly, cocoa powder will keep for about 3 years.

This is a hot take, but I don't think there's any need to buy high-end cocoa powder. My favorite brand to use is Hershey's, since it's budget-friendly and readily available in most major grocery stores. I'm not alone here—when I was living in New York City, I attended a cake-making class taught by famous wedding cake baker Ron Ben-Israel, who also swore by Hershey's.

vinegars

Vinegar has two main purposes in baking: to react with other ingredients to leaven batters, and to impart flavor. I like to keep both distilled white vinegar (which is neutral in taste and works well in recipes like red velvet cake, where vinegar is used as a leavener) and apple cider vinegar (which has a nice, tangy flavor that works well in pastry recipes) in my pantry cupboards. Store vinegar in its original packaging in a cool, dark place. Stored properly, vinegar will keep indefinitely as its acidic nature makes it self-preserving.

sprinkles

I always have bottles of all different shapes, sizes, and colors of sprinkles on hand. They're a fun, easy way to add texture and glamour to any dessert. Unfortunately, the truth is that most supermarket sprinkles taste like plastic (with the exception of the rainbow jimmies from the bulk bin section of Fairway Market in New York City—New Yorkers, these are the best sprinkles!). I've included some of my favorite sprinkle purveyors in Resources on page 287, but if you're feeling ambitious, you can make your own with the Overnight Homemade Sprinkles recipe on page 282. Store all sprinkles in their original packaging in a cool, dark spot to prevent them from fading in color. Store-bought sprinkles will keep for up to 1 year but will lose their flavor the longer they sit.

THE WEEKNIGHT BAKER'S SUBSTITUTIONS

How many times have you returned home from a trip to the grocery store, only to find that you forgot to buy one or two key ingredients for your weeknight baking project *again*? Because real talk: Despite my best attempts to stay organized, I still find myself missing ingredients for my projects every so often. In fact, it's happened frequently enough that I've learned how to substitute what's missing with what I already have at home. And while it's true that baking is notorious for precision and that you should use ingredients *exactly* as they are listed in recipes, there are places where you can be flexible . . . if you know the rules. And I'm here to teach them to you.

THE RULES FOR SUBSTITUTING BUTTER

Don't substitute margarine or other tub butters for real butter.

Although you can technically substitute margarine or other tub butters for real butter 1:1, please don't! Margarine and tub butters tend to be full of additional plant oils, skim milk, flavors, and colorings that don't have the same chemical structure as real butter. Not only will your baked goods be less flavorful, the recipe's *instructions* might not even work, either!

Take it from my experience: Once, during my early days of baking, I tried to make a pie crust with a tub butter spread. At the time, I didn't know that tub butter contained oil (which helps keep it soft even after being refrigerated). The dough never firmed up enough for me to be able to roll it out—it stuck to my rolling pin, counter, and hands. But still, I persevered, eventually using my hands to press the dough into the pie pan like I would for a tart shell. Despite my best attempts, the resulting crust tasted *terrible*. Why? Real butter has more water than oil. The water evaporates during the baking process to push the layers of pie dough apart to make a flaky crust. But because the tub butter I'd used for the crust contained more oil instead of water, none of this evaporation occurred. I was left with a dense crust with no flakiness. Stick with the real stuff for most of your baking projects—it's worth it, I promise.

You can substitute salted butter for unsalted butter . . . sometimes.

Butter is available both salted and unsalted; although baking recipes usually call for unsalted butter, most folks opt for the salted variety at the store because it tastes better and keeps longer in the fridge. Just between you and me, you can *probably* get away with using salted butter in most of the recipes in this book. But different brands add varying levels of salt to their salted butter, which means that the flavor of your dessert will vary widely depending on whatever brand of salted butter you happened to use. Baking with unsalted butter will give you more control over the final taste of your product, since you'll be adding the salt yourself. Why leave it up to chance?

So here are the rules I follow for myself: For baked goods with bold flavors like chocolate and peanut butter, salted butter will work just fine. But for vanilla-flavored items or in recipes with more delicate flavors (think: shortbread cookies, pie crusts, any kind of frosting or cream), stick with unsalted butter.

You can use cultured butter and sweet cream butter interchangeably.

Cultured butter is made from sour cream, which gives it a mild tang, whereas sweet cream butter is made from cream that hasn't been soured (but it's important to note that the cream hasn't been *sweetened*, either—it's confusing, I know!). You can use either variety in your baking, although some folks will argue that there's no point in using cultured butter since its subtle flavor will likely be overpowered by other ingredients. I personally like to think it gives my bakes that extra je ne sais quoi, but that might just be in my head. You do you.

You can use European butter and American butter interchangeably.

I like to travel, and one of my favorite things to do when I'm abroad in Europe is to treat myself to a hearty loaf of local bread with a generous serving of butter. I always felt like the butter there tasted better. I did some research and discovered that European butter contains more butterfat, which gives it a creamier taste and firmer consistency. While the minimum amount of butterfat for butter in the United States and Canada is 80%, most European butters must contain at least 82% butterfat (although it's not uncommon for European butters to have as much as 86%)! I recommend trying European-style butter if you're baking anything where butter is the main flavor component. Pound cakes, pie crusts, and shortbread cookies are recipes where it's worth the upgrade.

THE RULES FOR SUBSTITUTING CHOCOLATE

You can use milk chocolate and dark chocolate interchangeably . . . sometimes.

Milk chocolate and dark chocolate are often sold with a percentage on the package, which indicates how much of the bar, by weight, is made from cacao beans and cocoa butter. What's the difference between cacao and cocoa? All chocolate is made from the parts of a cacao tree. The unprocessed parts of this tree (like its pod, beans, and seeds) are typically referred to as "cacao," while the word "cocoa" is reserved for those same parts after they have been fermented, dried, and roasted in the first step to making chocolate. Typically, manufacturers refer to the two interchangeably as the same thing, with many favoring the term "cacao." However, in this book, I go against the norm and use the term "cocoa."

The higher the percentage, the darker and more bitter the chocolate will be. There's no standard baseline percentage for milk chocolate and dark chocolate; government and industry standards vary by country and market. In the United States, dark chocolate must contain a minimum of 35% cocoa—a surprisingly low percentage, considering that most brands have milk chocolate products that hover between 30% and 40% cocoa. In the ingredients lists in this book, you'll see that chocolate is usually accompanied with a note on what percent cocoa the chocolate should have. Higher cocoa percentages mean that there's less sugar in the chocolate, which I've accounted for by adding more sugar in the recipe. If you use a chocolate with a lower cocoa percentage, the chocolate will have more sugar and will likely make the dessert overly sweet. This works the other way, too: using an unsweetened bar with no sugar might lead to a bitter dessert with a rough, crumbly texture. So please, pay attention to those percentages!

That being said, you can get away with using the chocolate you prefer if it's being used in the recipe as a mix-in or a topping (for an example of a mix-in, check out the way chocolate is used in Chocolate Chip Cookies on page 115; for an example of a topping, check out the way chocolate is used in Banana Chocolate Chip Cake on page 91). But if the recipe instructs you to melt chocolate, stick with the type of chocolate that's specified in the ingredients list—any changes will affect the amount of sugar in the batter or dough, which will then change the taste and texture of your dessert completely.

You can use bittersweet and semisweet chocolate interchangeably, but avoid substituting unsweetened chocolate for either.

Some manufacturers make chocolate varieties specifically for baking that are labeled "bittersweet," "semisweet," or "unsweetened." You'll notice that there are usually no cocoa percentages on these bars—that's because there's no official benchmark for each designation. It's up to the manufacturers to determine how much cocoa to use, and percentages will vary greatly from brand to brand. I advise you to ignore these bars and stick with the ones that list their cocoa percentages so you know what you're getting. In a pinch, however, you can use either bittersweet or semisweet chocolate in the recipes in this book without too much consequence.

The one exception to this rule is unsweetened chocolate. Unsweetened chocolate is 100% cocoa, with no added sugar. Folks like to use unsweetened chocolate in baking for its intense flavor; on its own, however, it is quite bitter. Be careful when swapping in unsweetened chocolate for other types of chocolate—its lack of sugar makes it unpredictable to work with, and you'll likely end up with a baked good that isn't as smooth or sweet as you wanted it to be.

Be careful when substituting white chocolate for milk chocolate or dark chocolate.

Chocolate is made from the seeds of the fruit of the cacao tree; the seeds are harvested, fermented, dried, and roasted to develop flavor. After roasting, the beans are pulverized to create a paste called cocoa mass, which can be made into both cocoa powder (the same stuff we use in baking!) and cocoa butter (a vegetable fat made from pressing the cocoa mass). Cocoa butter is then mixed with milk powder, sugar, and even more cocoa to make chocolate.

Unlike its milk and dark counterparts, white chocolate is made without cocoa mass. Because of this, it cannot be substituted directly for dark or milk chocolate. Stick with my rule of thumb for substituting milk chocolate and dark chocolate—you can use or add white chocolate as a mix-in or topping. However, if you're following a recipe that requires you to melt dark or milk chocolate, you won't get the same results if you substitute white chocolate.

You can sometimes use natural unsweetened cocoa powder and Dutch-processed cocoa powder interchangeably, but always avoid using sweetened cocoa powder in baking recipes.

In the baking aisle of the grocery store, you'll find three types of cocoa powder: natural unsweetened, Dutch-processed (also known as Dutched or alkalized), and sweetened. Natural unsweetened cocoa powder is cocoa powder in its purest form, and is reddish brown in color. Dutch-processed cocoa powder is natural unsweetened cocoa powder that's been treated with an alkali solution to reduce its acidity level, turning its color almost black. Its lower acidity level means it will *not* react strongly with baking soda. If you swap out natural unsweetened cocoa for Dutch-processed in a recipe that uses baking soda as a leavener, there's a chance your baked good won't come out as light and fluffy as it should. Natural unsweetened cocoa powder is often used with baking soda in a recipe, while Dutch-processed cocoa powder is paired with baking powder. So if you ever see a recipe that doesn't specify which kind of cocoa powder to use, remember this rule: use natural unsweetened cocoa powder with baking soda, and Dutch-processed cocoa powder with baking powder. If your recipe contains both baking soda *and* baking powder, you'll likely be fine using either natural unsweetened or Dutch-processed cocoa powder.

As for sweetened cocoa powder, that stuff is best left for making hot cocoa. Sweetened cocoa powder is made by mixing unsweetened cocoa powder with sugar and other flavors. Using it in a recipe can have unpredictable results. Stick with natural unsweetened and Dutch-processed cocoa powders for baking!

You can absolutely substitute chopped chocolate bars for chocolate chips, and I recommend doing so for most recipes!

Allow me to be blunt: **stop using chocolate chips.** Chocolate chips are loaded with preservatives and stabilizers like paraffin, which helps the chips keep their structure during baking but gives the chocolate a waxy, plastic flavor. Stick with chocolate bars, which traditionally don't use the same additives as chocolate chips. Doing so will make your baking so much better.

I understand that sometimes, all you want is the chocolate chip cookie you loved as a kid—the kind made with chocolate chips. That's fine! Occasionally, I'll embrace the nostalgia, too. But know that not all chocolate chips are created equal. Try to find a good-quality brand with minimal preservatives and additives—Guittard, Valrhona, and even the readily available Ghirardelli are terrific. But if the back of that bag of chocolate chips lists more than six ingredients, *you can do better*.

THE RULES FOR SUBSTITUTING DAIRY AND OTHER FATS

You can use full-fat milk and cream interchangeably in most recipes.

Can I tell you a secret? With the exception of whipped cream and ganache (in which you should always use cream, no substitutes), full-fat milk and cream are pretty interchangeable and can be substituted for each other 1:1. The only thing to note is that cream has a higher fat content than milk—if you substitute cream for milk, you'll end up with a slightly heavier product, and vice versa.

Crème fraîche, sour cream, and yogurt can all be substituted for one another 1:1 in most recipes.

I've already explained how crème fraîche and sour cream can be easily substituted for each other in recipes (see page 10). Let me add that you can also use plain, unsweetened full-fat yogurt in place of crème fraîche or sour cream in recipes. However, yogurt is more acidic than both crème fraîche and sour cream, so your dessert will likely taste tangier. Just avoid using flavored yogurt (most flavored yogurts have a ton of added sugar and artificial flavors, leading to unpredictable results) or low-fat yogurt (similar to milk and cream, the full-fat stuff will just make your baked goods taste better).

You can use neutral-flavored oils (canola, grapeseed, vegetable, and more) interchangeably in any recipe without affecting flavor, but using flavored oils will change the way it tastes completely.

Although I call for canola oil throughout this book, you can use whatever neutral oil you have on hand. Good substitutions include regular vegetable oil, grapeseed oil, and peanut oil—none will affect the baked good's final taste and texture. But if the oil has a distinct flavor like coconut oil or olive oil, those flavors will also be present in your baked good.

THE RULES FOR SUBSTITUTING EGGS

Proceed with caution when substituting one size egg for another.

At grocery stores, you'll find eggs in four different sizes: medium, large, extra-large, and jumbo. Most recipes for baked goods, including the ones in this book, call for large eggs.

Egg sizes are determined by their weight by the dozen. In the United States, the USDA's official guidelines are:

Medium: 21 ounces per dozen (~1.75 ounces per egg)
Large: 24 ounces per dozen (~2.00 ounces per egg)
Extra-Large: 27 ounces per dozen (~2.25 ounces per egg)
Jumbo: 30 ounces per dozen (~2.50 ounces per egg)

In a pinch, you can get away with substituting medium or extra-large eggs for large. However, I wouldn't swap in medium eggs in a recipe that calls for jumbo eggs—or if I did, I'd add an extra medium egg to compensate for the difference in volume.

While it's no big deal to swap a few different-size eggs in a recipe that calls for one or two eggs, you'll likely start to notice a difference in recipes that use four or more eggs. I would proceed with caution and substitute egg sizes only if I really had no other options.

THE RULES FOR SUBSTITUTING FLOURS

You can substitute all-purpose flour for bread flour 1:1, and all-purpose flour for cake flour with a little math, but doing so will likely change the texture of your baked good.

I've already discussed how most flours are differentiated by their protein content on page 7. Here's a quick refresher: Bread flour contains more protein (between 14% and 16%), which helps develop the gluten, or structure, in crusty breads. Cake flour and pastry flour contain less protein (between 7% and 9%), which results in tender crumbs in cakes and pastries.

All-purpose flour gets its name because its protein level (between 10% and 12%) falls somewhere between that of bread flour and that of cake and pastry flours. In general, if a recipe calls for "flour," it's safe to assume that means all-purpose. Almost all the recipes in this book use all-purpose flour. The exception to this rule can be found in the Cakes chapter of this book, where all recipes use cake flour to ensure soft and tender cakes.

In a pinch, you can substitute all-purpose flour for bread flour 1:1 in most recipes, and all-purpose for cake flour with a little mathemagic (learn more on page 74). But a cake made with bread flour will turn out flatter and denser, and a bread made with cake flour will lack height and texture.

You can use bleached and unbleached flour interchangeably in most recipes.

Flour manufacturers often specify whether their flour is bleached or unbleached. Bleached flour has been treated with chlorine, which in theory makes the flour rise better, leading to airier textures and lighter crumbs in baked goods. However, I haven't noticed a difference in any of the recipes in this book when substituting one for the other. So my advice is to find a brand you like—whether bleached or unbleached—and don't worry about it too much unless a recipe specifically calls for one and explains why it's important.

Substituting whole wheat flour for all-purpose flour is doable, but takes a little bit of experimenting.

Whole wheat flours have gained significant street cred in our increasingly health-conscious world since they contain more protein, fiber, and nutrients than their refined counterparts. Unfortunately, the very same things that make whole wheat flours healthier weigh them down in dessert recipes—substituting the same amount of whole wheat flour for all-purpose flour in a recipe will result in a heavier, denser baked good. This may not be a bad thing, depending on what you're making. Cookies, bars, and loaf cakes like banana or pumpkin bread could actually benefit from whole wheat flour's nutty, hearty flavor. But for more delicate desserts like white cake or shortbread and sugar cookies, it's best to stick to the refined stuff.

To figure out whether a recipe will be delicious with whole wheat flour, I think about the color of its final product. Whole wheat flour will work well in desserts with brown or amber crumbs. But if the dessert has a white or pale-colored crumb, I stick with refined all-purpose or cake flour.

If you're ready to experiment with baking with whole wheat flour, start by replacing ⅓ to ½ cup of the all-purpose flour in the recipe and go from there. You can see this in practice in the Muffins and Scones recipes on page 220. I've replaced some of the traditional all-purpose flour with whole wheat flour and other alternative flours in many of those recipes.

THE RULES FOR SUBSTITUTING LEAVENERS

You can use active dry yeast and instant yeast interchangeably, but you'll need to change the way in which you activate the yeast and use it within the recipe.

While you can use active dry yeast and instant yeast pretty much interchangeably in most recipes, you'll need to change the way you work with the yeast depending on which type you use. The two types are activated at different temperatures, so read the manufacturer's instructions before you start (in general, active dry yeast is activated between 110° and 115°F, while instant yeast is activated between 120° and 130°F). In addition to different activation temperatures, active dry yeast is activated by soaking it in warm water with a little bit of sugar, whereas instant yeast can

be added directly to dry ingredients. Since I'm a weeknight baker, I *love* instant yeast—you get to skip a step, and it generally proofs faster than active dry yeast.

THE RULES FOR SUBSTITUTING SUGARS

I don't recommend substituting granulated sugar for brown sugar, and vice versa, in most recipes.

Many baking recipes call for both granulated *and* brown sugar. In these recipes, it's best to follow the ingredients exactly as they are written—while you can sometimes get away with using one for the other 1:1, in most recipes, you'll end up changing the flavor, texture, and even color of the baked good.

That being said, there's more leniency when it comes to recipes that use just *one* (but not both!) type of sugar. Good examples include recipes for pie fillings, custards, creams, and sauces. Here you can get away with using the type of sugar you prefer, but there's an exception to this rule. Substituting granulated sugar for brown sugar in a recipe that also uses baking soda might not work. The molasses or syrup in the brown sugar makes brown sugar more acidic than white sugar, which means it'll react better with baking soda (which is alkaline in nature). Granulated sugar isn't acidic, so it won't react with the baking soda in the same way.

Don't substitute confectioners' sugar for granulated sugar or brown sugar in recipes.

Confectioners' sugar is much finer than both granulated sugar and brown sugar, so you can't substitute it for either and get the same results. Take the creaming process of any recipe—beating granulated sugar and butter together results in a sandy, rough texture when you rub it between your fingers, whereas beating confectioners' sugar and butter together results in a silky-smooth texture similar to that of frosting. Use confectioners' sugar only when the recipe calls for it.

Research specialty brown sugars before substituting them for granulated sugar or standard brown sugar in recipes.

There is a wide variety of other brown sugars available in grocery stores and food specialty shops. The most common are Muscovado, turbinado, and Demerara. Muscovado is the darkest brown sugar available; it has a rich flavor similar to caramel, dates, and raisins, and it's soft and sticky like regular brown sugar. You can use it in any recipe that calls for brown sugar, but you'll likely need to increase the recipe's Bake Time by a few minutes. Muscovado sugar contains more moisture than regular brown sugar and will need more time to evaporate during the baking process.

Although turbinado and Demerara sugar look and taste like brown sugar, both are more similar to granulated sugar in texture. However, their granules are significantly larger, which means that both sugars are slower to dissolve and result in batters and doughs that take longer to bake. Because of this, I avoid using them in recipes and instead save these sugars for sprinkling on top of baked goods like loaf cakes and muffins, where their texture adds crunch.

It can be tricky to substitute liquid sweeteners like honey, agave syrup, and maple syrup for sugar in most recipes; however, if the recipe calls for one of these liquid sweeteners, go ahead and substitute the type you prefer 1:1.

Some bakers substitute honey, agave syrup, or maple syrup for sugars in their recipes for health reasons; however, getting the ratio right can be quite tricky, as you'll need to account for these sweeteners' extra liquid by either decreasing the liquid somewhere else in the recipe or increasing the dry ingredients. Then there's the fact that equivalent amounts of these sweeteners are significantly sweeter than sugar. But you can substitute these sweeteners for one another 1:1. Just note that if you use honey or maple syrup, you'll end up with those flavors in the dessert.

THE RULES FOR SUBSTITUTING SALT

You can't substitute table salt for kosher salt without reducing the amount of salt called for in the recipe.

Remember how on page 11, I said that you should use kosher salt, above all others, for all the recipes in this book? If it's an absolute emergency, you can use table salt, but you **must** reduce the recipe's indicated salt quantity by ½ teaspoon. Because table salt has smaller granules than kosher salt, a teaspoon of table salt will contain more granules. Your baked good will ultimately taste saltier than if you'd used the same quantity of kosher salt.

Don't use flaky salt in recipes (except to sprinkle it on cookies and bars as a finishing element).

Under no circumstance should you substitute flaky salt for kosher salt; its granules are much larger in size, making it unpredictable for use in recipes. It dissolves far less easily and could potentially leave pockets of salt in your doughs and batters. Flaky salt is best used as a finishing ingredient, especially for recipes with chocolate that is still warm and gooey from the oven (like the Single Lady Chocolate Chip Cookie on page 113).

THE WEEKNIGHT BAKER'S TOOLS

Back when I first started baking in college, making cupcakes and boxed-mix brownies in a tiny, ill-equipped dorm kitchen, I didn't have any of the fancy gadgetry that I own today. Instead, my dormmates and I were *fantastic* at improvising: we poured cream into mason jars and tossed the jar between us to whip cream; I made cakes with nothing but a fork to whisk the batter; and I portioned cookie dough by rolling it into balls between my palms like Play-Doh. While these methods worked, they also took much longer than the recipe would have ordinarily taken with the right equipment. Doing so made a huge mess that took twice as long to clean up, too.

My point: Good tools save you time in the kitchen. This chapter contains a list of the equipment I've tried and tested over the years that will help save time while baking.

aluminum foil

Use aluminum foil for storing baked goods in the freezer long-term. Wrapping baked goods in plastic wrap and then an extra layer of foil will prevent freezer burn and stop the goods from absorbing flavors and odors in the freezer.

bamboo skewers

The best way to tell when bars and cakes are done is to stick a long, thin bamboo skewer into their centers; if the skewer comes out with a few crumbs attached, it's ready! Keep a few of these on hand—you can even wash and reuse them, since bamboo has antibacterial properties.

bench scraper

A metal bench scraper with a dishwasher-friendly handle is the secret MVP in the baker's kitchen. It can function as a cutting tool (use it to divide doughs and chop up crumbs), a cake decorating tool (use it like an offset spatula to scrape frosting), and a cleaning tool (use it as a brush to sweep your counters).

blender

Some custard, batter, and cream recipes in this book call for a blender. When I lived in San Francisco and New York and didn't have room in my kitchen, I used an immersion blender to save space. While it did the job in a pinch, the results didn't compare to what you get by using a high-powered blender, which produces smoother batters, airier creams, and silkier custards in less time. I use a Wolf Gourmet blender, which I love, but a lower-priced brand and model will work just fine, too.

cake pans

My cupboard is stocked to the brim with cake pans of all shapes and sizes. These are the ones you'll need for the recipes in this book:

- 9 x 5-inch loaf pan
- 9 x 13-inch cake pan
- Three 8-inch round cake pans (opt for ones with sides that are 3 inches tall)
- Two 12-cavity muffin tins
- 8-inch square cake pan

For baking, *always* choose a light-colored pan over a dark one—dark colors absorb heat more quickly, causing the bottom and sides of baked goods to bake much faster than their centers. Some bakers swear by their glass pans, but I recommend metal since it conducts heat more efficiently and cools quickly when done. Glass pans stay warm for a long time, continuing to cook your food long after it's been pulled out of the oven, leading to overdone baked goods. Finally, it's also important to use cake pans with straight sides, as opposed to slanted sides. Although they take up much more space in your cupboard (since they're unstackable), they produce straight-sided cakes that are much easier to layer and frost. If you're just starting your own collection of cake pans, I recommend pans from Williams-Sonoma's Goldtouch® Nonstick line, which fit all of the parameters I just described.

chef's torch

Okay, indulge me for a moment—a chef's torch isn't a necessity, but it *is* fun to have in your kitchen. Aside from torching marshmallows and meringues, I like to have one for the wintertime, when "room-temperature" butter is still too cold for baking. When butter is too cold, it will be much harder to cream with sugar and eggs. So here's a neat trick: Blast the side of your stand mixer bowl with the chef's torch while beating butter and sugar. The torch helps the ingredients heat gently, softening the butter to the perfect temperature for baking. Just make sure your mixer bowl is made with a heatproof material (like stainless steel)!

cookie dough scoop

If there's one tool on this list that will significantly speed up your baking process, it's a cookie dough scoop. Before I invested in cookie dough scoops, I used my hands to roll cookie dough into balls like Play-Doh. It was fun but also took *forever*. A cookie dough scoop solves all these problems, portioning dough evenly and easily. It also works great for tasks like transferring thicker batters into cake pans. I recommend having two sizes: a 1-tablespoon cookie dough scoop and a 3-tablespoon cookie dough scoop.

digital candy thermometer

I use a candy thermometer when making curds, custards, and icings; although most recipes will instruct you to cook things to specific visual cues, you'll end up with more consistent results if you use a candy thermometer. Look for a digital one that gives an instant reading.

digital kitchen scale

When weeknight baking, a digital kitchen scale can save you a ton of time and cleanup; simply weigh out your ingredients into the same bowl, and reset the scale to zero before you add each ingredient (learn more on page 38). A good scale will cost less than $30 and offer readings in a variety of measurements like ounces, grams, and milliliters. I recommend the Primo Digital Kitchen Scale by Escali; I've had mine for many years now, and it shows no sign of stopping anytime soon.

double boiler

For mixtures that easily burn or scorch, use a double boiler. A double boiler is made up of two saucepans stacked one on top of the other. Fill the lower pan with a few inches of water, but not enough to touch the bottom of the upper pan. Bring the water to a boil. The resulting steam will heat what you're cooking in the upper pan very gently. You can invest in a real double boiler, but in a pinch, make your own by setting a glass or metal bowl on top of a saucepan filled with a few inches of water. Just be sure that, like a real double boiler, the water doesn't touch the bottom of the bowl.

fine-mesh sieve

There are some baking ingredients that get lumpy the longer they sit in the cupboard. You'll need to sift these ingredients to ensure that you don't end up with lumps in your baked good. The easiest and fastest way to sift is with a fine-mesh sieve: Invest in a large one, plop it over a big bowl, and dump the ingredient that needs to be sifted into it. Use a whisk to stir until the ingredient completely passes through the bottom of the sieve, lump-free. You'll also need a fine-mesh sieve for straining custard.

food processor

Some of the recipes in this book call for roughly chopped or grated ingredients; because those tasks are incredibly time-consuming, it's worth investing in a powerful food processor for those jobs. I'm partial to the Breville Sous Chef, which comes with a mini bowl for processing small quantities of ingredients. Whichever brand you choose, look for a food processor with dishwasher-friendly components to make cleanup easy.

stand mixer

Most recipes in this book were developed and written to be made with a stand mixer; you'll need to add more Work Time (see page 48) to each recipe if you're working with a handheld mixer, since it's not as powerful as a stand mixer. A stand mixer is one of the best investments you can make when it comes to baking. They're one of the most efficient tools in the kitchen and will save you countless hours when beating batter and kneading doughs, all while keeping your hands free for other tasks. The typical stand mixer comes with a set of three attachments: a paddle for beating, a dough hook for kneading, and a whisk. I use a KitchenAid 5-quart stand mixer, but you can use any brand you prefer.

paddle attachment with scraper

The only gripe I have with my stand mixer is that its paddle tends to miss ingredients at the bottom and sides of the bowl. I found myself frequently stopping the mixer and using a rubber spatula to scrape the stuck ingredients off the bowl so they could be beaten into the batter or dough. If you have a KitchenAid mixer, invest in their Flex Edge Beater paddle—this paddle has a flexible spatula along one side, which scrapes down the bowl as the paddle turns, reducing the need for you to stop the mixer and do it yourself.

knives

You'll need a good chef's knife or paring knife to prepare ingredients. A serrated knife is also especially useful for cutting clean slices of cakes and pastries; look for one with a flat tip to help cut through particularly crispy crusts.

microplane grater

A Microplane grater is the fastest and easiest way to zest citrus fruits. You can also use it to grate cheese and shave tough spices like cinnamon sticks, nutmeg seeds, and more.

microwave

A microwave is a weeknight baking godsend. It can bring ingredients to room temperature quickly without getting any pots or pans dirty;

be sure to check out How to Bring Common Baking Ingredients to Room Temperature Quickly on page 41 to learn more.

measuring cups

Measuring cups are likely the most controversial thing I'm recommending for your drawers. Unlike kitchen scales, which allow you to measure ingredients by weight, measuring cups measure by volume (for a deeper dive on this issue, see page 35). Although I encourage you to use a scale when you bake, I prefer to use volume measures in very specific circumstances (like in my Any Kind of Fruit Pie on page 205). Stick with measuring cups made of a material like stainless steel—they'll last a lifetime.

In addition to having a set of measuring cups, which are typically only used to measure out dry ingredients like flour and sugar, I encourage you to have a liquid measuring cup as well. A liquid measuring cup looks like a mini pitcher, complete with a handle and a spout. Technically, liquid and dry measuring cups measure the same volume, but pouring a liquid ingredient into a dry measuring cup is a pain—you'll need to fill it to the very brim, and then transfer it to wherever it needs to go without spilling. In contrast, liquid measuring cups have lots of extra room for the liquid to slosh around without spilling. For the most accurate measure, set the liquid measuring cup on a flat surface and squat down so that the measuring line is at eye level—pour in the ingredient until the bottom of its meniscus reaches just above the desired marking.

measuring spoons

Unlike measuring cups, measuring spoons are an essential and totally uncontroversial tool in the baker's kitchen since volume measurements are much more precise than weight measurements for small quantities of ingredients. Because unless you're working with a jeweler's scale, most home kitchen scales simply aren't precise enough to measure ¼ teaspoon of a fine ingredient like baking powder. The scale will round up or down by a gram—that means that at any point between 0.51 grams and 1.49 grams, the scale is going to read the same figure!

I recommend sourcing a set of measuring spoons with rectangular heads that can fit in the openings of smaller spice jars. Most measuring spoons come with four measures (1 tablespoon, 1 teaspoon, ½ teaspoon, ¼ teaspoon), but it's worth it to find a set that comes with an extra measure for ⅛ teaspoon— you'll need it for the Single Lady Chocolate Chip Cookie recipe on page 113.

metal scoops

Although most dry ingredients like flour and sugar come in resealable bags, I like to store my dry ingredients in airtight plastic containers to extend their shelf-life. I then give each container its own metal scoop. The scoop will be forever assigned to that ingredient, living in the same container and saving me the hassle of washing spoons and scoops each time I bake.

mixing bowls

A good mixing bowl has tall sides (which help prevent ingredients from flying everywhere as you mix them) and a rimmed lip (which helps you pour batters into pans more accurately). I recommend keeping a mix of glass and metal bowls in your cupboard. Glass mixing bowls are nonreactive, which make them great for storing food long-term and for mixing acidic ingredients. Look for ones that are heatproof and oven safe, as recipes in this book will occasionally ask you to cook or even bake ingredients in a glass bowl. Metal mixing bowls are perfect for use in a homemade

double boiler (see page 28), as they conduct heat evenly and efficiently.

nonstick cooking spray

Greasing your baking pans will prevent cakes, cookies, and bars from sticking to the pan when turned out or sliced. I like using nonstick cooking spray for the job: it's fast, easy, and skips the mess of using flour and butter. Don't be afraid to use a good amount of spray, and choose a spray made from a neutral oil like canola or vegetable to ensure that it doesn't affect the flavor of your baked good.

offset spatula

While spatulas for cooking have a rectangular square head, offset spatulas have a thin, blunt blade perfect for spreading and scraping. Before I bought an offset spatula, I used butter knives and spoons to spread batters across pans and frosting across cakes. My first offset spatula was an absolute game changer and got the job done much faster and neater than any of my makeshift tools. Invest in both a short and long offset spatula with sturdy metal blades.

oven thermometer

Most modern ovens have internal thermometers. But these degrade over time, giving you temperatures that are several degrees off. I discovered this the hard way: for two weeks after moving into a new apartment in San Francisco, I burned everything I baked. I finally bought an oven thermometer and discovered that the oven ran 100 degrees warmer than what it read on its panel. Yikes.

A good oven thermometer will come with a hook, magnet, or clip that will allow you to place it in the oven; I like to hang mine on the center rack (right underneath where I place my pans) for the most accurate readings.

pastry brush

You'll need a pastry brush for glazing pie crusts with egg wash. Opt for a silicone one that you can easily throw in the dishwasher; they last a long time, whereas old-fashioned pastry brushes with natural bristles need to be washed by hand and start shedding their bristles after a few months.

parchment paper

I use parchment paper almost every time I bake. Lining your pans with parchment paper will ensure that your cakes and bars come out of their pans easily; plus, really good, thick parchment paper will absorb any grease or oil from cookies and will save you from having to scrub your pans.

Although parchment paper is readily available at most grocery stores, it is often sold in rolls, and never lays flat when cut. Instead, I like to use parchment paper sheets, which are pre-cut to fit standard sheet pan sizes and stored flat like sheets of printer paper. Parchment paper sheets are available online from King Arthur Flour's digital store; see Resources on page 287 for more information.

pie pan

Pie recipes in this book are made with 9-inch pie pans. Be sure to use a thin aluminum pan with a wide rim, which prevents pie crusts from slipping and shrinking (to learn more, see page 191).

pie weights

Pie weights are used when parbaking unfilled pie crusts (like the Silkiest Pumpkin Pie on page 217); the pie weights keep the crust from puffing up and help prevent the crust from sliding down the edges of the pie pan. Although you can buy ceramic pie weights online, I prefer to use coins from my change jar to save space in my kitchen drawers. Line the pie crust with aluminum foil and pour in the loose change, spreading it out so that it's weighted toward the edges of the crust as opposed to the center. You can also use dried beans or uncooked rice with the same results.

piping bag and piping tips

A piping bag with a tip is one of the easiest ways to decorate a cake; you can squeeze out different patterns and dots for fast decoration (learn more on page 109). I recommend starting with a writing tip, a star tip, a petal tip, and a set of couplers (plastic knobs that attach to the end of the piping bag and allow you to switch piping tips easily).

plastic wrap

Many of the recipes in this book can be baked, decorated, assembled, or even served later if they are stored properly in the refrigerator or freezer. Wrapping your batters, doughs, and baked goods in plastic wrap will protect many of your recipes from going stale and absorbing other flavors during storage. Look for professional-grade plastic wrap, which is available at bulk stores like Costco or online from Amazon. Professional-grade plastic wrap is reusable and thicker than what's usually available at supermarkets, and adheres really well to almost any surface.

pots and pans

A few of the recipes in this book require a saucepot, a saucepan, or a cast-iron skillet. It's best to use pots and pans that are light in color (to allow you to see visual cues like color changes) and have heavy bottoms (to prevent whatever you're cooking from scorching easily). When it comes to cast-iron skillets, buy one that you want to keep forever since its cooking surface will become nonstick and smoothen over time.

rolling pin

I'm partial to heavy rolling pins made out of marble (which also helps keep pastry dough cool), but others prefer lighter pins made out of wood, or tapered ones with no handles. Figure out the style of rolling pin you like best and keep that one in your kitchen—there's no right or wrong answer here! Visit a specialty store like Williams-Sonoma or Sur La Table to check out the different varieties, and don't be afraid to plop a pin down on a surface and pretend to roll out dough. You want something that feels good in your hands and is heavy but still easy to maneuver.

rotating cake stand

A rotating cake stand is handy for decorating cakes (learn more on page 107). Look for a sturdy one with a heavy metal base that isn't easily moved when nudged; you can find a selection of rotating cake stands on Amazon.

rubber spatulas

Even with a stand mixer doing most of the work, you'll still need a handful of rubber spatulas for additional scraping and mixing. These are distinct from cooking spatulas, which are stiff and meant for flipping food in a pan. Rubber spatulas instead have a flexible head that can reach the corners of baking pans and can easily follow the contours of a bowl. Look for one made from a heatproof and dishwasher-friendly material like silicone.

sheet pans

Rimmed metal pans are called a variety of different names: baking sheets, jelly-roll pans, sheet pans. They're all the same thing. I call them sheet pans because that's what professional kitchens call them and doing so makes me feel like a pro, too. They come in a range of sizes, but the ones used most often in this book are half sheet pans (13 x 18 inches) and quarter sheet pans (9 x 13 inches). I recommend keeping a pair of each size in your cupboard. Similar to cake pans, choose light-colored sheet pans made from a sturdy but lightweight aluminum material that won't warp when baked—the commercial-grade varieties on Amazon do the trick.

Note that sheet pans are distinct from cookie sheets; sheet pans have a rim, while cookie sheets are rimless, with the exception of one side that also functions as a handle. I avoid cookie sheets since they tend to be flimsier than standard sheet pans and tend to burn the bottoms of my cookies.

storage containers

Storage containers allow you to keep your ingredients and baked goods fresh. For storing bulk ingredients like flour and sugar, invest in large, airtight containers like OXO's POP Containers. I also store smaller, more fragrant ingredients like chocolate and spices in widemouthed glass Ball or Kerr jars since glass doesn't absorb colors, flavors, and odors like plastic can. For the baked goods themselves, I recommend keeping a mix of glass and plastic airtight snapware containers from Pyrex and OXO to keep everything fresh for several days after baking.

tart pan

A tart pan is distinct from a pie pan and has fluted edges and a removable bottom. Similar to my advice for cake pans, look for a light-colored tart pan made from aluminum. Although most recipes in this book call for an 8-inch round tart pan, you can use a 5 x 14-inch rectangular tart pan in its place.

timer

For years, I used my cell phone to time how long baked goods stayed in the oven; when I did, I often found myself forgetting to set the timer. Once I invested in a timer specifically for baking, I almost never forgot. Go for a small, portable one with a magnetic back that you can stick on the oven or the fridge. For baking, I prefer an electronic one that can count down to the very last second.

whisks

Opt for a standard, dishwasher-friendly balloon whisk or French whisk (which is just a longer, narrower balloon whisk). While I prefer metal whisks, I also keep a silicone-coated one around for when I need to whisk anything in a nonstick pot or pan—uncoated metal whisks have the potential to scrape the nonstick coating off the pan.

wire racks

Cooling your baking pans on wire racks will help them come to room temperature more quickly and efficiently than cooling them on a trivet. Wire racks allow air to circulate underneath the pan, helping to prevent anything from overcooking and/or getting soggy. Most wire racks have round wiring that can make indentations or weird moldings on delicate cakes and cookies; look for a rack with flat slats like Crate & Barrel's wire rack.

zip-top bags

Zip-top bags are an easy way to store leftover cookie dough, frosting, and more in the freezer. Use thicker, heavy-duty gallon-size bags designed for long-term use. If storing something for an extended period of time, I like to double bag the item and wrap the whole thing in an extra layer of aluminum foil. Most bags can be reused a few times—just give them a quick rinse and be sure to dry completely before reusing.

volume and weight measures,

or how i learned to stop worrying about measuring cups and love the digital scale

In The Weeknight Baker's Tools, I encourage you to keep both measuring cups *and* a digital scale in your cupboard. Some might argue that having both is redundant, since both tools measure ingredients. But there's one major difference between them—measuring cups measure by volume, whereas digital scales measure by weight. And that's not the same thing! Volume is a measure of how much *space* an ingredient takes up, whereas weight is a measure of how *heavy* an ingredient is.

To understand what that *really* means, imagine two boxes, each the same size, both packed to the brim and sealed shut in the same way. However, one is filled with fluffy marshmallows for your next baking project, while the other is filled with pretty enameled cast-iron skillets for your kitchen. Intuitively, you know that the box filled with cast-iron skillets is going to be *much* heavier than the one filled with marshmallows. That means they have different weight measures, yet because both occupy the same size box, *they have identical volume measures*. Crazy, right?!

Now let's apply that in the kitchen. A cup of flour and a cup of milk have the same volume, but will have different weights: my 1-cup measure of flour weighs 4.5 ounces, whereas my 1-cup measure of milk weighs almost twice as much—8 ounces! To make matters even more confusing, the weight of the same volume of a dry ingredi-

ent can vary considerably depending on how the cup was filled. Somebody who scoops flour into a measuring cup and packs it down will likely have a cup of flour that weighs more than somebody who simply scoops the flour into the cup and levels it off once it's filled. This is why bakers *love* measuring by weight with a digital scale instead of by volume with measuring cups. It's much more reliable, since it completely eliminates the inconsistencies that come from using measuring cups and volume measures.

That being said: I get it. Using a digital scale seems like a big deal. Most folks, myself included, start out baking with measuring cups. That's why I've taken care to include both volume *and* weight measurements for all the recipes in this book. But if you're looking to take your baking to the next level, you **need** to start using a digital scale.

There are a couple of exceptions to this rule: as I explained on page 30, measuring spoons are far more efficient than their cup counterparts. And there are some recipes, like those for fruit pie fillings, where it's really just not all that important to have an exact weight measure of the ingredient (learn more on page 49). But here's a good rule for using weight measurements: if the recipe calls for more than a few tablespoons of the ingredient, break out the scale and measure by weight instead of volume.

THE WEEKNIGHT BAKER'S TECHNIQUES

This is probably the most embarrassing thing I will write in this book, but here we go: Sometimes, when I'm baking in the kitchen, I talk out loud and explain why I do things the way I do to my cat. Over time, I found myself waxing poetic about the same techniques over and over again. I eventually realized that these talking points were the foundation of my weeknight baking. Without further ado, consider the points below your crash course on my best time-saving techniques.

READ EVERY RECIPE CAREFULLY AND IN FULL.

Reading a recipe in full before starting any of its steps is the best way to ensure success any time you bake. I speak from experience—for many years, I'd just dive headfirst into the recipe without reading it in full. I often found myself rushing to prep ingredients midway through the recipe or, worse, discovering that the recipe I was baking to satisfy my need for dessert right then actually required me to chill the batter or dough for 24 hours before baking it. Don't forget to take note of the equipment and ingredients list, too—often, you may be instructed to use an ingredient at two (or more!) different points in the recipe, sometimes in different quantities each time. Reading a recipe in full will eliminate surprises and minimize mistakes.

SPOT SHORTCUTS WITHIN THE RECIPE ITSELF.

Although most recipes generally follow a similar format (a lesson I learned after years of reading many, many recipes), there are a few steps you can do out of order to save a few minutes here and there:

Preheat the oven as you prep the ingredients.

Heating the oven to the temperature needed for the recipe takes time and is often the first step in my recipes. It's best to be efficient about it—multitask by turning on your oven as you read the recipe in full and prep the ingredients.

If you see an ingredient that requires heating or cooling in some way as part of its prep, prep that ingredient first.

Most recipes list ingredients in the order they're used in the recipe; as a result, beginner bakers will find themselves going down the list and measuring and preparing the ingredients accordingly. I recommend reading the ingredients list in full first to see if any ingredients like butter or chocolate need to be melted. If so, start there. Then you can multitask: while that ingredient is melting, prep the rest of the ingredients. The best part is that the ingredient will usually have finished melting around the time you finish prepping everything else!

When recipes ask for an ingredient to be melted and cooled, that usually means the melted ingredient should be slightly warm to the touch but no longer hot, at a temperature between 85° to 90°F. To cool a melted ingredient quickly, pour it into a liquid measuring cup set on a wire rack. Pouring the ingredient into a different vessel than the one in which it was melted in will allow it to lose heat quickly and cool faster, and the wire rack allows air to circulate around the measuring cup, which also speeds cooling.

Similarly, if you see an ingredient that needs to be boiled, start your prep with that ingredient. It's the same multitasking logic for ingredients that need to be melted and cooled. If the recipe calls for the boiled ingredient to be steaming hot for use in the recipe, make sure to keep it covered with a pot lid (or a heatproof plate) to prevent it from cooling too quickly while you work through the recipe.

BE EFFICIENT IN PREPPING YOUR INGREDIENTS BY USING A DIGITAL SCALE.

There are many arguments as to why you should use a digital scale when you bake, the chief one being that it's the most accurate method for measuring and guarantees consistent results each time (see more on page 35). But real talk: That wasn't what finally made me switch to a scale. Instead, I switched because I was too lazy to wash more dishes than I needed to.

With a measuring scale and the following techniques, you can use just two bowls for prepping most recipes:

If the recipe instructs you to eventually combine the ingredients together, you can weigh them all in the same bowl.

Most recipes instruct you to weigh out dry ingredients, then combine them in the same bowl to add to the batter or dough later at the same time. If a recipe instructs you to do this, weigh out the ingredients into the same bowl. Set a large bowl (or the size indicated in the recipe) on the scale, tare the scale so it reads "0," then add your first ingredient to the bowl until the scale registers the desired weight. Tare the scale again and continue adding ingredients, resetting the scale to zero after you've added each one. Doing so eliminates the need to use a different measuring cup each time!

Similarly, if a recipe instructs you to eventually combine all wet ingredients together, you can also just weigh them all into the same bowl. Just be more mindful and read the recipe completely before doing so—while it's more common to mix the dry ingredients of a recipe together all at once, wet ingredients sometimes get added in different stages throughout the recipe.

If the recipe instructs you to cream butter and sugar together, measure them into your stand mixer bowl.

Most recipes, especially recipes for cookies and cakes, will instruct you to combine butter and sugar in the bowl of your stand mixer and cream them together. Save yourself a bowl and simply weigh out those ingredients in your mixer bowl ahead of time.

IF YOU HAVE TO USE MEASURING CUPS, USE THEM PROPERLY AND EFFECTIVELY.

The correct way to fill a dry measuring cup is to spoon the dry ingredient into the measuring cup until it forms a small mound within the cup. Use a butter knife or bench scraper to level off the mound so that the ingredient is flush with the top edges of the measuring cup. If you're measuring a dry ingredient that has a tendency to clump or get packed down (like flour, confectioners' sugar, or cocoa powder), you'll need to aerate these dry ingredients first by whisking them in their bags or containers before scooping them into the measuring cup.

If you're using a liquid measuring cup, set the measuring cup on a flat, stable surface. Squat down so the measuring cup's markings are at eye level. Pour in the liquid until the bottom of the meniscus reaches just above the desired marking on the measuring cup. If you're working with a sticky liquid like honey or corn syrup, lightly spray the measuring cup with cooking spray—the sticky liquid will slide right out of the measuring cup and leave nothing behind when it's time to add it to the recipe.

FIND THE COMMON DENOMINATOR IN MEASURING CUPS AND SPOONS.

Another way to save time cleaning up is to find the common denominator between the quantities of ingredients, and use that measure to prep all ingredients. For instance, if a recipe calls for 1 cup flour, ½ cup chocolate chips, and ¼ cup nuts, I usually reach for the ¼ cup measure and use it to measure out one ¼ cup of nuts, two ¼ cups of chocolate chips, and four ¼ cups of flour. You'll need to do some basic math, sure, but it's the fun kind that will make you feel smart and wonder why your teachers never taught you fractions this way in school.

The same rule applies for measuring spoons: If a recipe calls for 1 teaspoon of vanilla extract and ½ teaspoon of kosher salt, I'll reach for the ½ teaspoon to measure both. Measure the dry ingredients before the wet ingredients (if you start with the wet ingredients, the dry ingredients will stick to the measuring spoon). You can apply this same theory if your recipe calls for both tablespoons and teaspoons; just remember that 3 teaspoons equal 1 tablespoon.

DON'T WASTE YOUR TIME SIFTING FLOUR.

You've likely come across a recipe that asks you to sift an ingredient (usually flour, cocoa powder, or confectioners' sugar) before starting. You'll be relieved to find that in this book, I rarely ask you to sift ingredients, and especially not flour. Why? I think sifting flour is often a waste of time. Don't get me wrong—sometimes it's necessary to sift flour! If your bag of flour has been sitting in the cupboard too long and you find it has developed clumps, by all means, *sift away*.

But traditionally, recipes ask you to sift ingredients as a way to aerate them and guarantee consistency between cup measurements, since cups of unsifted flour will vary widely in weight depending on how tightly the flour was packed in the bag. And back in the day, wheat milling techniques weren't as streamlined as they are now. Flour was ground to inconsistent sizes, leading to temperamental results in recipes. Sifting the flour helped promote consistency in recipe results by removing the larger particles that could potentially cause densely textured baked goods or even ones that would sink in the middle. But modern techniques have improved significantly since then, and now produce refined and clump-free flours that don't need to be sifted.

That being said, take a look in the bag or container of flour before you start. If your flour has been sitting untouched for several months, then yeah, you'll probably need to sift it. But there's a shortcut, too: if you don't already, store your flour in a large, airtight container instead of its original bag. Use a fork or whisk to stir the flour before measuring it. It's *much* easier than having to sift the entire bag of flour.

And finally, if you're making a dessert with an incredibly light batter that needs to be folded—by all means, sift your ingredients! But, if you're working with a batter that can be mixed in a stand mixer, most of those flour clumps will likely work themselves out in the mixing process.

DON'T BE AFRAID TO LEAVE INGREDIENTS ON THE COUNTER TO BRING THEM TO ROOM TEMPERATURE.

The official guidelines from the United States Department of Health & Human Services is that most refrigerated and perishable foods can be left at room temperature, out of the sun, for up to 2 hours; if it's a 90°F day or hotter, that time frame narrows to 1 hour.

Between you and me, I *bend* those guidelines. Because a lot of my baking happens in the evening, I bring my butter and eggs to room temperature by removing them from the fridge right before I head off to work. I keep these ingredients in a cool, dark corner of the kitchen, far from any sunlight or residual heat from appliances. By the time I get home from my 8-hour workday, the ingredients are at room temperature. But know that my house runs cold, usually with a temperature between 60° and 65°F. If you're the kind of person who likes to keep your heat high (say, 80°F), your eggs might spoil if left at room temperature for 8 hours.

There's a little more leeway when it comes to butter. Butter can be kept at room temperature for up to 3 days; store it in an airtight container on the counter, away from sunlight and any heat-emitting appliances. I recommend keeping butter at room temperature if you're planning on tackling a recipe within the next few days. Otherwise, it's best to keep butter in the refrigerator to prevent it from turning rancid. If stored properly, butter will keep in the refrigerator for up to 1 month and in the freezer for up to 1 year. Butter can absorb odors, so if you're planning on storing it long-term, wrap the sticks in an extra layer of plastic wrap, place them in a zip-top bag, and store them in the refrigerator or freezer as far away from the meat and produce drawers as you can. To thaw frozen butter, place the butter in the refrigerator the day before you plan to use it. Butter has gone bad when it smells like the odors of your fridge and, when sliced, the outside of the butter is a slightly different color than the inside.

I'm more cautious when it comes to other dairy products like milk and cream. Right when I get home, I'll remove those products from the fridge and then cook myself a quick dinner or maybe hit the gym. By the time I'm done, an hour or two later, the ingredients will be at room temperature.

How to bring common baking ingredients to room temperature quickly.

So you read the section above but you *still* forgot to bring everything to room temperature. It happens to the best of us! Here are some of my secrets to bring common baking ingredients to room temperature quickly:

butter

It can take anywhere from 30 minutes to an hour for refrigerated butter to soften to room temperature. Speed things up by cutting the butter into 1-inch cubes: Take a stick of butter and halve it lengthwise. Flip the butter on its side and halve it lengthwise again. At this point, you should have four long columns of butter. Hold the columns together and slice crosswise into 1-inch pieces. Each piece will be a rough cube.

Place the butter cubes in a microwave-safe bowl and microwave at 20% power in 10-second intervals until the butter cubes have softened (it really shouldn't take more than 20 seconds or so). If you don't have a microwave, you can place the butter cubes in a double boiler over medium-low heat for around 1 minute. Just be careful to keep an eye on the butter, because once it gets going, it melts fast!

Perfectly softened butter should still be slightly cool to the touch. The butter cubes should hold their shape when lightly poked. If you want to be technical about it, use a digital thermometer—a thermometer inserted into one of the butter cubes should read between 65° and 70°F, which is generally the range people mean when they say "room temperature" for ingredients.

eggs

To bring whole eggs to room temperature quickly, fill a small or medium bowl with warm water. You want the temperature to feel like a warm bath (one that's not too hot—you don't want to end up accidentally cooking the eggs!). Carefully place the eggs in the water and let them sit for 5 to 10 minutes. If you do this at the beginning of prepping a recipe, the eggs will be at room temperature right as you finish prepping the rest of your ingredients (especially since most recipes in this book require 5 to 10 minutes of ingredient prep).

If you're working with a recipe that calls for the eggs to be separated into whites and yolks, it's easier to separate them while the eggs are still cold—at room temperature, yolks break easily. To bring egg whites and yolks to room temperature, separate the cold eggs, placing the whites and yolks in separate thick ramekins. Set the ramekins in a cake pan and pour very hot water (not warm water this time—the heat needs to penetrate the ramekins) into the pan until the water reaches halfway up the sides of the ramekins. Let sit for 5 to 10 minutes.

buttermilk, cream, and milk

Buttermilk, cream, and milk are easy to bring to room temperature quickly: simply pour the amount needed for the recipe into a microwave-safe container and heat at 20% power in 10-second intervals until the liquid has warmed to room temperature. Just be careful not to leave in the microwave unattended for long periods—when warmed, cream has a tendency to foam, and buttermilk has a tendency to separate (though giving it a good whisking before using it in the recipe solves this easily). If you don't have a microwave, heat the amount needed in a small saucepan over medium-low heat for a minute or so, swirling the pan every 10 seconds.

crème fraîche, sour cream, and yogurt

Cultured dairy like crème fraîche, sour cream, and yogurt is a bit trickier to bring to room temperature quickly; they take on a funky odor when warmed in the microwave. My solution is low tech. I scoop out the amount needed for the recipe and place it in a heatproof bowl. I then place the heatproof bowl on top of my oven, close to where it vents heat (most ovens have a "hot spot" on the surface of its range where this occurs). As the oven preheats, it should warm the dairy to room temperature.

If you have a fancy oven that doesn't emit heat this way, you can always warm up the dairy in a double boiler. Cook over medium-low heat for 1 minute, whisking continuously to prevent it from scorching.

BELIEVE IN THE POWER OF PREP AND PREP AHEAD.

Prep your ingredients by measuring them out and ensuring that they're all at the right temperature before you proceed with *any* of a recipe's steps. Keep an eye out for ingredients that need to be melted or boiled, fruit that needs to be peeled and sliced, spices that need to be ground, and chocolate and nuts that need to be chopped—these tend to be the more time-consuming tasks in ingredient prep.

If you find yourself tackling a baking recipe with a ton of ingredients that need to be prepped beforehand, don't be afraid to do these far ahead of the recipe itself. Chopped nuts and chocolate and ground spices will keep for six months to a year if stored properly (store chopped nuts in the freezer, and chopped chocolate and ground spices in a cool, dark, dry place away from major heat sources). There's also no need to limit yourself to only the quantity required for the recipe; you can prep in bulk to ensure you'll have some on hand the next time you want to make the recipe. I frequently apply this long-term Prep Ahead philosophy in my kitchen: if I know I'm making chocolate chip cookies multiple times in the span of a few weeks (I have a sweet tooth, what can I say?), I take 10 to 15 minutes to chop one of those mega Pound Plus blocks of chocolate from Trader Joe's. The chopped chocolate will stretch over several recipes, and I won't have to chop chocolate again until I run out of this batch.

For more perishable ingredients like fruit, you can still prep up to a few days beforehand. Depending on how ripe your fruit is, prepped fruit will keep in an airtight container in the fridge for up to 3 days. If you're working with a fruit that tends to turn brown (apples, pears, and bananas are all likely to oxidize), squeeze half a lemon over the fruit and give it a good toss before storing. Don't panic too much if the fruit oxidizes—if you're baking the fruit into a pie or a crisp, it's likely to turn brown and lose its color in the oven anyway.

TIMING IS EVERYTHING, UNTIL IT'S NOT— DON'T FORGET TO RELY ON VISUAL CUES.

What if a recipe tells you it takes 3 minutes to cream butter and sugar, but you find that it's plenty fluffy a minute into the creaming process? What if it tells you it takes 40 minutes to bake a cake, but you open the oven door after 40 minutes and find that the batter is still completely raw? Well, trust your gut. Stop creaming earlier; leave the cake in the oven longer. When it comes to baking, there are a ton of variables at play, and recipe writers like myself aren't always going to know what they are and how to account for them. It could be a 90°F day, which means that your butter is meltier than usual and creaming faster than it did on the winter day when I developed the recipe. Or your batter is still raw because you forgot about the importance of an oven thermometer (see page 32) and are now unknowingly baking a cake at a temperature lower than what the recipe actually calls for. That's why it's important to pay attention to the visual cues provided in the recipe—they can be more accurate than timing cues, and will help guide you through all the unknowns.

UNDERSTAND THE DIFFERENCE BETWEEN ACTIVE AND PASSIVE TIME IN RECIPES, AND FIGURE OUT HOW TO USE THE LATTER TO YOUR ADVANTAGE.

Here's the dirty little secret about baking: the most time-consuming element of baking recipes is the act of baking the good itself. Everything else—prepping ingredients, mixing batter, kneading dough, and whatever else—usually doesn't take long at all. And most baking recipes can be divided into three units of time: Prep Time, Work Time, and Bake Time.

Although I'll be going into this in more detail on page 47, a quick summary is this: Prep Time refers to how long it takes to prep the ingredients, Work Time is how long you'll be working through the steps of the recipe, and Bake Time is how long the batter or dough spends in the oven. Both Prep Time and Work Time are "active"—time when you're *actively* working by prepping ingredients, mixing batters and doughs, and following the recipe's steps. But Bake Time is "passive time"—you're not really doing anything but waiting for your recipe to finish baking.

Although Bake Time is usually the only explicit form of passive time in baking recipes, train yourself to watch out for more hidden throughout recipes. Instructions related to bringing ingredients to specific temperature are usually a good clue—waiting for something to be melted, cooled, or boiled qualifies as passive time. Anything that needs to be creamed or whisked with a stand mixer for extended periods of time is also considered passive time. Take advantage of that passive time by multitasking: prep whatever comes next in the recipe (you'll notice that some of the tips on the previous pages advise you to do exactly this) or clean a few dishes.

So when you see me telling you throughout this book that you'll have a baked good ready with less than 15 minutes of work, that means you're only *actively* working for 15 minutes. **But it doesn't necessarily mean that your baked good will be ready to eat in 15 minutes.** You'll need to account for passive time, too.

RECIPES: BEFORE YOU START

PREP, WORK, AND BAKE TIME

Each recipe will have an estimate for *Prep Time*, *Work Time*, and *Bake Time*.

PREP TIME

Maybe you've heard the term *mise en place* before. It's a fancy French culinary term that roughly translates to "put in place." This refers to the setup required before cooking—the organizing and arranging of ingredients and tools needed to follow a recipe before you get started with its first step. But I'm not that fancy, so I just call this process "Prep Time" throughout the book.

Thankfully, it's rare that you'll need to do *that* much prep for baking recipes. Unlike cooking, which often requires you to do things such as peel, chop, and process ingredients like vegetables and meat, most baking ingredients already come prepped! Unless you're a super DIYer who likes to mill your own flour and grind your own confectioners' sugar, most of the prep needed for one of my recipes is simply the act of reaching into your pantry and fridge for ingredients and measuring out what is needed for the recipe. **As a result, most of my recipes only require 5 to 10 minutes of Prep Time.**

Note that Prep Time happens *before* you start the first step of the recipe. Read the ingredients list in full before even reading the steps. Be sure to take note of anything that has a comma after it, because that means the ingredient requires an extra step of prep aside from measuring it. For instance, "2 pounds ripe apples, peeled, cored, and diced into 1-inch cubes" means you'll weigh out the apples, then peel, core, and dice them. Alternately, watch out for instructions like this one: "12 ounces peeled bananas." That means you'll be peeling the bananas first, then weighing them.

Are you the sort of person who reads this and thinks, "Pssh, prep time! I don't need prep time, I'll grab and measure the ingredients as I follow the steps"? Ahh, yes. I used to live on the edge, just like you. And I have countless stories of how I discovered, halfway through the recipe, that I didn't actually have enough of an ingredient on hand and ended up with a lackluster baked good that was missing an egg or half a stick of butter. Sometimes I failed to make it at all since it turned out I was missing *several* key ingredients and didn't realize until I was already three-quarters of the way through the recipe. Or I could tell you about all the times I ended up overmixing a batter because I was distracted by frantically trying to prep the next ingredient to throw in. So trust me on this one—the few minutes of prep beforehand is worth it and will make your baking process go much smoother than without it.

WORK TIME

"Work Time" is the time, after you've finished gathering your ingredients, when you start actively going through the steps in the recipe. For this book, I timed each of the recipes from the moment I started the first step right to the moment after I placed the baked good in the oven and set the timer.

You'll notice that most recipes in this book have Work Times that range from 15 to 20 minutes. This is weeknight baking, after all! There will be a handful of recipes in which the Work Time will be longer; in those instances, you'll have the option of either breaking down the recipe in steps so you're only actively working for 15 minutes each night over 3 nights, or just committing to the full 45 minutes to get it done. The choice is yours—live the life you want.

BAKE TIME

"Bake Time" is the easy one: it starts from the moment you place your batter or dough on the oven rack and ends right when you pull the finished baked good from the oven. The accuracy of every recipe's Bake Time will depend on your oven and how accurate its temperature is. Since most ovens run too hot or too cold, I suggest getting an oven thermometer (see page 32) to know what you're working with and calibrate the oven to the right temperature yourself by adjusting the oven temperature up or down based on the oven thermometer's reading. Because if the oven runs too hot, you might accidentally burn your baked good. If it runs too cold, you'll be sitting around waiting for a recipe that takes way longer than what the Bake Time promised. I don't want one of my 30-minute recipes to turn into a 3-hour endeavor!

Note that while these times are approximations, they're *pretty good* approximations—my testers and I made each recipe *at least* five times and timed it every step of the way to make sure we were getting consistent results. But realistically, there are some things I just don't know about. Like what if your kitchen is the size of a football field? Or you keep your ingredients up three flights of stairs? So just give or take a few minutes for each estimate, and try not to hate me if it's too far off.

CUPS VERSUS OUNCES

The recipes in this book contain measurements in both volume (in cups) and weight (in ounces). I've already encouraged you multiple times to measure your ingredients by weight as opposed to by volume. But here I'm going to talk about the few times throughout the book where I *don't* provide weight measures for certain ingredients.

I don't provide weight measures for fruit used in a pie or tart recipe (see Any Kind of Fruit Pie on page 205 as an example). That's because the weight measures for the same volume of fruit will vary significantly due to a number of variables. Take strawberries—are you using organic ones from the local farmers' market? If so, they'll likely be smaller and weigh less than the ones you can buy in the grocery store shipped all the way from another country. Are they in season? If they are, they will be juicier and plumper, weighing more than the same kind during the wintertime. And what about different strawberry varieties? Are you using smaller Hood strawberries or larger Ventana strawberries? Are you stressed out yet?

Because of all these factors, it doesn't make much sense to provide weight measures for fruit— with one exception. In instances where the fruit is used in the recipe to play a crucial role in the baked good's crumb and texture, it absolutely makes sense to have weight measurements. Banana Bread (page 57) is one such recipe—too much banana will cause the loaf to collapse in the middle, while too little will result in a dry and bland bread. But for recipes where the fruit doesn't have any impact on the recipe's structural integrity (like when it's used as a filling for Any Kind of Fruit Pie on page 205, or a topping for Choose-Your-LOE Berries and Cream Tart on page 185), volume measurements are just fine.

OUNCES VERSUS FLUID OUNCES

In baking, there are two major units of weight: grams and ounces. I use the latter in this book, which is a little controversial since the word *ounce* can be confusing as a unit of measure. It is frequently used to denote two different types of measures: ounces, a measurement of weight, and fluid ounces, a measurement of volume.

I've already discussed how volume and weight measures are different (see page 35 if you need a refresher). But when it comes to ounces and fluid ounces, it's a common mistake to conflate the two as the same thing. Because a cup of water happens to equal both 8 fluid ounces in volume *and* 8 ounces in weight, it's easy to think that the two can be used interchangeably. This is flat-out incorrect—water (and other fluids with a density similar to water, like milk and vinegar) is the exception rather than the rule. To understand this, just think of 1 cup of flour and 1 cup of milk.

Whereas they'll both have the same volume (8 fluid ounces), 1 cup of flour weighs 4.5 ounces and 1 cup of milk weighs 8 ounces.

So in this book, when you see a liquid ingredient with an ounce measure next to it, **that ounce measure will always refer to the weight of the liquid and *not* its volume (fluid ounces)**. If you measure a liquid ingredient by volume in a liquid measuring cup, it's likely that the ingredient's *volume* in fluid ounces will be similar to its *weight* in ounces. But always remember that that's the exception rather than the rule.

INGREDIENT TEMPERATURES

Most of the recipes in this book will have ingredients listed with certain temperature cues like "whole milk, **at room temperature**" or "**very cold** unsalted butter." If it's an ingredient that's kept in the fridge (like butter, milk, or eggs) and you don't see a temperature cue next to it, **you can use the ingredient straight from the fridge, still chilled.** Neat, right? Because I know how time-consuming it can be to bring ingredients to room temperature, I experimented to see if I could get the same results with cold ingredients as with those ingredients at room temperature. I discovered that in some recipes you can, and in some you definitely *cannot*—so if an ingredient has a specific temperature noted (usually "boiling hot," "at room temperature," or "very cold"), pay attention! That means the temperature of the ingredient *really* matters in that recipe (especially if it's in **bold**), and anything otherwise will lead to batters and doughs that won't mix properly and will curdle or melt if the ingredients aren't at the specified temperatures.

"**Boiling hot**" means freshly boiled; prep that ingredient first and cover it with a pot lid or a heatproof plate to keep it hot as you prep the rest of the ingredients (as directed on page 38). "**At room temperature**" means the ingredient needs to be softened to room temperature, which is ideally at 70°F (although you can get away with a range between 65° and 75°F). "**Very cold**" ingredients should be coming from the coldest part of your fridge; to be extra safe, attend to it first by sticking it in the freezer for 5 to 10 minutes as you prep the rest of the ingredients. Just don't forget that it's there!

LOAF CAKES

Loaf cakes are the perfect weeknight baking project. They come together with just 20 minutes of Work Time and are so moist and flavorful on their own that no frosting is required. Many loaf cakes keep well at room temperature. They taste even better the day after they're baked, with flavors that deepen the longer they sit.

Despite all these great weeknight baking qualities, I didn't always love baking loaf cakes. Although I've always found loaf cake batter a breeze to mix together, it was a completely different ball game once I placed it in the oven. Most loaf cake recipes tend to bake unevenly—the edges will brown far quicker than the center, leaving the baker to choose between a cake with a slightly burnt bottom and sides versus one with perfect edges but an underbaked center.

It became my mission to solve this issue. I made many different loaf cake recipes to showcase on *Hummingbird High*, experimenting with oven temperatures and altering Bake Times, all with no luck. One day, I failed to follow my own advice on prepping ingredients (see page 44) and found myself missing a half stick of butter for a pound cake recipe. Instead of running to the store, I decided to reduce the rest of the ingredients in the recipe to match the amount of butter I had on hand. Doing so would make a smaller loaf, sure, but one that would be enough to satisfy my craving. When I pulled it out of the oven, I was surprised to find that I'd baked the perfect loaf: moist and flavorful in the center, and more important, with no burnt bottom or edges.

I realized then that the loaf cake recipes I'd previously tried produced more batter than what was actually needed for a reasonable size loaf. That excess batter was causing the bottoms and edges of my loaf cakes to burn, since all that batter took too long to bake in one pan. I decided to apply this theory to some of my favorite loaf cake recipes, reducing the ingredient quantities to make less batter. It worked! All came out perfectly, with no overdone edges in sight.

Along the way, I also discovered that the right cake pan is crucial in delivering a perfectly baked loaf cake. Enamelware, glass, and ceramic pans don't perform as well as more traditional bakeware like professional, insulated metal cake pans. These are pans made from two layers of metal with a layer of air sandwiched in between them. The layer of air acts as an insulator, preventing the bottom and edges of your loaf cake from burning.

Alas, I know that professional cake pans are a luxury. So there are ways to hack it at home without having to buy a new set. You can place your loaf pan on a sheet pan when baking; the extra layer of metal helps insulate the bottom of the loaf cake. Even better, if you've purchased your loaf pan as a stackable set of two, you can double them up to re-create a "professional" insulated pan. Cool, right?

After I figured out these tricks, my loaf cakes came out perfect each time. Loaf cakes quickly became one of my favorite weeknight baking projects—and I hope they'll become one of yours, too.

classic pound cake

When I find myself craving a yellow cake but don't want to put in the time and energy to make one from scratch, I make this classic pound cake. Pound cake gets its name from its ratios—traditional pound cake recipes call for a pound of each of its main ingredients (flour, sugar, butter, eggs). The recipe steps are straightforward and the batter comes together quickly. The best part? With a smear of Nutella or peanut butter, a slice of classic pound cake tastes like your favorite yellow cake with frosting.

ACTIVE TIME

25 minutes

prep time: **5 minutes**
work time: **20 minutes**
bake time: **60 minutes**

makes one 9 x 5-inch loaf cake

NOTE: Because this recipe uses so few ingredients, each ingredient must be the very best quality you can find. This is one where it's worth sourcing high-quality European butter (I'm partial to Vermont Creamery's European-style cultured butter).

1⅔ cups (7.5 ounces) all-purpose flour

1 teaspoon kosher salt

1¼ cups (10 ounces) unsalted butter, at room temperature

1¼ cups (8.75 ounces) granulated sugar

1 teaspoon pure vanilla extract

5 large eggs

1. Position a rack in the center of the oven and preheat the oven to 350°F. Spray a 9 x 5-inch loaf pan with cooking spray and line it with parchment paper, leaving a 2-inch overhang on the long sides. Spray the parchment, too.

2. In a medium bowl, whisk together the flour and salt.

3. In the bowl of a stand mixer fitted with the paddle attachment, beat the butter on medium-low until smooth and creamy, about 1 minute. Add the sugar and vanilla; increase the mixer to medium-high and beat until light, fluffy, and doubled in volume, about 5 minutes, using a rubber spatula to scrape down the bottom and sides of the bowl as necessary. Reduce the mixer to low and add the eggs one at a time, adding the next egg only after the previous one has been fully incorporated, scraping down the bottom and sides of the bowl after each addition. With the mixer on low, gradually add the dry ingredients and beat until just combined. Scrape down the bottom and sides of the bowl once more, and beat on low for an additional 30 seconds.

4. Pour the batter into the prepared pan and use an offset spatula to smooth the top. Set the loaf pan on a sheet pan and bake for 60 to 65 minutes, or until a skewer inserted into the center of the cake comes out with a few crumbs attached. Cool on a wire rack. Serve warm or at room temperature. The cake can be stored at room temperature, wrapped tightly in plastic wrap, for up to 3 days.

variation

lemon pound cake

Make the pound cake as directed, but add the zest of 2 medium lemons to the butter and sugar when creaming. Proceed as directed, but substitute 1 teaspoon lemon extract for the vanilla. This variation does not significantly affect Prep, Work, or Bake Time.

banana bread

I know that whenever I buy a bunch of bananas, I always end up with one or two left over, ripened a few days past their prime. It's easy to take these bananas and throw them into a satisfying, tasty batter for banana bread. Furthermore, banana bread is a great weeknight baking project because it uses ingredients most of us already have on hand.

Because there are a million recipes for banana bread, I knew mine had to punch above its weight in terms of flavor. As a result, my recipe uses about ½ cup more fruit than most, but doesn't ask you to cook, strain, or mash the bananas beforehand like other recipes. I find these steps to be unnecessary, yielding little extra flavor but adding lots of extra mess and Work Time—a definite no-no for weeknight baking projects. A touch of sour cream, however, ensures that the loaf stays incredibly moist the next day; in a pinch, you can substitute crème fraîche or yogurt for the sour cream.

ACTIVE TIME

23 minutes

prep time: **8 minutes**

work time: **15 minutes**

bake time: **60 minutes**

makes one 9 x 5-inch loaf cake

NOTE: This recipe works best if you use incredibly ripe, spotted, and *almost* black bananas. If you bought bananas specifically for this recipe, check out Bananas About Bananas on page 61 for neat tricks on how to ripen them quickly and store any extras for future baking projects.

NOTE: Bananas are listed in the recipe by weight, not volume or size. Why? It's risky *not* to include exact measures for banana bread. Too little banana, and your bread will turn out dry, flavorless, and maybe even soapy tasting (banana's natural acidity helps neutralize the baking soda in the recipe, so without enough fruit, the banana bread will taste like baking soda!). But too much banana, and your bread might take forever to bake or collapse in the center. For best results, first peel the bananas, then use a digital scale to weigh the naked fruit. For those of you who need volume measurements, that's 1½ cups mashed bananas, from around 3 large bananas.

2 cups (9 ounces) all-purpose flour

1 teaspoon baking soda

1 teaspoon kosher salt

½ cup (4 ounces) unsalted butter, at room temperature

1 cup tightly packed (7.5 ounces) dark brown sugar

2 large eggs

½ cup (4 ounces) sour cream

1 tablespoon pure vanilla extract

12 ounces very ripe peeled bananas

1. Position a rack in the center of the oven and preheat the oven to 350°F. Spray a 9 x 5-inch loaf pan with cooking spray and line it with parchment paper, leaving a 2-inch overhang on the long sides. Spray the parchment, too.

2. In a medium bowl, whisk together the flour, baking soda, and salt.

3. In the bowl of a stand mixer fitted with the paddle attachment, combine the butter and sugar. Beat on medium-high until light, fluffy, and doubled in volume, 3 to 5 minutes, using a rubber spatula to scrape down the bottom and sides of the bowl as necessary. Reduce the mixer to low and add the eggs one at a time, adding the next egg only after the previous one has been fully incorporated, scraping down the bottom and sides of the bowl after each addition. Add the sour cream and vanilla all at once and beat on low until combined. Gradually add the dry ingredients and beat until just combined. Add the bananas a handful at a time and beat until broken into pieces and distributed evenly throughout the batter, about 1 minute. Scrape down the bottom and sides of the bowl once more, and beat on low for an additional 30 seconds.

4. Pour the batter into the prepared pan and use an offset spatula to smooth the top. Set the loaf pan on a sheet pan and bake for 60 to 65 minutes, or until a skewer inserted into the center of the banana bread comes out with a few crumbs attached. Cool on a wire rack. Serve warm or at room temperature. The banana bread can be stored at room temperature, wrapped tightly in plastic wrap, for up to 3 days.

variations

instagram babe banana bread

This is an impressive variation that makes a beautiful banana bread with barely any extra work. Use a sharp knife to slice an extra peeled banana (there's no need to weigh it!) in half lengthwise. Pour the batter into the prepared loaf pan and place the banana halves, cut-side up, on top. Bake as directed. Take a shot for Instagram when it's out of the oven; watch the likes roll in. This variation does not significantly affect Prep, Work, or Bake Time.

chocolate banana bread

Proceed with the recipe as directed, but add ½ cup (4 ounces) roughly chopped dark chocolate (at least 65% cocoa) to the batter after adding the bananas. Mix until the chocolate is evenly distributed throughout the batter, then pour the batter into the prepared loaf pan. Sprinkle another ½ cup (4 ounces) roughly chopped chocolate over the batter, then bake as directed. This variation adds about 5 minutes of Prep Time for chopping the chocolate.

peanut butter cup banana bread

You know those mini peanut butter cups at Trader Joe's? I'm obsessed with them. I can eat an entire bucket in one sitting, easily. But I'd rather not, so I try to use them up in my baked goods—like banana bread. Proceed with the recipe as directed, but add 1 cup (8 ounces) mini peanut butter cups to the batter after adding the bananas. Bake as directed. This variation does not significantly affect Prep, Work, or Bake Time.

Don't live near a Trader Joe's and/or have no idea what I'm talking about? No worries! Quarter some regular-size peanut butter cups and use those instead. This variation adds about 5 minutes of Work Time, to chop the peanut butter cups.

bananas about bananas
everything you wanted to know about baking with bananas

on ripening bananas

The riper your bananas are, the sweeter and more flavorful your banana bread will be. You want your bananas to be *really* ripe; they're ready to be baked with when they are super spotty and almost black.

There are a ton of tips available online about how to ripen your bananas faster; I've tried most and am sorry to report that many don't work and just create more mess for you to clean up. I have a couple tricks up my sleeve, too, but unfortunately, these tricks still take time—there's no magic bullet for ripening bananas quickly.

That being said, there *are* ways to speed up the process: If your bananas are attached together at the stem, pull them apart to separate them. Place all the bananas in a paper bag and seal. Store in a warm spot for a few days—once you open the bag, you'll have riper bananas! Bananas release ethylene gas, which controls the fruit's ripening process, and much of that gas is released at the stem. Separating the bananas allows this gas to release faster, and sealing the bag traps the gas and speeds up the ripening process. You can stick other fruits (avocados, pears, apples, etc.) in the bag, and they'll ripen faster, too.

on freezing bananas

If your bananas get *too* ripe and you're unable to use them immediately, freeze them! You can freeze bananas with or without their peels, but I prefer the former because they last longer that way and aren't as susceptible to freezer burn. I put bananas, skin and all, in a gallon-size zip-top bag (to make sure they don't impart their flavor to anything else in the freezer) and freeze them. Don't panic if the peel turns entirely black—that's totally normal, and the fruit inside remains edible and unaffected.

When using frozen bananas in any recipe, transfer them to the fridge, still in their bag, and thaw them overnight. Alternatively, you can thaw them on your counter at room temperature for a few hours. Remove them from their bag and place them on a plate; as the bananas thaw, they'll release a seemingly large amount of liquid. Don't throw it out! Simply dump the fruit and its liquid into a bowl and whisk them together before incorporating the banana into the recipe as directed. That banana juice is actually the secret to the very best banana bread, keeping it extremely moist and flavorful.

on mashing bananas

A lot of recipes for banana bread instruct you to mash your bananas before using them. Here's a secret: If you've ripened your bananas properly, *you don't need to do that.* Save yourself some time (and another dirty dish)! Your stand mixer or even a handheld electric mixer will easily smash through ripe bananas without difficulty; I like to throw them in last, letting the mixer break them down and distribute them perfectly throughout the batter.

choose-your-own pumpkin spice bread

I first discovered this recipe when I was living a few blocks from the famous San Francisco bakery Tartine. In the fall, I'd brave the long line, ignore their famous croissants, and instead opt for a slice of their seasonal pumpkin loaf bread. It was light and fluffy, and tasted like pumpkin pie. When I moved away, I bought a copy of their cookbook just so I could make the loaf bread and get my fix in my new city. I was pleasantly surprised to find that the recipe came together quickly and was perfect for weeknight baking; unlike most loaf cakes, it used oil instead of butter, skipping the need to cream butter and sugar together. The oil also kept the loaf flavorful and moist for much longer, perfect for savoring a slice to get me through my weekday mornings.

I've since customized their recipe with my own mix of pumpkin spice, and you can, too! If you choose to make your own spice blend, just be sure to add another 5 minutes or so to the Prep Time, since the recipe assumes you've already mixed your pumpkin spice.

 **ACTIVE TIME**

20 minutes

prep time: **5 minutes**

work time: **15 minutes**

bake time: **60 minutes**

makes one 9 x 5-inch loaf cake

1¾ cup plus 1 tablespoon (8.15 ounces) all-purpose flour

1 recipe Classic Pumpkin Spice, Vanilla Pumpkin Spice, Chai Pumpkin Spice, or Actually Spicy Pumpkin Spice (page 67)

1½ teaspoons baking powder

½ teaspoon baking soda

1 teaspoon kosher salt

1 cup plus 2 tablespoons (9 ounces) canned pumpkin puree

1 cup (8 ounces) canola oil

2 teaspoons pure vanilla extract

1⅓ cups (9.35 ounces) plus 2 tablespoons granulated sugar

3 large eggs

1. Position a rack in the center of the oven and preheat the oven to 350°F. Spray a 9 x 5-inch loaf pan with cooking spray and line it with parchment paper, leaving a 2-inch overhang on the long sides. Spray the parchment, too.

2. In a medium bowl, whisk together the flour, pumpkin spice, baking powder, baking soda, and salt.

3. In the bowl of a stand mixer fitted with the whisk attachment, combine the pumpkin puree, oil, vanilla, and 1⅓ cups (9.35 ounces) of the sugar. Whisk on medium-low until just combined, about 1 minute, using a rubber spatula to scrape down the bottom and sides of the bowl as necessary. Add the eggs one at a time, adding the next egg only after the previous one has been fully incorporated, scraping down the bottom and sides of the bowl after each addition. With the mixer on low, gradually add the dry ingredients and whisk until just combined. Scrape down the bottom and sides of the bowl once more, and whisk on medium for an additional 15 seconds.

4. Pour the batter into the prepared pan and use an offset spatula to smooth the top. Sprinkle with the remaining 2 tablespoons sugar. Set the loaf pan on a sheet pan and bake for 60 to 65 minutes, or until a skewer inserted into the center of the cake comes out with a few crumbs attached. There will still be patches of sugar on top, but that's totally okay, I promise! In fact, that's the look you want. Cool on a wire rack. Serve warm or at room temperature. The cake can be stored at room temperature, wrapped tightly in plastic wrap, for up to 3 days.

variations

pumpkin brûlée bread

This is a really impressive variation that requires barely any extra work. When you pull your pumpkin bread out of the oven, there should still be patches of granulated sugar on top. Cool for 20 to 30 minutes on a wire rack, then use a chef's torch to brûlée the patches of sugar until melted and golden brown. Serve immediately. This variation does not significantly affect Prep, Work, or Bake Time.

toasted coconut pumpkin bread

Proceed with the recipe as directed, but use melted coconut oil instead of canola oil in the recipe. In the final step, substitute 2 tablespoons coconut sugar for the granulated sugar; combine the coconut sugar and ¼ cup (about 0.5 ounces) large raw coconut flakes in a small bowl. Sprinkle the mixture over the batter. Bake as directed. This variation does not significantly affect Prep, Work, or Bake Time.

brown butter pumpkin bread

Brown butter adds an extra nutty flavor to this bread, and its intensity will mute the flavor of the spices. If you want your bread to maintain the same level of spice, I suggest increasing the pumpkin spice in the recipe by a half.

Before starting the recipe, you'll need to brown 1 cup (8 ounces) unsalted butter following the instructions on page 161 and let it cool. Proceed with the recipe as directed, but use the brown butter instead of the canola oil in the recipe. This variation adds about 10 minutes of Work Time.

an ode to the grind
everything you wanted to know about grinding your own spices

Over time, spices lose their flavor, and a lot of spices you buy preground in bottles from the grocery store are actually years old and ultimately flavorless. As a result, many cookbooks and recipes will encourage you to grind whole spices yourself. But doing so is meticulous work that takes time. And we're weeknight baking over here, remember? There are a couple of solutions:

prep your spices ahead

Make your spice blend a few days before you plan to make your recipe. Keep the freshly ground spices in an airtight container (a small mason jar or a small zip-top bag will work perfectly here). But let me warn you that it can be time-consuming and potentially dangerous work, especially if you're using a Microplane grater to shave small, hard spice pods. Invest in an electric spice grinder to speed up the process (Cuisinart makes a wonderful model with dishwasher-safe parts). In a pinch, a coffee grinder will do, but be sure to grind some raw rice in it beforehand to clean out any lingering coffee (and after, to clean out any spices if you plan on using it for coffee once more).

visit a local spice shop

Visit a local spice shop and ask them to grind the spices for you. Lots of spice shops have fancy machinery that will be more efficient than whatever spice grinder you have at home. This cuts down on the effort required (though not necessarily the time, since you have to find a local spice shop). Alternatively, a lot of spice shops have bulk bins that have the spices already preground. Don't be afraid to ask when it was all processed or ask for something freshly ground if necessary.

shop smart

Can't find a local spice shop? No problem. When shopping for spices in the grocery store, check the "sell by" date to get an idea of when the spice was ground. Try to find a "sell by" date that's furthest ahead of the current date. That usually means the spice was processed more recently.

don't worry

Shrug your shoulders and don't stress out about it. Let me be honest with you—between juggling my day job and my blog, I didn't always have the time to grind my own spices. And my cakes still came out great. Yours will, too.

pumpkin spice
(and all its variations)

I'll admit it: I wasn't always a fan of pumpkin spice. It was only when a friend of mine pointed out that I'd only ever tried it in Starbucks' Pumpkin Spice Lattes that I realized I should probably give it a chance. So one day, I rifled through my spice drawer and decided to make my own.

There are no strict rules here. But I think cinnamon and nutmeg are an absolute must. Everything else can come and go, depending on your preferences. Want a pumpkin spice that's less spice and more pumpkin? Easy—go heavy on the vanilla, light on everything else. Want a pumpkin spice that's actually spicy? Add lots of ginger and a touch of allspice and white pepper. I've included some basic recipes for you to start with, but I hope you eventually make this recipe your own.

 ACTIVE TIME

<5 minutes

prep time: **<5 minutes**
work time: **<5 minutes**

each makes about
3 tablespoons

CLASSIC PUMPKIN SPICE

5 teaspoons ground cinnamon

2 teaspoons ground nutmeg

¼ teaspoon ground cloves

VANILLA PUMPKIN SPICE

4 teaspoons ground cinnamon

2 teaspoons vanilla bean powder

¼ teaspoon ground cloves

¼ teaspoon ground nutmeg

CHAI PUMPKIN SPICE

1 tablespoon ground cardamom

2 teaspoons ground cinnamon

1 teaspoon ground ginger

½ teaspoon ground cloves

½ teaspoon ground nutmeg

ACTUALLY SPICY PUMPKIN SPICE

1 tablespoon ground cinnamon

1 tablespoon ground ginger

½ teaspoon ground white pepper

¼ teaspoon ground allspice

¼ teaspoon ground nutmeg

In a small bowl, whisk together the spices. Pour into a small, airtight container (like a mason jar), and store in a cool, dark place for up to 3 months.

loaf cakes 2.0

As a frequent weeknight baker, I often found myself with a pile of leftover baked goods getting stale on my counter. It seemed like a shame to throw anything out, so I began repurposing them as ingredients in other recipes as a way to make them tasty again. Since loaf cakes retain a lot of their flavors several days after they've been baked, they were the perfect candidates for these baking experiments. Here are my favorite ways to "revive" stale loaf cakes.

prep time: **<5 minutes**
work time: **none!**
bake time: **none!**

CAKE TOAST

Got leftover loaf cake on your counter that's going stale fast? Make cake toast! The toaster browns and crisps the slice of loaf cake, making it the perfect vehicle for butter and jam.

Toast a slice of loaf cake in your toaster on its lowest setting. A toaster oven would work best, but regular toasters work just fine, too. Just watch the timer—too long in the toaster, and the loaf cake might dry out too much. Serve with a pat of butter or your favorite breakfast spread like jam, jelly, peanut butter, or Nutella.

prep time: **<5 minutes**
work time: **5 minutes**
bake time: **none!**

makes 4 servings

CAKE FRENCH TOAST

One of my favorite restaurants in New York, Russ & Daughters Cafe, serves a custardy babka French toast with crispy edges. The French toast is made with slightly stale babka slices that they cook on the griddle. A lightbulb went off in my head: What if I took slices of my leftover loaf cake and did something similar?

2 large eggs

1 tablespoon heavy cream

Pinch of kosher salt

1 tablespoon unsalted butter, plus more for serving

4 thick (around 2-inch) slices stale loaf cake

Maple syrup, for serving

1. In a small shallow bowl, whisk together the eggs, cream, and salt.

2. In a medium, nonstick skillet, melt the butter over medium heat. Working quickly, dip one side of a slice of loaf cake into the egg mixture and allow the mixture to soak about halfway through the cake slice; flip and repeat with the other side. Allow any excess egg mixture to drip off the slice, then place in the pan. Cook until crisp and golden brown, about 2 minutes per side. Transfer the French toast to a plate and repeat with the remaining slices. Serve immediately, with maple syrup and butter.

CAKES

A few years ago, the start-up that I worked for held a talent show to showcase their employees' hobbies. For an hour and a half, we gathered to watch as many of us demonstrated a range of secret talents: a group of coworkers had formed a band and sang about life at our company; another coworker displayed a slideshow of the neon signs he liked to photograph; another described the scavenger hunt he'd designed for his young son, complete with a hand-drawn map, a metal detector, and buried treasure somewhere along the Oregon Coast shoreline.

I remember feeling intimidated after watching all my talented coworkers. For my presentation, I brought in a layer cake I'd made for my blog, which to me didn't seem all that special compared to their projects. I shakily approached the podium and held up the cake for everybody to see. Because it was almost Easter, I'd decorated the cake with a pale blue cream cheese frosting and used a paintbrush to fleck it with chocolate, similar to the surface of a robin's egg. As I explained how I'd achieved this effect, the crowd actually went wild (though I will say copious amounts of beer had been distributed), with my coworkers literally jumping up from their seats and begging for slices of the cake. I ended up winning a prize.

So if I had to pick the baked good that made me known as a serious baker among my friends, family, coworkers, and blog readers, I'd probably say it would be cake. Throughout the years, I've made a variety of different layer cakes, from classics like yellow cake with rich, dark chocolate frosting, to quirkier ones like a birthday cake topped with cotton candy, a Vietnamese iced coffee cake complete with coffee swirls, and a black-and-white cake inspired by the East Coast bomb cyclone of 2018. Baking and decorating cakes is my way of expressing creativity and having some fun, especially after several very dry hours of staring at numbers and code in the office.

But here's the funny thing about my cakes: although they look like the result of a full day's worth of work in the kitchen, they usually take me about an hour of work *at most* over a few evenings. That's because I break up the work—I've included the timeline on page 76 so you can, too. Cakes make for great weeknight baking because their timeline can be flexible. They're made with parts that store well in the refrigerator and freezer, allowing you to start and stop working on the recipe to fit your schedule.

But wait, there's more! *Their format* can be flexible, too: each recipe in this chapter can be made as a sheet cake, a double-layer cake (and in some cases, a triple-layer cake), or cupcakes. The best part? Most traditional cake recipes produce cakes that dome when baked; that dome usually needs to be sliced off with a serrated knife so the tops of the cake layers are level when you stack them to create a layer cake. But because my cake recipes hardly dome, you skip this step completely! This applies to cupcakes as well; although a small dome is traditional on cupcakes, I find that it's easier to frost flat-top cupcakes, both by hand and with a piping bag. I'm confident you will, too.

As always, the right tools are crucial here. If using a stand mixer, it's worth investing in a paddle beater with a scraper (see page 29). When using a stand mixer, ingredients sometimes stick to the bottom and sides of the bowl, requiring you to stop the mixer every so often and use a rubber spatula to scrape down the bowl to incorporate those ingredients. But a paddle beater with a scraper does this job fairly well, and you'll need to scrape the bowl only three times: once after the butter and sugar have been creamed, once after the eggs have been added, and a final time after the dry ingredients have been mixed in.

Finally, when making layer cakes, you're looking for two layers of equal size. Choose two cake pans from the same brand to make this easy. I like to use a digital scale to measure out equal amounts of batter into each pan, too. I've even included the approximate weight of the batter for each recipe to help you do the same. The easiest way to do this is to set a prepared cake pan on a digital scale, and tare it to "0." Pour batter into the pan until the scale registers the weight listed in the recipe. Repeat with the second cake pan. For cupcakes, use a liquid measuring cup or a cookie dough scoop to portion the batter evenly.

CAKE FLOUR VERSUS ALL-PURPOSE FLOUR

You'll notice that each recipe in this chapter uses cake flour. Cake flour has a much lower protein content than all-purpose flour and will result in a softer crumb; it's my secret ingredient to making the lightest and airiest cake possible. However, I *totally* get that it's annoying to store two different types of flour in your pantry. And that's fine—we can work with that!

There are ways to make your own cake flour at home with all-purpose and cornstarch, but I don't recommend that. We're weeknight baking, after all, and I don't want to add another step to your Prep and Work Times, since homemade cake flour formulas usually involve a lot of time-consuming sifting. Instead, I'm going to teach you how to convert each recipe to use all-purpose flour instead. It involves some basic math, sure, but at least it doesn't involve any sifting or last-minute trips to the grocery store.

Behold the golden rule:

1 cup cake flour = 1 cup all-purpose flour minus 2 tablespoons

What does that mean, exactly? Most recipes in this chapter use 2 cups of cake flour. If you were to swap out 2 cups of cake flour for the equivalent value of all-purpose flour, you would use 2 cups minus 4 tablespoons of all-purpose flour. If you translate that quantity to regular ingredient-speak, that would equal 1¾ cups of all-purpose flour (since 4 tablespoons = ¼ cup).

Note that the golden rule works well for whole quantities like 2-cup or 3-cup measures. But if the recipe calls for cake flour in fractional quantities like 2¼ cups or 3⅓ cups, it can get a little bit trickier. So perhaps it's easier to think about this relationship in mathematical ratios. A cup of cake flour is equal to 7/8 cup of all-purpose flour; multiplying the cup measure of cake flour by 0.875 (the decimal value of 7/8) will get you its equivalent cup measure of all-purpose flour. And to spare you from having to convert that value into the appropriate cup measure, you can just multiply that value by the weight of a cup of all-purpose flour (4.5 ounces) to get the amount of flour needed for the recipe!

That mathemagic looks like this:

(0.875 × cups of cake flour called for in the recipe) × 4.5 = ounces of all-purpose flour needed

To go back to the example above, if you multiply 2 cups of cake flour by 0.875, you get 1.75 (or 1¾ cups), which matches the values given by the golden rule. From there, determine how many ounces of all-purpose flour you'll need:

1.75 × 4.5 = 7.85 ounces all-purpose flour

If only my math teachers had told me that paying attention in class would save me many, many trips to the grocery store in my adult years.

weeknight baking layer cake schedule

DAY 1: BAKE AND FREEZE THE CAKES!

Most of the recipes in this chapter require only 15 minutes of Work Time; the real time-consuming parts are the Bake Time (which, depending on the kind of cake you're making, can be as long as 45 minutes) and waiting for the cake to cool before storing it.

If you're making the cake several days before you're planning to serve it, my advice is to freeze the cake and then frost it the night before serving. Never, ever store unfrosted cake in the refrigerator—refrigerating it dries it out quickly, whereas freezing it actually stops the drying process (more on that in a minute).

I like to wait until my cakes have cooled completely to freeze them, but if you're strapped for time, you can freeze them when they're still warm but cool enough to touch (usually after 15 to 20 minutes of cooling). There's actually a school of bakers who swear by this technique, arguing that it leads to an extra-moist cake since it traps escaping steam. However, I wouldn't recommend freezing a cake while it's still HOT—there's a chance that throwing a hot cake (or anything hot!) in the freezer will lower the unit's core temperature and cause other frozen foods to thaw, potentially causing a food safety issue.

Before you stick a cake in the freezer, you'll need to turn it out of its pan and remove the parchment paper. Wrap it carefully in a layer of plastic wrap, ensuring that every inch of its surface area is covered tightly. If you've got multiple cake layers, you'll need to wrap each one individually—wrap two together, and they'll stick. Once you've wrapped the cake once, wrap it tightly *again* in another sheet of plastic wrap. It may seem like a lot, but trust me—it's the best guard against freezer burn.

If you're planning to freeze your cake for longer than a few days, I recommend adding a layer of aluminum foil over the double layer of plastic wrap. Cake is especially susceptible to absorbing odors and flavors from other items in the freezer; aluminum foil will help prevent this. I like to use a heavy-duty marker to write the cake's flavor and the date it was made directly on the aluminum for identification purposes—in general, unfrosted cakes will keep in the freezer for up to 1 year. Set the wrapped cake flat in the freezer and freeze overnight; the next day, when it's frozen solid, you can store it on its side or on top of some other frozen items if you need to save room in your freezer. Just make sure it's really frozen solid or it might warp before you have a chance to decorate it.

In addition to keeping your cake fresh and moist, freezing has other advantages. A frozen cake is easier to frost than one at room temperature, since crumbs are less likely to separate from the cake and get mixed into the frosting. To thaw a frozen cake, you'll need to plan ahead—the day before you're planning to frost the cake, remove it from the freezer, remove and discard *only* the aluminum foil layer, then thaw the plastic-wrapped cake in the refrigerator overnight.

DAY 2: MAKE THE FROSTING AND APPLY A CRUMB COAT!

Frosting a warm or hot cake is a big no-no; steam escaping the cake will cause the frosting to melt. I usually like to wait until the second day to frost my cake. So go ahead and make that frosting now.

After making the frosting, I divide the batch into two parts: two-thirds to save for decorating (place this frosting in an airtight container and refrigerate overnight), and one-third to use now for a crumb coat. A crumb coat is a thin layer of frosting that's spread over the naked cake to trap crumbs. If you've ever tried to frost a cake without a crumb coat, you'll know that crumbs can shake loose from the cake and get caught in the frosting, leaving your cake with unsightly bumps. The crumb coat seals in any crumbs, allowing you to apply thicker and smoother layers of frosting later.

To apply a crumb coat, first stack your cakes, layering frosting between each cake to keep them together (for more in-depth instructions, see page 107). Then cover the surface of the entire layer cake with a thin layer of frosting—this is the crumb coat. Use just enough frosting to cover the entire cake completely. Refrigerate the cake overnight. I usually don't bother covering the cake with plastic wrap since I find that the frosting does a good enough job of sealing the moisture in; however, if that makes you nervous, chill the cake for 15 to 20 minutes to allow the frosting to solidify before covering it loosely with plastic wrap.

DAY 3: FINISH FROSTING AND EAT!

We made it to Day 3! Remove the frosting from the fridge. Transfer the frosting to the bowl of a stand mixer fitted with the paddle attachment and beat on medium-low to soften it before use. If you've found that the frosting isn't quite spreadable yet, follow any of the methods on page 97 to thaw the frosting to your ideal spreadability. Finish frosting the cake.

an expedited layer cake schedule

All right, I hear ya. Don't have three days to make one cake? What about two days? Bake the cake on Day 1—if you're planning on frosting it the next day and serving it immediately, there's no need to freeze it. Just wrap it tightly in two layers of plastic wrap and leave it at room temperature overnight.

Apply the crumb coat per Day 2's instructions. To make your life easier, you can stick the cakes in the freezer for 15 to 20 minutes before applying the crumb coat to help seal in any loose crumbs. After coating, refrigerate the cake for 15 to 20 minutes, or until the crumb coat is set. Try poking it gently with your finger; if you don't leave an indentation in the frosting, it's time for the next step. Remove the cake from the refrigerator and use the rest of the frosting to cover it completely, decorating it however you like.

Note that with this expedited schedule, you'll be doubling the amount of Work Time on Day 2. There will also be more passive waiting time if you choose to freeze the cake beforehand and as you wait for the crumb coat to set before frosting the cake completely.

yellow cake

 ACTIVE TIME

20 minutes

SHEET CAKE

makes one 9 x 13-inch cake

prep time: **5 minutes**

work time: **15 minutes**

bake time: **35 minutes**

LAYER CAKE

makes one 8-inch
double-layer cake

prep time: **5 minutes**

work time: **15 minutes**

bake time: **40 minutes**

CUPCAKES

makes 32 cupcakes

prep time: **5 minutes**

work time: **15 minutes**

bake time: **30 minutes**

After the talent show (see page 73), once word had officially gotten around the start-up about my baking prowess, my coworkers would occasionally ask me to bake for special occasions and company events. The most requested recipe was a classic birthday cake; teams would often want to surprise one of their members on his or her birthday with the perfect yellow layer cake covered in rich and creamy chocolate frosting. Some confessed to me that they'd tried to make their own version at home—from a random recipe online or from a box mix—and had been disappointed by its taste. Many asked for my yellow cake recipe, as well as for any tricks and tips.

A good yellow cake is light and buttery, with a sunny crumb that holds up well under layers of thick frosting—like this recipe! The brown sugar and oil keep the cake moist and flavorful longer, which is incredibly helpful if you find yourself building the cake over a few days per the Weeknight Baking Layer Cake Schedule (page 76).

2 cups (8 ounces) cake flour

1 teaspoon baking powder

1 teaspoon kosher salt

⅔ cup (5.35 ounces) unsalted butter, at room temperature

1⅔ cups (11.65 ounces) granulated sugar

⅓ cup tightly packed (2.5 ounces) dark brown sugar

4 large eggs

⅔ cup (5.35 ounces) canola oil

⅔ cup (5.35 ounces) buttermilk

1 tablespoon pure vanilla extract

1. Position a rack in the center of the oven and preheat the oven to 350°F. Prepare your cake pan of choice: If making a sheet cake or layer cake, generously spray the sheet pan or cake pans with cooking spray and line the bottom(s) with parchment paper (cut to fit, if using round pans). Spray the parchment, too. If making cupcakes, line two muffins tins with paper liners.

2. In a medium bowl, whisk together the flour, baking powder, and salt.

3. In the bowl of a stand mixer fitted with the paddle attachment, combine the butter and sugars. Beat on medium until light, fluffy, and doubled in volume, 3 to 4 minutes, using a rubber spatula to scrape down the bottom and sides of the bowl as necessary. Reduce the mixer to low and add the eggs one at a time,

NOTE: If making cupcakes, this recipe will yield more than 24 cupcakes. If you own only two muffin tins, follow the instructions to bake and cool as many cupcakes as you can in the tins, and repeat the recipe instructions to fill and bake the remaining batter into cupcakes.

adding the next egg only after the previous one has been fully incorporated, scraping down the bottom and sides of the bowl after each addition. With the mixer on low, slowly pour in the oil, followed by the buttermilk and vanilla, and beat until the mixture is smooth, 3 to 4 minutes. Gradually add the dry ingredients and beat until just combined. Scrape down the bottom and sides of the bowl once more, and beat on low for an additional 30 seconds.

4. Pour the batter into the prepared pan(s). If making a sheet cake, bake for 35 to 40 minutes. If making a layer cake, note that this recipe makes around 43 ounces of batter; pour 21.5 ounces into each cake pan and bake for 40 to 45 minutes. If making cupcakes, use a cookie dough scoop to fill each paper liner two-thirds of the way; bake for 30 to 35 minutes. When done, the top of the cake should bounce back when gently pressed and a skewer inserted into the center of the cake should come out with a few crumbs attached. Cool completely in the pan(s) on a wire rack before frosting.

PAIRS WELL WITH:
Chocolate Buttercream Frosting (page 103); Chocolate Fudge Frosting (page 104)

chocolate cake

 ACTIVE TIME

20 minutes

SHEET CAKE

makes one 9 x 13-inch cake

prep time: **10 minutes**

work time: **10 minutes**

bake time: **35 minutes**

LAYER CAKE

makes one 8-inch
double-layer cake

prep time: **10 minutes**

work time: **10 minutes**

bake time: **35 minutes**

CUPCAKES

makes 24 cupcakes

prep time: **10 minutes**

work time: **10 minutes**

bake time: **20 minutes**

The first time I made chocolate cake on a weeknight, it was a disaster. I had volunteered to bring a cake for my coworker's baby shower, and I wanted to impress. Instead, hours after I began, I found myself in the kitchen, covered in flour and cocoa powder, staring at two sunken layer cakes. I'd only skimmed the recipe beforehand, and mistakenly assumed that its complicated steps like sifting the flour and cocoa powder twice and pushing the cake batter through a sieve would result in a better cake. Nope.

After that, I made it my mission to develop a reliable chocolate cake recipe. Throughout the years, I tried and experimented with many recipes, but always found myself coming back to the same one: Ina Garten's. Ina's cake is chocolaty without being overly sweet and has the softest, moistest crumb you can imagine. It comes together with minimal equipment (no stand mixer needed for this one, folks!), saving you a few minutes of Work Time and cleanup time. It was the perfect weeknight baking recipe without me needing to drastically change any steps or ingredients!

Note that the Prep Time for this recipe is almost as long as its Work Time; that's because you'll need a fresh cup of hot coffee here, and water does take time to boil (unless you have an electric kettle, in which case, Prep Time will go by fairly fast). In the past, when I'm super crunched for time, I've bought bottles of cold brew coffee and heated what I needed for the recipe in the microwave; I wish you could skip this step, but it's essential that you bring the coffee to a boil since its high temperature will "bloom" the cocoa powder in the batter, giving the cake a dark, rich color and deeper chocolate flavor. To save on Prep Time, boil the water to make the coffee first. You'll have time to prep the rest of the ingredients while the water comes to a boil.

2 cups (8 ounces) cake flour

2 cups (14 ounces) granulated sugar

¾ cup (2.25 ounces) natural unsweetened cocoa powder, sifted if lumpy

2 teaspoons baking soda

1 teaspoon baking powder

1 teaspoon kosher salt

1 cup (8 ounces) buttermilk

½ cup (4 ounces) canola oil

2 large eggs

2 teaspoons pure vanilla extract

1 cup (8 ounces) **boiling hot** coffee

1. Position a rack in the center of the oven and preheat the oven to 350°F. Prepare your cake pan of choice: If making a sheet cake or layer cake, generously spray the sheet pan or cake pans with cooking spray and line the bottom with parchment paper (cut to fit, if using round pans). Spray the parchment, too. If making cupcakes, line two muffin tins with paper liners.

2. In a medium bowl, whisk together the flour, sugar, cocoa powder, baking soda, baking powder, and salt.

3. In a large bowl, whisk together the buttermilk, oil, eggs, and vanilla. Gradually whisk in the dry ingredients until just combined. Slowly pour in the coffee. The batter will be fairly runny; use a rubber spatula to scrape down the bottom and sides of the bowl. Use the rubber spatula to finish mixing until smooth and well combined, 2 to 3 minutes more.

4. Pour the batter into the prepared pan(s). If making a sheet cake, bake for 35 to 40 minutes. If making a layer cake, note that this recipe makes around 44 ounces of batter; pour 22 ounces into each cake pan and bake for 35 to 40 minutes. If making cupcakes, pour the batter into a large liquid measuring cup and use it to fill each paper liner two-thirds of the way; bake for 20 to 25 minutes. When done, the top of the cake should bounce back when gently pressed and a skewer inserted into the center of the cake should come out with a few crumbs attached. Cool completely in the pan(s) on a wire rack before frosting.

PAIRS WELL WITH:
Classic American Buttercream Frosting (page 99); Chocolate Buttercream Frosting (page 103); Chocolate Fudge Frosting (page 104); Cream Cheese Frosting (page 100); Nut Butter Frosting (page 106)

a modern red velvet cake

 ACTIVE TIME

20 to 23 minutes

SHEET CAKE

makes one 9 x 13-inch cake

prep time: **8 minutes**

work time: **12 minutes**

bake time: **35 minutes**

LAYER CAKE

makes one 8-inch
double-layer cake

prep time: **8 minutes**

work time: **15 minutes**

bake time: **35 minutes**

CUPCAKES

makes 24 cupcakes

prep time: **8 minutes**

work time: **15 minutes**

bake time: **20 minutes**

NOTE: Red food coloring is essential for this recipe. It's available in most grocery stores in individual large bottles or in a small bottle as part of a pack of four colors. The red food coloring in a pack will be *just* enough for this recipe. I suggest buying the large bottle so you always have some on hand for spontaneous baking projects!

Boxed mixes can make a pretty good version of both vanilla and chocolate cakes. But red velvet? Not so much. Unhappy with the boxed-mix version, I wanted to teach myself how to make red velvet cake. It was the first thing I taught myself how to bake from scratch during my sophomore year in college.

What makes a good red velvet cake? Once, when I was visiting New York, I came across a red velvet cake slice from a now closed barbecue restaurant in Morningside Heights. This cake just knocked it out of the park. It had an incredibly moist and light crumb, with notes of citrus to complement the red velvet's subtle chocolate and buttermilk flavors. I created this red velvet cake recipe as an homage to that slice (RIP).

When making this cake, it's especially important to prep the baking soda and vinegar in their own separate ramekins. You'll combine the two ingredients in the final step of the recipe. When you do, the mixture will bubble and hiss—throw it immediately into the batter and mix, mix, mix. This helps give the cake a light and airy texture that is unique to red velvet. Although the recipe's steps are slightly more complicated than what I would ordinarily have you do for a weeknight baking project, this recipe is a perfect candidate for the Weeknight Baking Layer Cake Schedule (page 76), as its cocoa and citrus notes intensify overnight.

2 cups (8 ounces) cake flour

2 teaspoons natural unsweetened cocoa powder, sifted if lumpy

¾ teaspoon baking powder

½ teaspoon kosher salt

1⅓ cups (9.35 ounces) granulated sugar

Zest of 1 small to medium orange (about 1 tablespoon)

6 tablespoons (3 ounces) unsalted butter, at room temperature

⅓ cup (2.65 ounces) canola oil

2 large eggs

1 tablespoon red food coloring

1 tablespoon pure vanilla extract

1 cup (8 ounces) buttermilk

1 teaspoon baking soda

1 teaspoon distilled white vinegar

1. Position a rack in the center of the oven and preheat the oven to 350°F. Prepare your cake pan of choice: If making a sheet cake or layer cake, generously spray the sheet pan or cake pans with cooking spray and line the bottom(s) with parchment paper (cut to fit, if using round pans). Spray the parchment, too. If making cupcakes, line two muffin tins with paper liners.

2. In a medium bowl, whisk together the flour, cocoa powder, baking powder, and salt.

3. In the bowl of a stand mixer fitted with the paddle attachment, combine the sugar and orange zest. Use your fingers to rub the zest into the sugar—this will infuse the sugar with oils from the zest. Add the butter and oil and beat on medium until light, fluffy, and doubled in volume, 2 to 3 minutes, using a rubber spatula to scrape down the bottom and sides of the bowl as necessary. Reduce the mixer to low and add the eggs one at a time, adding the next egg only after the previous one has been fully incorporated, scraping down the bottom and sides of the bowl after each addition. Add the food coloring and vanilla and beat until the batter is a uniform red color.

4. With the mixer on low, gradually add the dry ingredients in three parts, alternating with the buttermilk, beginning and ending with the dry ingredients. Beat until the last of the dry ingredients are just combined. Scrape down the bottom and sides of the bowl once more and beat for 30 seconds.

5. Working quickly, place the baking soda in a small ramekin, add the vinegar, and whisk—the mixture will start to bubble and fizz almost immediately. With the mixer on low, pour the vinegar mixture into the cake batter and increase to medium, beating for an additional 30 seconds.

6. Pour the batter into the prepared pan(s). If making a sheet cake, bake for 35 to 40 minutes. If making a layer cake, note that this recipe makes around 34 ounces of batter; pour 17 ounces into each cake pan and bake for 35 to 40 minutes. If making cupcakes, use a cookie dough scoop to fill each paper liner two-thirds of the way; bake for 20 to 25 minutes. When done, the top of the cake should bounce back when gently pressed and a skewer inserted into the center of the cake should come out with a few crumbs attached. Cool completely in the pan(s) on a wire rack before frosting.

PAIRS WELL WITH:
Classic American Buttercream Frosting (page 99); Cream Cheese Frosting (page 100)

white wedding cake

 **ACTIVE TIME**

18 to 23 minutes

SHEET CAKE

makes one 9 x 13-inch cake

prep time: **8 minutes**

work time: **10 minutes**

bake time: **35 minutes**

LAYER CAKE

makes one 8-inch
double-layer cake

prep time: **8 minutes**

work time: **15 minutes**

bake time: **40 minutes**

CUPCAKES

makes 34 cupcakes

prep time: **8 minutes**

work time: **15 minutes**

bake time: **25 minutes**

NOTE: If making cupcakes, this recipe will yield more than 24 cupcakes. If you own only two muffin tins, follow the instructions to bake and cool as many cupcakes as you can in the tins, and repeat the recipe instructions to fill and bake the remaining batter into cupcakes.

A wedding photographer friend of mine once confessed that most wedding cakes were actually made from a combination of boxed mix and shortening. That explained a lot; although most of the wedding cakes I've eaten looked beautiful, their flavor left a lot to be desired. It also explained why good friends of mine skipped the professional bakeries and asked me to make their wedding cakes instead.

Wedding cakes are actually fairly simple to make—even on a weeknight. All you need is a great white cake base recipe (like this one!). This recipe makes more batter than the others in this chapter, and that's to allow you to customize your layer cake accordingly. Bake the batter in two 8-inch pans for a rustic look, or three 8-inch pans for a more classic one (if using three 8-inch pans, just be sure to reduce the Bake Time to 25 to 30 minutes).

NOTE: It's especially important that your butter, milk, and egg whites are warmed to room temperature—this batter will curdle if some of the ingredients are colder than others. If you're short on time, check out my tips on how to bring your ingredients to room temperature quickly on page 41!

NOTE: For this recipe, you'll need to use clear vanilla extract. This helps keep the cake perfectly white. You can use the regular stuff, especially if that's what you have on hand (we're weeknight baking, after all)—however, the cake will look more yellow than white.

3 cups (12 ounces) cake flour

2 cups (14 ounces) granulated sugar

4½ teaspoons baking powder

1 teaspoon kosher salt

1 cup (8 ounces) unsalted butter, cut into 1-inch cubes, **at room temperature**

1⅓ cups (10.65 ounces) whole milk, **at room temperature**

5 large egg whites, **at room temperature**

1 tablespoon clear artificial vanilla extract

1. Position a rack in the center of the oven and preheat the oven to 350°F. Prepare your cake pan of choice: If making a sheet cake or layer cake, generously spray the sheet pan or cake pans with cooking spray and line the bottom(s) with parchment paper (cut to fit, if using round pans). Spray the parchment, too. If making cupcakes, line two muffin tins with paper liners.

PAIRS WELL WITH:
Classic American
Buttercream Frosting
(page 99)

2. In the bowl of a stand mixer fitted with the paddle attachment, combine the flour, sugar, baking powder, and salt. Beat on low until just combined, about 15 seconds. Add the butter all at once and beat on low until the mixture has the texture of coarse meal, with pea-sized pieces of butter throughout, about 3 minutes. Add 1 cup (8 ounces) of the milk all at once and increase the mixer to medium. Beat until the batter is light and fluffy, about 2 minutes, using a rubber spatula to scrape down the bottom and sides of the bowl as necessary. While the batter is mixing, whisk together the egg whites, remaining ⅓ cup (2.65 ounces) milk, and vanilla in a large liquid measuring cup. Reduce the mixer to low and add the egg white mixture in two or three additions, scraping down the bottom and sides of the bowl after each addition, then beat until just combined.

3. Pour the batter into the prepared pan(s). If making a sheet cake, bake for 35 to 40 minutes. If making a layer cake, note that this recipe makes around 50 ounces of batter; pour 25 ounces into each cake pan and bake for 40 to 45 minutes. If making cupcakes, use a cookie dough scoop to fill each paper liner two-thirds of the way; bake for 25 to 30 minutes. When done, the top of the cake should bounce back when gently pressed, and a skewer inserted into the center of the cake should come out with a few crumbs attached. Cool completely in the pan(s) on a wire rack before frosting.

banana chocolate chip cake

After I mastered banana bread, I wondered if there was anything else I could do with the week's leftover bananas. And since you now know I love layer cakes, I decided to try a banana layer cake. This is the result, and it's one of my favorite recipes; it has the flavor of my banana bread recipe (page 57), but with the light crumb and texture of my favorite yellow cake (page 79).

While this recipe comes together quickly, it does require a little more mixing than the other cakes in this chapter, thanks to all the buttermilk and oil in the recipe. Making sure that all your ingredients are at room temperature will considerably speed up the mixing process. And of course, make sure to use the ripest, spottiest bananas you have on hand, since more spots means more banana flavor (see Bananas About Bananas on page 61, if yours aren't quite there yet).

To make this cake extra special, I studded it with chocolate chips. Be sure to use mini ones, as regular-size chocolate chips tend to sink in the batter. There's also some creative leeway here; you can either stir the chips into the batter or sprinkle them on the top of the cake. Either method works well for both the sheet cake and the layer cake variations. For cupcakes, I like to stir three-quarters of the chocolate chips into the batter, reserving the final quarter for sprinkling on top.

NOTE: Bananas are listed in the recipe by weight, not volume or size—learn why on page 57. For best results, first peel the bananas, then use a digital scale to weigh the naked fruit. For those of you who need volume measurements, that's 1 cup mashed bananas, from around 2 large bananas.

2 cups (8 ounces) cake flour

¾ teaspoon baking powder

½ teaspoon baking soda

½ teaspoon kosher salt

6 tablespoons (3 ounces) unsalted butter, **at room temperature**

1 cup (7 ounces) granulated sugar

1 large egg, **at room temperature**

½ cup (4 ounces) buttermilk, **at room temperature**

2 tablespoons canola oil

1 teaspoon pure vanilla extract

8 ounces very ripe peeled bananas

1 cup (6 ounces) mini chocolate chips

1. Position a rack in the center of the oven and preheat the oven to 350°F. Prepare your cake pan of choice: If making a sheet cake or layer cake, generously spray the sheet pan or cake pans with cooking spray and line the bottom(s) with parchment paper (cut to fit, if using round pans). Spray the parchment, too. If making cupcakes, line two muffin tins with paper liners.

SHEET CAKE

makes one 9 x 13-inch cake

prep time: **8 minutes**

work time: **15 minutes**

bake time: **35 minutes**

LAYER CAKE

makes one 8-inch
double-layer cake

prep time: **8 minutes**

work time: **15 minutes**

bake time: **30 minutes**

CUPCAKES

makes about 20 cupcakes

prep time: **8 minutes**

work time: **15 minutes**

bake time: **22 minutes**

PAIRS WELL WITH:
Chocolate Buttercream
Frosting (page 103);
Chocolate Fudge Frosting
(page 104); Cream Cheese
Frosting (page 100); Nut
Butter Frosting (page 106)

2. In a medium bowl, whisk together the flour, baking powder, baking soda, and salt.

3. In the bowl of a stand mixer fitted with the paddle attachment, combine the butter and sugar. Beat on medium-high until light, fluffy, and doubled in volume, 2 to 3 minutes, using a rubber spatula to scrape down the bottom and sides of the bowl as necessary. Reduce the mixer to low and add the egg; increase the mixer to medium-high and beat until light and fluffy, another 1 to 2 minutes. With the mixer on low, slowly pour in the buttermilk, oil, and vanilla; increase the mixer to medium-high and beat until the batter is almost white and doubled in volume, about 5 minutes. Don't worry too much about overmixing at this stage—keep going until the batter is completely smooth.

4. Stop the mixer and scrape down the bottom and sides of the bowl with a rubber spatula. With the mixer on low, add the bananas a handful at a time and beat until broken into pieces and distributed evenly throughout the batter, about 1 minute. Gradually add the dry ingredients and beat until just combined. Scrape down the bottom and sides of the bowl once more, and beat on low for an additional 30 seconds. Add three-quarters of the chocolate chips (if that's the mix-in method you've chosen) and beat for about 30 seconds to distribute them throughout the batter.

5. Pour the batter into the prepared pan(s). Sprinkle the top of the batter with the remaining chocolate chips (or all of them, if that's the mix-in method you've chosen). If making a sheet cake, bake for 35 to 40 minutes. If making a layer cake, note that this recipe makes around 31.5 ounces of batter; pour 15.75 ounces into each cake pan and bake for 30 to 35 minutes. If making cupcakes, use a cookie dough scoop to fill each paper liner two-thirds of the way; bake for 22 to 25 minutes. Because of the chocolate chips, it can be hard to tell when the cake is done—look at the edges of the cake and see if they're golden brown. A skewer inserted into the center of the cake should come out with a few crumbs attached. Cool completely in the pan(s) on a wire rack before frosting.

peanut butter brown sugar cake

 ACTIVE TIME

13 to 18 minutes

SHEET CAKE

makes one 9 x 13-inch cake

prep time: **8 minutes**

work time: **5 minutes**

bake time: **40 minutes**

LAYER CAKE

makes one 8-inch
double-layer cake

prep time: **8 minutes**

work time: **8 minutes**

bake time: **45 minutes**

CUPCAKES

makes 30 cupcakes

prep time: **8 minutes**

work time: **10 minutes**

bake time: **25 minutes**

Of all the cakes I made for this book, this was the only one that I never got sick of eating—no matter how much I ate. This cake is so moist that it doesn't even need any frosting, but works wonderfully with chocolate fudge or a dollop of crème fraîche or whipped cream (or Crème Fraîche Whipped Cream on page 275).

This recipe comes from my friend Molly Yeh. Molly is a food blogger, too, and we spend an embarrassing amount of time texting each other about baking. Usually it's to brainstorm goofy ideas ("Do you think a yogurt taco sounds good?" "No, Molly."); other times, it's to swap tips and tricks ("How do I avoid resting this dough overnight if I want cookies right now?" "More flour, maybe?"). When she heard I was looking for the perfect peanut butter cake recipe, she recommended the "Party Trick" peanut butter cake from her book *Molly on the Range*. She described it as "idiot-proof" and "hangover-proof," which I interpreted as "perfect for weeknight baking."

I made a few changes to make her recipe even more weeknight baking–friendly: I used brown sugar not only to enhance the cake's molasses flavor, but also to help keep it moister overnight. This recipe works best with the natural, unsweetened kind of peanut butter (the kind with the oil on top that needs to be stirred and refrigerated after opening). Be sure to use room-temperature peanut butter—chilled peanut butter won't incorporate into the batter properly. If you're pulling your peanut butter straight from the fridge, give it a quick zap in the microwave to make sure it's soft.

2¼ cups (9 ounces) cake flour

2 cups tightly packed (15 ounces) dark brown sugar

1½ teaspoons baking powder

1½ teaspoons baking soda

1½ teaspoons kosher salt

1 cup (9.5 ounces) unsweetened creamy natural peanut butter

1 cup (8 ounces) buttermilk

¾ cup (6 ounces) water

½ cup (4 ounces) canola oil

2 large eggs

2 teaspoons pure vanilla extract

NOTE: If making cupcakes, this recipe will yield more than 24 cupcakes. If you own only two muffin tins, follow the instructions to bake and cool as many cupcakes as you can in the tins, and repeat the recipe instructions to fill and bake the remaining batter into cupcakes.

PAIRS WELL WITH:
Chocolate Buttercream Frosting (page 103); Chocolate Fudge Frosting (page 104); Cream Cheese Frosting (page 100); Nut Butter Frosting (page 106)

1. Position a rack in the center of the oven and preheat the oven to 350°F. Prepare your cake pan of choice: If making a sheet cake or layer cake, generously spray the sheet pan or cake pans with cooking spray and line the bottom(s) with parchment paper (cut to fit, if using round pans). Spray the parchment, too. If making cupcakes, line two muffin tins with paper liners.

2. In a medium bowl, whisk together the flour, brown sugar, baking powder, baking soda, and salt.

3. In the bowl of a stand mixer fitted with the whisk attachment, combine the peanut butter, buttermilk, water, oil, eggs, and vanilla. Whisk on low until the mixture is smooth and caramel in color, about 1 minute. Gradually add the dry ingredients, using a rubber spatula to scrape down the bottom and sides of the bowl as necessary. Take extra care here—a small amount of peanut butter always sticks to the bottom. Whisk on low until just combined.

4. Pour the batter into the prepared pan(s). If making a sheet cake, bake for 40 to 45 minutes. If making a layer cake, note that this recipe makes around 54 ounces of batter; pour 27 ounces into each cake pan and bake for 45 to 50 minutes. If making cupcakes, use a cookie dough scoop to fill each paper liner two-thirds of the way; bake for 25 to 30 minutes. When done, the top of the cake should bounce back when gently pressed and a skewer inserted into the center of the cake should come out with a few crumbs attached. Cool completely in the pan(s) on a wire rack before frosting.

variation

tahini brown sugar

Tahini is a creamy condiment made from ground sesame seeds. It has a rich, nutty flavor and is slightly less sweet than peanut butter. Although it's often used in Middle Eastern cuisine, and mostly in savory dishes like hummus and baba ghanoush, tahini appears more and more often in desserts and sweets recipes.

Substitute 1 cup (9 ounces) well-stirred tahini for the peanut butter. Proceed with the recipe as directed. This variation does not significantly affect Prep, Work, or Bake Time.

FROSTINGS

No cake is complete without a healthy portion of frosting or icing on top, and the recipes in this chapter were written with the weeknight baker in mind. Not only do they allow you to customize every cake recipe in this book to your own personal taste, but they're incredibly fast to make—almost all require only 5 minutes of Work Time. To make your life even easier, all the frostings in this chapter can also be made in advance of making the cake itself:

HOW TO CHILL AND THAW FROSTING FOR FUTURE USE

To refrigerate frosting, simply transfer it to an airtight container with a lid. Press a sheet of plastic wrap directly against the surface of the frosting to prevent a skin from forming, then cover with the lid. Frosting will keep in the refrigerator for up to 1 week.

To freeze frosting, transfer it to a zip-top bag, pressing as much air out of the bag as possible before sealing. Place the bag of frosting in a second zip-top bag and seal; freeze overnight. Once the frosting has frozen solid, wrap the bag tightly in a layer of aluminum foil to prevent the frosting from absorbing any odors or flavors and return it to the freezer. Frosting will keep in the freezer for up to 1 year. To thaw frozen frosting, you'll need to plan ahead—two days before you plan to use it, transfer the frosting to the refrigerator and let it thaw overnight, then follow any of the methods below to bring it to a spreadable consistency.

Even after thawing, you'll need to allow refrigerated frosting to warm up a bit before using it; a frosting straight from the fridge will still be stiff and difficult to work with. You want frosting to be melted enough that it will spread with little resistance (similar to the consistency of creamy peanut butter), but not so much that it's runny and dripping off the cake. You can bring chilled frosting to the proper consistency in a number of ways:

the lazy-but-time-consuming way
Remove the container from the fridge and let it sit at room temperature for at least 1 hour (I take the lid off but leave the plastic wrap pressed against the surface of the frosting—if the frosting was frozen and thawed in the fridge overnight, remove the outer bag and the foil). If I'm weeknight baking, I actually remove the frosting from the refrigerator in the morning, leave it in a dark, cool spot in my kitchen, and head to the office; by the time I'm back, the frosting is the perfect consistency. Although this method is pretty low effort, it is unfortunately time-consuming and might not work if you keep your kitchen temperature cooler than 70°F.

the tech-heavy way

A faster way to warm your chilled frosting is in the microwave. Transfer the frosting to the bowl of a stand mixer fitted with the paddle attachment, reserving about ¼ cup (you can just eyeball it, there's no need to be precise here) in a separate smaller bowl. Microwave the ¼ cup of frosting on medium-low in 10-second intervals for about 1 minute total, until it gets a little runny. Add the warm frosting to the bowl of the stand mixer and beat on medium until the entire batch is soft and smooth again, about 2 minutes. If I'm rushed, this is my method of choice—it uses fewer dishes than the Pastry School Way (see below), but it can also be unpredictable: some frostings melt faster than others, so you really need to keep an eye on it in the microwave. And remember, the microwave's power setting is your friend—low and slow is the way to go here!

the pastry school way

If you don't have a microwave, you can heat up the entire batch of frosting in a double boiler. Scrape the frosting into a double boiler and heat over medium-low heat for about 5 minutes, using a heatproof rubber spatula to stir the frosting as it heats. At first, the frosting will be stiff, but it will soften after 2 to 3 minutes. Transfer the frosting to a stand mixer fitted with the paddle attachment and beat on medium until smooth and soft again, about 2 minutes.

classic american buttercream frosting

In the baking world, there are many types of buttercream, each with their own nationality: American, French, German, Italian, Swiss, and so on. Although the ingredients of each are basically the same, the methods for making them vary and yield different results. For weeknight baking, I tend to stick with American buttercream, as it's the easiest and fastest to make. That, and it's a sweet and simple frosting that will remind you of the birthday cakes of your childhood. The most time-consuming part of this recipe involves sifting the confectioners' sugar—but don't skip it! Skipping this step will result in lumpy frosting.

 ACTIVE TIME

10 minutes

prep time: **<5 minutes**
work time: **5 minutes**

makes about 4 cups

1 cup (8 ounces) unsalted butter, **at room temperature**

4 cups (16 ounces) confectioners' sugar, sifted

2 tablespoons whole milk

2 teaspoons pure vanilla extract

Pinch of kosher salt

In the bowl of a stand mixer fitted with the paddle attachment, beat the butter on medium-low until smooth and creamy, about 1 minute. Reduce the mixer to low and add the confectioners' sugar 1 cup at a time, beating until combined. Scrape down the bottom and sides of the bowl with a rubber spatula. Add the milk, vanilla, and salt all at once and beat on low just to incorporate the liquid. Scrape down the bottom and sides of the bowl once more, then beat on medium-high until the frosting is creamy and smooth, 2 to 3 minutes. Use immediately or follow the storage instructions on page 97. The frosting will keep in the refrigerator for up to 1 week or the freezer for up to 1 year.

cream cheese frosting

If you're looking for something with a little more complexity than American buttercream, look no further than cream cheese frosting. Adding cream cheese to a batch of American buttercream gives it a tang that complements cakes with deep flavors like chocolate and red velvet. Similar to American buttercream, this recipe comes together in just 5 minutes. Make sure both the cream cheese and the butter are at room temperature for the smoothest and silkiest texture. Don't be afraid to give both ingredients a quick 10- to 15-second zap in the microwave to warm them up!

ACTIVE TIME

10 minutes

prep time: **<5 minutes**
work time: **5 minutes**

makes about 5 cups

1½ cups (12 ounces) cream cheese, **at room temperature**

1 cup (8 ounces) unsalted butter, **at room temperature**

4½ cups (18 ounces) confectioners' sugar, sifted

2 tablespoons whole milk

1 teaspoon pure vanilla extract

¼ teaspoon kosher salt

In the bowl of a stand mixer fitted with the paddle attachment, combine the cream cheese and butter. Beat on medium-low until soft and creamy, about 1 minute. Scrape down the bottom and sides of the bowl with a rubber spatula. With the mixer on low, gradually add the confectioners' sugar, milk, vanilla, and salt and beat until smooth. Scrape down the bottom and sides of the bowl once more, then beat on medium-high until the frosting is creamy and smooth, 2 to 3 minutes. Use immediately or follow the storage instructions on page 97. The frosting will keep in the refrigerator for up to 1 week or the freezer for up to 1 year.

chocolate buttercream frosting

Although many chocolate frosting recipes ask you to do complicated and time-consuming things like tempering chocolate or folding it into meringue, the truth is, you can make a perfectly dreamy chocolate frosting with simple pantry ingredients. For this recipe, use either natural unsweetened cocoa powder or the Dutch-processed variety; the latter will give the frosting a darker color and a milder chocolate taste. Making the frosting ahead of time per the Weeknight Baking Layer Cake Schedule (page 76) also allows the cocoa powder to fully bloom, infusing the frosting with even more flavor as it sits in the fridge.

ACTIVE TIME
10 minutes

prep time: **<5 minutes**
work time: **5 minutes**

makes about 4 cups

1 cup (8 ounces) unsalted butter, **at room temperature**

3½ cups (14 ounces) confectioners' sugar, sifted

½ cup (1.5 ounces) natural unsweetened or Dutch-processed cocoa powder, sifted

¼ cup (2 ounces) whole milk

1 teaspoon pure vanilla extract

¼ teaspoon kosher salt

In the bowl of a stand mixer fitted with the paddle attachment, beat the butter on medium-low until soft and creamy, 2 to 3 minutes. Scrape down the bottom and sides of the bowl with a rubber spatula. With the mixer on low, gradually add the confectioners' sugar, cocoa powder, milk, vanilla, and salt and beat until combined. Scrape down the bottom and sides of the bowl once more, then beat on medium-high until the frosting is creamy and smooth, 2 to 3 minutes. Use immediately or follow the storage instructions on page 97. The frosting will keep in the refrigerator for up to 1 week or the freezer for up to 1 year.

chocolate fudge frosting

If you're ready to take your chocolate frosting to the next level, meet your new favorite recipe. This chocolate fudge frosting uses melted chocolate for a thicker, silkier texture, just like chocolate fudge. However, unlike with traditional fudge recipes, there's no need to fuss with a candy thermometer. You don't even need a stand mixer! All you need to do is throw the ingredients into a food processor, and voilà: the lightest, smoothest chocolate frosting in the world. This is weeknight baking at its best.

 ACTIVE TIME

20 minutes

prep time: **5 minutes**

work time: **15 minutes**

makes about 5 cups

6 ounces unsweetened chocolate, from a high-quality chocolate bar, hand broken into pieces

4½ cups (18 ounces) confectioners' sugar, sifted

1½ cups (12 ounces) unsalted butter, **at room temperature**

6 tablespoons (3 ounces) whole milk

1 tablespoon pure vanilla extract

¼ teaspoon kosher salt

1. In a food processor, pulse the chocolate for a few seconds at a time until chopped into 1- to 2-inch pieces. Transfer the chocolate to the top of a double boiler or to a heatproof bowl set over a medium, heavy-bottomed saucepan filled with a few inches of simmering water (be sure the bottom of the bowl does not touch the water). Cook over medium heat, using a heatproof rubber spatula to stir the mixture and scrape the sides of the bowl occasionally, until the chocolate has melted, about 10 minutes. Set the top of the double boiler or the bowl on a wire rack and let the chocolate cool while you prep the other ingredients.

2. In the food processor, combine the confectioners' sugar, butter, milk, vanilla, and salt. Pour in the melted chocolate and pulse briefly to combine, then process until the frosting is creamy, smooth, and light brown in color, about 5 minutes. Scrape down the bottom and sides of the bowl with a rubber spatula, then process for an additional 30 seconds. Use immediately or follow the storage instructions on page 97. The frosting will keep in the refrigerator for up to 1 week or the freezer for up to 1 year.

nut butter frosting

Since weeknight baking means using what's on hand, I wanted to include a frosting recipe to use what is in people's pantries. Most households usually have some type of peanut butter or another nut butter like almond butter in their cupboards for use in breakfasts and snacks. You can use whatever nut butter you have in your pantry in this recipe, be it peanut butter, almond butter, or even Nutella. Just make sure the nut butter is at room temperature and well-stirred, especially if you prefer natural brands that need to be refrigerated after opening. I usually pop the nut butter in the microwave to make sure it's the perfect temperature, heating the nut butter in 10-second intervals until it's melty and very spreadable. This recipe uses almond extract to amplify the nut butter's flavor—but if you're in a pinch and find you don't have any in your pantry, vanilla extract will work just as well.

ACTIVE TIME

10 minutes

prep time: **<5 minutes**
work time: **5 minutes**

makes about 4 cups

1½ cups (12 ounces) unsalted butter, **at room temperature**

½ cup (4.75 ounces) unsweetened creamy natural nut butter of your choice

2 teaspoons almond extract

½ teaspoon kosher salt

4 cups (16 ounces) confectioners' sugar, sifted

2 tablespoons whole milk

In the bowl of a stand mixer fitted with the paddle attachment, combine the butter, nut butter, almond extract, and salt. Beat on medium-low until soft and creamy, 1 to 2 minutes. Scrape down the bottom and sides of the bowl with a rubber spatula. With the mixer on low, gradually add the confectioners' sugar and milk and beat until combined. Scrape down the bottom and sides of the bowl once more, then beat on medium-high until the frosting is creamy and smooth, 2 to 3 minutes. Use immediately or follow the storage instructions on page 97. The frosting will keep in the refrigerator for up to 1 week or the freezer for up to 1 year.

weeknight layer cake decorating techniques

You've just read two entire chapters on how to make all kinds of cakes and frostings. Great! At this point, you have everything you need to make a delicious cake. But you might also be wondering, *How on earth do I make my cake look good?*

In the age of Instagram, Pinterest, and blogs, you can find tons of photos of amazing homemade cakes with elaborate structures, colors, and all kinds of decorations. I make some myself, blogging about cakes that look like cherry blossom trees in bloom and pink galaxies with edible gold constellations. But usually, those cakes are my week*END* baking projects. If I find myself tasked with making a cake on a weeknight (like that time I promised my coworker a birthday cake the next day and completely forgot about it until the night before—*my bad*), I use the following techniques. Each requires few tools and results in a beautifully decorated cake in 20 minutes or less.

assembling a layer cake

To make a layer cake, you'll need at least two cake layers (or more, if you're feeling fancy) made with your favorite cake recipe and one batch of your favorite frosting from this book. Start by placing one of the cake layers on the plate you plan to serve it on. Take an offset spatula and drop about ½ cup of the frosting right in the middle of the top of the cake. Spread it evenly all over the top, just like you would spread butter on toast. There's no need to frost the sides of the cake yet, but don't worry if some frosting accidentally ends up there—we'll fix it later.

Place your second cake layer on top of the first, adjusting it if it's crooked—the layers should be stacked evenly on top of each other. If you're working with more than two layers, go ahead and repeat the previous step with as many layers as you're using. If not, give yourself a pat on the back—you've just assembled a double-layer cake! Wasn't that a breeze? It's time to decorate.

weeknight baking offset spatula designs

For the following designs, you'll need a long offset spatula and a rotating cake stand. In a pinch, you can always use a lazy Susan by setting the cake on a serving platter, then placing it on an upside-down bowl on the lazy Susan's center. You'll be able to rotate the cake this way.

NAKED CAKE

A naked cake is a layer cake with a thin coating of frosting on its sides and top; the frosting is so sheer that you can still see the cake's crumb underneath.

To frost a naked cake, start with an assembled layer cake. Drop a medium dollop of frosting in the center of the top of the cake. Use an offset spatula to spread the frosting over the top of the cake, just like when you assembled the layer cake. Next, apply a large dollop of frosting to the side of the cake. Spread it in a thin layer over the sides of the cake. If using a rotating cake stand, you can spread the frosting easily by holding the length of the offset spatula's blade against that dollop of frosting as you rotate the stand—doing so will spread the frosting in a thin, even layer. Add additional dollops of frosting as needed and spread until a thin layer of frosting covers the sides of the cake. It's up to you to use however much frosting you want, but know that you should still be able to

see generous amounts of cake through the frosting. Be sure to freeze any leftover frosting you have (see page 97) for your next naked cake!

RUSTIC SWIRLS

These swirls are probably my favorite cake decorating technique. It's incredibly easy, and it results in a beautiful cake each time.

To decorate a cake with rustic swirls, start with a crumb-coated cake (see page 77). Transfer the cake to a serving plate and use an offset spatula to spread a thick, even layer of frosting all over the top and sides of the cake, adding a little bit of frosting at a time. Then use the spatula to make large, random sweeping motions across the frosting on the top and sides of the cake; the sweeping motions will create the swirls. Don't overthink it! For this method, a little work goes a long way. I promise it'll be beautiful no matter what you do.

weeknight baking piping bag designs

I used to think that piping bags were only used by pastry chefs in professional kitchens. But they are actually one of the fastest ways to decorate cakes at home, too.

To fill a piping bag with frosting, snip the corner of the bag to make a hole big enough for the top of the piping tip. Slide in the tip so that the narrow end is facing out; if you're planning on filling multiple bags with different frosting colors, I recommend using a coupler (learn more on page 33), which will allow you to transfer the tip from bag to bag easily. Place the piping bag tip down in a tall, empty glass and fold the upper half of the bag down around the glass to hold the bag open. Fill the bag with frosting, making sure to leave at least 4 inches at the top of the bag. Fold the bag back up around the frosting, and use your hands to push all the frosting down toward the tip to eliminate any air pockets. Twist the bag shut like you would the end of a candy wrapper and secure the top with a rubber band. To pipe, hold the bag with your hand just below the rubber band and apply pressure from the top, working your way down the bag as it gradually empties.

STAR BORDERS

I love this design—not only does it make your cake look like it came from a professional bakery, but it also takes a grand total of 5 minutes to pipe these seemingly complicated star borders.

Start with an assembled layer cake covered in a thin layer of frosting, similar to the naked cake design. Fit a piping bag with a large star tip and fill the bag with your favorite frosting—this design works best with the buttercream and cream cheese frostings in this book.

To pipe a star border, hold the tip perpendicular to the top of the cake. Using even pressure, pipe little dots of frosting around the edge of the top of the cake. If you're feeling ambitious, you can also pipe a border around the bottom edge of the cake. Don't forget the sprinkles!

QUICK-AND-EASY CASCADING ROSES

Although not as elaborate as some of the buttercream roses and flowers you see on wedding cakes, these quick-and-easy roses are still beautiful, especially when made with a pastel frosting.

Start with an assembled layer cake covered in a thin layer of frosting, similar to the naked cake design. Fit a piping bag with a large open star tip (in particular, Wilton 1M or Ateco #824 work well here) and fill it with your favorite frosting recipe—this design works best with the buttercream and cream cheese frostings in this book.

To pipe cascading roses, hold the tip perpendicular to the cake's surface. Using even pressure, pipe frosting in a tight, round spiral, starting from the center and working your way out. Release the pressure just as you complete the spiral to create a tail that tapers off, and release *all* pressure before you pull the tip away completely. Make smaller roses by looping the spiral of frosting once around itself, and larger ones by looping two or three times around itself.

DROP
COOKIES

I love drop cookies, the kind made from doughs that don't require you to roll them out with a rolling pin. In many ways, they're the ultimate weeknight baking project: they come together quickly, and any leftovers (baked cookies *or* unbaked cookie dough!) store well.

Cookie dough freezes wonderfully, and actually tastes better the longer it sits. There's research that states that resting your cookie dough will lead to a more delicious cookie. Time in the freezer allows the flour and sugar to absorb more flavors from the other ingredients in the dough.

It also means you can just stick the prepped cookie dough in the freezer and bake it whenever it's most convenient for you. With a batch of frozen cookie dough in your freezer, you can have a warm cookie in your hands in an astonishingly short amount of time, anytime. Different cookie doughs freeze and bake in different ways, so I've included specific instructions on how to bake from frozen with each recipe.

To set yourself up for success with the following recipes, be sure to invest in a 3-tablespoon cookie dough scoop for the job—not only will it speed up the Work Time for each recipe, but you'll end up with perfect, even cookies each time.

And finally, most of the cookie recipes in this book will seem like they instruct you to pull the cookies out of the oven too early, with the centers still soft and the edges hardly set. THIS IS NOT A MISTAKE. This is how you make cookies with gooey centers and crisp edges! Pull the pan out right as the cookies start to set; leave it untouched on a wire rack for 20 minutes to allow the residual heat from the pan to finish baking the cookies to perfection. It'll be hard to resist, but I promise the wait for the perfect cookie is worth it.

single lady chocolate chip cookie

prep time: **<1 minute**
work time: **5 minutes**
bake time: **12 minutes**

makes 1 giant chocolate chip cookie

Although my boyfriend Erlend and I have been dating since college, there were a couple of times during our relationship when we had to go long-distance. It wasn't easy—after a long day at the office, I would come home to video chat with Erlend and spend the rest of the night quietly by myself. To pass the lonely evenings, I found myself in the kitchen baking once more.

The problem was, with Erlend in another city, I found myself with piles of baked goods that I couldn't finish on my own. I started to figure out ways to scale down recipes to make small batches just for me. Cookies in particular worked well: I baked one or two portions at a time and froze everything else for whenever the next craving hit. Still—an entire batch of cookies usually took 15 to 20 minutes to mix. And there were nights when I wanted something faster.

Enter this chocolate chip cookie recipe. This recipe comes together in 5 minutes, uses one bowl, and produces a 4-inch-wide monster of a cookie. There's a good chance you won't even need to go to the store to make it, since you likely have all the ingredients in your pantry. Why? It uses oil and water in place of butter and eggs. That saves you a bunch of time, eliminating the need to wait for butter to come to room temperature. Use whatever oil you have on hand for a custom cookie—neutral ones like canola and grapeseed oil make a classic chocolate chip cookie, whereas olive oil and coconut oil produce more unique flavors. Whatever chocolate you have in your snack drawer also works well in these cookies. Chop up your favorite chocolate bar to use in place of the chocolate chips for a molten chocolaty cookie. Unlike all other recipes, which call on you to prep a whole list of ingredients before you start, the only thing you'll need to prep here is chocolate—because this cookie uses such small quantities of each ingredient, it's actually faster to measure them out as you use them.

Finally, I do have one rule for this recipe: **the cookie must be eaten the day it's made, within 30 minutes of being pulled out of the oven.** It's best warm, after 10 to 15 minutes of cooling on a wire rack, when the cookie is just *barely* set. It should be messy to eat, in the best way possible. Think: crisp edges with a warm, gooey center and puddles of melted chocolate. Once it's fully cooled, this cookie will taste a little cakey and a little oily, which I wouldn't have you eat because you deserve better than that. Besides, this is your instant gratification cookie. Why wait?

1½ teaspoons granulated sugar

1½ teaspoons tightly packed dark brown sugar

NOTE: For this recipe, it's especially important that you follow the ingredient quantities exactly as they are written. Because it produces just one serving, any variance in the ingredient quantities—no matter how small and seemingly insignificant—will result in a dramatically different cookie. A ⅛-teaspoon measure doesn't usually come with your average teaspoon set but can be purchased individually from Amazon. Don't try to eyeball this one—too much baking soda will lead to a weird, puffy cookie.

1 tablespoon oil

2 teaspoons water

¼ teaspoon pure vanilla extract

3 tablespoons plus 1 teaspoon all-purpose flour

⅛ teaspoon baking soda

⅛ teaspoon kosher salt

1 ounce dark chocolate (between 60% and 70% cocoa), from whole fèves or a high-quality chocolate bar, chopped into ½- to 1-inch pieces

Flaky salt, for garnish

1. Position a rack in the center of the oven and preheat the oven to 350°F. Line a quarter sheet pan with parchment paper.

2. In a medium bowl, combine the sugars, oil, water, and vanilla. Use a rubber spatula to mix together until moistened. Add the flour, baking soda, and salt and mix until just combined, about 1 minute. Add the chocolate and mix until evenly distributed throughout the dough, about 30 seconds.

3. Scrape the dough into a mound in the center of the prepared pan. It will be a little bit shinier than traditional cookie dough, but that's totally okay, I promise! If your mound is a little messy, you can use the spatula to press it into a rough circle. There's no need to worry about appearances here—this is for you, and only you.

4. Bake for 12 minutes, or until the edges are set but the center is still gooey. Cool on the pan on a wire rack for 10 minutes, or until the edges and bottom of the cookie are set and feel firm to the touch. Sprinkle with flaky salt and devour while warm, completely and shamelessly.

chocolate chip cookies

Chocolate chip cookies were one of the first baked goods I taught myself how to make from scratch. I loved personalizing my cookies with my favorite chocolate and ingredients—check out the Chocolate Chip Cookie Mix-Ins on page 118, which allow you to use whatever's in your pantry to make the chocolate chip cookies of your dreams!

Beyond the mix-ins, my ideal chocolate chip cookie has barely crisp edges, a chewy and fudgy center, and a generous amount of melty chocolate. This recipe makes cookies that are exactly that. And it's genius in other ways, too, like in that it calls for *melted* butter. Not only does melted butter lead to denser, chewier cookies, but it saves you a ton of time, since there's no need to sit around waiting for the butter to come to room temperature. I like to melt the butter in a pan, which allows me to keep a close eye on it as I prep the rest of the ingredients. You can also melt the butter in the microwave—just be sure to heat it at low power and monitor the butter so that it doesn't overheat. There should be no sizzling, crackling, or popping as it melts.

I've written this recipe for maximum efficiency to save you as much time as possible as you go through its steps. There's little prep required beyond dicing the butter before you melt it. As the butter melts, you'll gather the rest of the ingredients and eventually add them directly to the warm butter. Just be sure to add the ingredients in the order they're listed. It's especially important to mix the sugars into the melted butter before adding the egg; the sugars will help bring the temperature of the butter down to prevent the egg from accidentally scrambling.

ACTIVE TIME

15 minutes

prep time: **<5 minutes**
work time: **15 minutes**
bake time: **10 minutes**

makes about 16 cookies

½ cup (4 ounces) unsalted butter, cut into 1-inch cubes

1 recipe Chocolate Chip Cookie Mix-In of your choice (page 118)

1⅔ cups (7.5 ounces) all-purpose flour

½ teaspoon baking powder

½ teaspoon baking soda

1 teaspoon kosher salt

¾ cup tightly packed (5.65 ounces) dark brown sugar

¼ cup (1.75 ounces) granulated sugar

1 large egg

2 teaspoons pure vanilla extract

1. In a medium, heavy-bottomed saucepan, melt the butter over low heat, about 10 minutes. Stir regularly to prevent butter from getting too hot—at no point should the butter sizzle, crackle, or pop.

2. While the butter melts, position a rack in the center of the oven and preheat the oven to 350°F. Line two half sheet pans with parchment paper.

3. Prepare the ingredients for the mix-in of your choice in a food processor. Pulse for a few seconds at a time until roughly chopped.

4. In a medium bowl, whisk together the flour, baking powder, baking soda, and salt. In the bowl of a stand mixer fitted with the paddle attachment, combine the sugars.

5. Once the butter has melted completely, pour it over the sugar in the mixer bowl and beat on low until just combined. Add the egg and vanilla and beat until just combined. Use a rubber spatula to scrape down the bottom and sides of the bowl. With the mixer on low, gradually add the dry ingredients and beat until just combined. Scrape down the bottom and sides of the bowl once more, and beat on low for an additional 30 seconds. Increase the mixer to medium-low, add the mix-in all at once, and beat until the mix-in is evenly distributed throughout, about 1 minute.

6. Use a 3-tablespoon cookie dough scoop to portion the cookie dough into balls, placing them at least 3 inches apart on the prepared sheet pans. Bake one pan at a time for 10 minutes, or until the edges have set but the centers are still gooey. The cookies will look puffed when you pull them out of the oven, but will fall and crack into the perfect cookies as they cool. Cool the cookies on the pan on a wire rack for 20 minutes, or until the edges and bottoms of the cookies have set and feel firm to the touch. Repeat with the remaining cookie dough (or freeze it to bake later). Serve warm or at room temperature. The cookies can be stored in an airtight container or zip-top bag at room temperature for up to 3 days.

bake later

Make the dough and form it into balls as directed. Follow the instructions on page 121 to freeze the dough. When ready to bake, position a rack in the center of the oven and preheat the oven to 350°F. Line a half sheet pan (or two, depending on how many cookies you're making) with parchment paper. Place the cookie dough balls at least 3 inches apart on the prepared sheet pan(s) and set aside at room temperature to thaw as the oven preheats. Bake one pan at a time for 12 to 15 minutes, or until the edges have set but the centers are still gooey. Cool and serve as directed.

chocolate chip cookie mix-ins

To make really good chocolate chip cookies, you need really good, high-quality chocolate. And real talk: Chocolate chips don't qualify. Most chocolate chips, with some exceptions, are made with poor-quality chocolate mixed with stabilizers like paraffin wax (yep, the kind of wax used to make candles—that's what lets the chips hold their shape when baked). In my opinion, the best chocolate chip cookies *don't actually use chocolate chips* and instead use chopped bar chocolate. Chopped chocolate melts into the cookie, swirling throughout the dough. I recommend using your favorite chocolate bar: chop it into 1- to 2-inch pieces, or use a food processor to help with the task. To save even more time, you can also buy fèves (little 1½-inch discs of chocolate) from chocolate makers like Callebaut, Guittard, and Valrhona. Although they're a little on the spendy side, I like to splurge because these discs are the perfect size and shape to use for cookies, saving me the time and effort of chopping chocolate for the recipe.

I've included some of my favorite mix-ins for cookie dough below; each will work wonderfully in the Chocolate Chip Cookies recipe on page 115 and allow you to customize your chocolate chip cookies. There are recipes for those with a major sweet tooth, and those looking for more complex and unique flavors. Don't be afraid to play around with textures, too—although I instruct you to roughly chop the chocolate in the recipe, you can chop everything up into larger pieces (or even keep the fèves whole!) if chunky cookies are your thing.

⏱ ACTIVE TIME

5 minutes

prep time: **<5 minutes**
work time: **<5 minutes**

each makes enough for
1 recipe of chocolate chip
cookies

CLASSIC CHOCOLATE CHIP

4 ounces dark chocolate (at least 60% cocoa), from whole fèves or a high-quality chocolate bar, hand broken into pieces

4 ounces extra-dark chocolate (at least 70% cocoa), from whole fèves or a high-quality chocolate bar, hand broken into pieces

TRIPLE CHOCOLATE CHIP

3 ounces extra-dark chocolate (at least 70% cocoa), from whole fèves or a high-quality chocolate bar, hand broken into pieces

3 ounces milk chocolate (at least 35% cocoa), from whole fèves or a high-quality chocolate bar, hand broken into pieces

3 ounces white chocolate, from whole fèves or a high-quality chocolate bar, hand broken into pieces

DARK CHOCOLATE AND HAZELNUT

6 ounces extra dark chocolate (at least 70% cocoa), from whole fèves or a high-quality chocolate bar, hand broken into pieces

½ cup (2.5 ounces) roasted and salted hazelnuts

ROASTED WHITE CHOCOLATE AND MACADAMIA

6 ounces Valrhona Dulcey white chocolate, from whole fèves or a high-quality chocolate bar, hand broken into pieces

½ cup (2.5 ounces) roasted and salted macadamia nuts

MILK CHOCOLATE AND TOFFEE

6 ounces milk chocolate (at least 35% cocoa), from whole fèves or a high-quality chocolate bar, hand broken into pieces

2 ounces chocolate toffee chunks (from a candy bar like Skor or Heath)

CHOCOLATE CHIP CANDY BAR

4 ounces dark chocolate (at least 60% cocoa), from whole fèves or a high-quality chocolate bar, hand broken into pieces

2 ounces M&M's or other similar candy-coated chocolate drops (I'm partial to the ones from Trader Joe's)

2 ounces mini dark chocolate nonpareils

how to freeze cookie dough to bake later

I mentioned on page 113 that I started freezing cookie dough to prevent myself from eating too many cookies at once. But there were other added benefits, too—I always had cookie dough on hand to bake when friends came over. We'd watch a movie, drink wine, and eat freshly baked cookies without having to deal with the time, mess, and cleanup of making them from scratch. All I needed to do was preheat the oven, pop a couple of the frozen dough balls on a sheet pan, and we'd have fresh baked cookies in 15 minutes. Similarly, when I knew there was a celebration coming up at the office, I'd arrive that day with a bag of cookies. My coworkers were impressed, thinking I'd spent all night baking, but really, all I'd done was bake the stash of cookie dough in my freezer.

Note that while you can freeze a lot of cookie doughs, there are rules. Freezing doughs that are thinner and batter-like, like those for madeleines or pizzelles, won't work—which is why you won't find a recipe for either cookie in this book. And because the cookie dough has been frozen, you'll need to adjust baking times—don't miss the Bake Later instructions at the end of every cookie recipe.

To freeze drop cookie dough, you're going to need a few tools: a 3-tablespoon cookie dough scoop, a quarter sheet pan, parchment paper, and a zip-top bag. Proceed with your favorite cookie recipe as directed, except skip the part about preheating the oven (unless, of course, you want one or two cookies right away). Line the sheet pan with parchment paper. Use the scoop to portion the cookie dough into balls, placing them on the prepared pan as you go. Cover loosely with plastic wrap and freeze for 1 hour or until they're hard enough to be transferred to the zip-top bag without losing their shape. You could just leave them on the pan, but storing them in a bag will leave more room in your freezer. Make sure you close the bag tightly—if not stored properly, butter can absorb flavors from the freezer that will make your cookies taste like whatever else is in there. Cookie dough will keep in the freezer for up to 1 year, but is best within the first 3 months.

oatmeal cookies

As a kid, I hated raisins. I was always disappointed when my mom would pack me a small box of raisins with my lunch, and I begged her for the candies and cookies that my classmates got instead. She rarely relented, and I was stuck with my little box for most of preschool and kindergarten.

As a college student, when I began to bake more, I realized I was avoiding recipes with raisins, like oatmeal cookies. I claimed I didn't like their flavor, but in retrospect, I'm pretty sure it was the raisins I was avoiding (childhood habits die hard!). Because when my boyfriend Erlend *insisted* that I give oatmeal cookies another chance by making them to his specifications—without raisins, and with chocolate instead—I was hooked.

This recipe makes an oatmeal cookie that you can customize with mix-ins made from pantry items and beyond. There's a Classic Oatmeal Raisin Mix-In for the traditionalists out there, but I encourage you to explore the other options, too. Want something for the holidays? Try the Oatmeal, Cranberry, and White Chocolate Mix-In. Looking to impress? Chop up some fancy crystallized ginger and use it instead of dried fruit.

Like the other drop cookie recipes in this chapter, this recipe is easy and fast, with a Work Time of just 10 minutes. After adding the oats, you'll need to use a rubber spatula to scrape the bowl a few more times than you would for other doughs—oats have a tendency to get stuck at the bottom of the mixer bowl.

ACTIVE TIME

15 minutes

prep time: **5 minutes**
work time: **10 minutes**
bake time: **15 minutes**

makes about 20 cookies

1 recipe Oatmeal Cookie Mix-In of your choice (page 125)

1¼ cups (5.65 ounces) all-purpose flour

1½ teaspoons ground cinnamon

1½ teaspoons baking soda

¾ teaspoon kosher salt

⅔ cup (5 ounces) tightly packed dark brown sugar

⅓ cup (2.35 ounces) granulated sugar

¾ cup (6 ounces) unsalted butter, **at room temperature**

1 large egg

1½ teaspoons pure vanilla extract

1¾ cups (6.15 ounces) old-fashioned rolled oats

1. Position a rack in the center of the oven and preheat the oven to 350°F. Line two half sheet pans with parchment paper.

2. Place the mix-in of your choice in a shallow bowl and toss to combine.

3. In a medium bowl, whisk together the flour, cinnamon, baking soda, and salt.

4. In the bowl of a stand mixer fitted with the paddle attachment, combine the sugars and butter. Beat on medium-high until light, fluffy, and doubled in volume, 2 to 3 minutes, using a rubber spatula to scrape down the bottom and sides of the bowl as necessary. Reduce the mixer to low, add the egg and vanilla, and beat until combined. Scrape down bottom and sides of the bowl. With the mixer on low, gradually add the dry ingredients and beat until just combined. Add the oats all at once and beat on low until combined, scraping down the bottom and sides of the bowl as needed to fully incorporate oats. Add the mix-in all at once and beat on medium-low until the mix-in is evenly distributed throughout, about 1 minute.

5. Use a 3-tablespoon cookie dough scoop to portion the cookie dough into balls, placing them at least 3 inches apart on the prepared sheet pans. Bake one pan at a time for 15 minutes, or until the edges have set but the centers are still gooey. Cool the cookies on the pan on a wire rack for 20 minutes, or until the edges and bottoms of the cookies have set and feel firm to the touch. Repeat with the remaining cookie dough (or freeze it to bake later). Serve warm or at room temperature. The cookies can be stored in an airtight container or zip-top bag at room temperature for up to 3 days.

bake later

Make the dough and form it into balls as directed. Follow the instructions on page 121 to freeze the dough. When ready to bake, position a rack in the center of the oven and preheat the oven to 350°F. Line a half sheet pan (or two, depending on how many cookies you're making) with parchment paper. Place the cookie dough balls at least 3 inches apart on the prepared sheet pan(s). Bake one pan at a time for 18 to 20 minutes, or until the edges have set but the centers are still gooey. Cool and serve as directed.

oatmeal cookie mix-ins

Oatmeal cookies are traditionally made with raisins, which, as you know, I'm not the world's biggest fan of. If you agree with me and want to try something new, know this: you can substitute any kind of dried fruit for the raisins for an updated twist on the classic oatmeal cookie. When writing this recipe, I spent a lot of time exploring my supermarket's dried fruit and nut aisle to see what would work best. Dried cherries and cranberries ended up being my favorites, but I encourage you to experiment! In general, if it's a fruit that can be used in granola or trail mix, it's fair game for these cookies.

⏱ **ACTIVE TIME**

5 minutes

prep time: **<5 minutes**

work time: **<5 minutes**

each makes enough for
1 recipe of oatmeal cookies

CLASSIC OATMEAL RAISIN

1 cup (5.5 ounces) raisins

OATMEAL CHOCOLATE CHIP

8 ounces dark chocolate (at least 70% cocoa), from whole fèves or a high-quality chocolate bar, chopped into ½- to 1-inch pieces

OATMEAL, CRANBERRY, AND WHITE CHOCOLATE

1 cup (6 ounces) dried cranberries

3 ounces white chocolate, from whole fèves or a high-quality chocolate bar, chopped into ½- to 1-inch pieces

OATMEAL, CHERRY, AND PISTACHIO

1 cup (5 ounces) dried cherries

½ cup (2.5 ounces) shelled pistachios

OATMEAL AND CRYSTALLIZED GINGER

½ cup (3.5 ounces) crystallized ginger, chopped into ¼- to ½-inch pieces

snickerdoodles

What. The. Heck. Is. A. Snickerdoodle?

Once, on a slow week at work, I found myself in an internet spiral as I tried to find the answer to that seemingly innocent question. A few cookbooks claim that snickerdoodles are German in origin, pointing out that the cookie's name comes from the German word *schneckennudel*. Others trace its origin to New England's tradition of whimsical cookie names. I ended my Google search as clueless as I had started it.

There was one consolation, though—I learned that snickerdoodles are basically sugar cookies, but with one important distinction: sugar cookies are leavened with baking powder, whereas snickerdoodles use cream of tartar. Traditionally, snickerdoodles are flavored with cinnamon, which I'll admit is not my favorite flavor in the spice rack. Since weeknight baking means making the recipe work for you, I began to experiment—bakers flavor sugar cookies with different extracts and mix-ins all the time. Why not snickerdoodles, too?

Which leads me back to this recipe. It produces classic snickerdoodles with a buttery soft center and crisp edges. But I also included ways to make these snickerdoodles your own, too. Stick with the traditional cinnamon sugar, or go for something new, like my personal favorite variation, raspberry sumac sugar. Like the other cookie recipes in this section, you can freeze the cookie dough and bake it later to fit your schedule, but I like baking a big batch to share over a few days—these cookies taste even better the day after they're made, as they soften and absorb more flavors from their topping.

ACTIVE TIME

20 minutes

prep time: **5 minutes**
work time: **15 minutes**
bake time: **10 minutes**

makes about 20 cookies

1 recipe Snickerdoodle Topping of your choice (page 129)

2¾ cups (12.35 ounces) all-purpose flour

2 teaspoons cream of tartar

1 teaspoon baking soda

½ teaspoon kosher salt

1½ cups (10.5 ounces) granulated sugar

1 cup (8 ounces) unsalted butter, **at room temperature**

2 large eggs

2 teaspoons pure vanilla extract

1. Position a rack in the center of the oven and preheat the oven to 400°F. Line two half sheet pans with parchment paper.

2. Prepare or place the snickerdoodle topping in a shallow bowl.

3. In a medium bowl, whisk together the flour, cream of tartar, baking soda, and salt.

4. In the bowl of a stand mixer fitted with the paddle attachment, combine the sugar and butter. Beat on medium-high until light, fluffy, and doubled in volume, 2 to 3 minutes, using a rubber spatula to scrape down the bottom and sides of the bowl as necessary. Reduce the mixer to low and add the eggs one at a time, adding the next egg only after the previous one has been fully incorporated. Add the vanilla and beat until just combined. Scrape down the bottom and sides of the bowl. With the mixer on low, gradually add the dry ingredients and beat until just combined. Scrape down the bottom and sides of the bowl once more, and beat on low for an additional 30 seconds.

5. Use a 3-tablespoon cookie dough scoop to portion the cookie dough into balls. Roll each in the snickerdoodle topping, covering them completely. Place the coated cookies at least 3 inches apart on the prepared sheet pans. Bake one pan at a time for 10 minutes, or until the edges have set but the centers are still gooey. The cookies will look puffed when you pull them out of the oven, but will fall and crack into the perfect cookies as they cool. Cool the cookies on the pan on a wire rack for 20 minutes, or until the edges and bottoms of the cookies have set and feel firm to the touch. Repeat with the remaining cookie dough (or freeze it to bake later). Serve warm or at room temperature. The cookies can be stored in an airtight container or zip-top bag at room temperature for up to 3 days.

bake later

The dough CANNOT be frozen with the topping, so save the work of making the topping for the day you plan to bake the cookies.

Make the cookie dough as directed. After scooping the cookie dough, lightly moisten your hands and give each cookie dough ball a quick tap with your palm to flatten it slightly—doing so will help the cookies flatten as they bake after being frozen. Follow the instructions on page 121 to freeze the dough. When ready to bake, position a rack in the center of the oven and preheat the oven to 400°F. Line a half sheet pan (or two, depending on how many cookies you're making) with parchment paper. In a shallow bowl, make the Snickerdoodle Topping of your choice. Roll each cookie dough ball in the snickerdoodle topping, covering them completely. Place the cookie dough balls at least 3 inches apart on the prepared sheet pan(s). Bake one pan at a time for 12 to 14 minutes, or until the edges have set but the centers are still gooey. Cool and serve as directed.

snickerdoodle topping

For a more modern take on the classic snickerdoodle, I suggest using spices and ingredients that add a bit of flash and color: freeze-dried fruit, matcha, black sesame seeds, and sprinkles. Freeze-dried fruit can be found in the dried fruit and nuts aisle of grocery stores like Whole Foods and Trader Joe's, while ingredients like black sesame seeds, matcha, and sumac can be found at specialty spice shops and Asian or Middle Eastern grocery stores.

ACTIVE TIME

5 minutes

prep time: **<5 minutes**

work time: **<5 minutes**

each makes enough for
1 recipe of snickerdoodles

CLASSIC SNICKERDOODLE TOPPING

¼ cup (1.75 ounces) granulated sugar

2 tablespoons ground cinnamon

BLACK SESAME SNICKERDOODLE TOPPING

¼ cup (1.75 ounces) granulated sugar

2 tablespoons black sesame seeds, finely processed

CARNIVAL SNICKERDOODLE TOPPING

½ cup (4 ounces) rainbow nonpareil sprinkles

MATCHA SNICKERDOODLE TOPPING

¼ cup (1.75 ounces) granulated sugar

1 tablespoon matcha green tea powder

RASPBERRY SUMAC SNICKERDOODLE TOPPING

¼ cup (1.75 ounces) granulated sugar

2 heaping tablespoons freeze-dried raspberries, finely processed

2 teaspoons ground sumac

ROLL-OUT COOKIES

Roll-out cookies—the kind of cookies with dough that is rolled with a rolling pin and stamped with cookie cutters—have never been my favorite thing to bake. As a weeknight baker, I find them too time-consuming: Recipes instruct you to make the dough, let it rest, roll out the dough, and let it rest again. And this is before even baking the cookies! I've commiserated with many bakers—and everyone I know has a story about a batch of roll-out sugar cookies that kept them up until three in the morning.

To add further insult to injury, I also make a huge mess every time I bake a batch of roll-out cookies. Most recipes ask you to flour your counter, and then proceed to tell you to roll out a slab of dough the size of a small rug. I always found those instructions hilarious, especially when I lived in shoebox apartments in San Francisco and New York, where my IKEA coffee table doubled as my kitchen counter. I'd stay up past midnight to finish baking and decorating a batch of roll-out sugar cookies, and then spend another hour cleaning flour out of unexpected places like underneath the dish rack or behind my ears.

So when I set out to develop my own recipe for roll-out cookies, I wanted to see if it was possible to make them without pulling an all-nighter or creating a disaster area. To do so, I broke all the traditional roll-out cookie recipe rules:

RULE 1: FOR THE BEST ROLL-OUT COOKIES, THE DOUGH NEEDS TO BE CHILLED AND RE-CHILLED MULTIPLE TIMES THROUGHOUT THE RECIPE.

Many traditional recipes instruct you to make the dough, chill it, roll it out, cut out cookies, chill the cutouts, and then bake them. It's a lot of steps, and over the years, I've learned that you can eliminate almost half of them and still get perfect cookies every time.

Many recipes tell you to chill the dough immediately after mixing it together. This is because most instruct you to use butter that's softened to room temperature. Softened butter will cause the dough to stick to your counter as you roll it out. However, almost all the recipes in this chapter use cold butter, either straight from the fridge or even chilled for a few minutes in the freezer. Using cold butter results in a dough that's still firm enough to be rolled out into a slab immediately after mixing without sticking.

However, after rolling out the dough, this is when it's worth chilling the slab for longer, either for a full hour or overnight. You'll be using the slab to cut out your cookies. The fully chilled dough leads to sharper shapes, and you can bake any cutouts immediately without them losing their shape in the oven since they're still cool from the fridge. There is no need to re-chill the cutouts, saving you time once more.

RULE 2: USE A FLOURED WORK SURFACE TO ROLL OUT YOUR COOKIES.

Most recipes instruct you to roll out your cookies on a floured work surface, like your kitchen countertop, to help prevent the cookie dough from sticking to the counter. While this method works, it can be pretty inconsistent. On a warm day, you'll need to use more flour, which can dry out your dough and lead to tough cookies. It's also hard to tell how much flour you actually need until it's already too late, when you've stamped out your cookie shapes only to find that half of them are stuck on the counter. Oh, and sometimes the dough sticks to the rolling pin, too, even if you've sprinkled a generous amount of flour there.

So, what if I told you there's an easier, more consistent way to roll out the dough, and that it involves almost no mess?

Instead of rolling out the dough on a floured surface, sandwich the dough between two large sheets of parchment paper. The bottom sheet will prevent the dough from sticking to the counter, while the top sheet will prevent the dough from sticking to the rolling pin. With this method, there are no floured surfaces to wipe and clean. You can even reuse the parchment paper to line your sheet pans when it comes time to bake the cookies. And if the dough does stick to the parchment after you've rolled it out, no problem—scoot the flat parchment sandwich onto a sheet pan and stick it in the fridge to chill the dough until it's ready to work with again.

RULE 3: ROLL-OUT COOKIES NEED SPECIALIZED TOOLS LIKE COOKIE CUTTERS.

If you're baking for a special occasion, I encourage you to buy all the cute cookie cutters you want and stamp your heart out. But cookie cutters can take up a lot of valuable real estate in the kitchen. So if you're looking to declutter, it turns out that you don't actually *need* cookie cutters—in fact, I like to turn roll-out cookies into slice-and-bake ones. Here's how:

Once you've made the cookie dough, divide it in two. Shape each portion into a rough log and wrap each in plastic wrap. And now comes the fun part—it's time to pretend we're back in preschool. Use your hands to roll the dough as you would clay or Play-Doh, rolling it back and forth in quick motions until it forms a circular log that is about 1½ inches in diameter. If the dough feels soft, stick it in the fridge for about 10 minutes. Then unwrap a log, take a sharp knife, and slice the log crosswise into ½-inch-thick discs. Voilà! Roll-out cookies made without cookie cutters.

In addition to this slice-and-bake method, there are other tricks and hacks you can use to get cute cookie shapes without ever needing cookie cutters. Be sure to check out the recipe for Almost-

No-Mess Shortbread Cookies on page 141 to learn how to get perfectly square cookies without any waste.

As there are so many ways to shape and stamp your dough, the Work Time for the recipes in this chapter will vary depending on how you choose to roll and cut your cookies. And be warned: Using cookie cutters will usually take longer. But don't worry! You can split that work up over several days with my Weeknight Baking Roll-Out Cookie Guide.

weeknight baking roll-out cookie schedule

DAY 1: MAKE AND SHAPE THE DOUGH!

Follow the recipe instructions to make, roll out, and cut the dough. Place the cookies on parchment paper–lined sheet pans, leaving 1 to 1½ inches between them. Cover each pan loosely with plastic wrap. Refrigerate overnight.

DAY 2: BAKE AND COOL THE COOKIES!

Remove and discard the plastic wrap and follow the recipe instructions to bake the cookies. Cool the cookies completely on the pans on wire racks. If your cookies don't need to be iced (like the Almost-No-Mess Shortbread Cookies on page 141 or Black-and-White Chocolate Chunk Shortbread Cookies on page 145), go ahead and eat one! However, if you're making A Roll-Out Sugar Cookie Recipe That Actually Has Your Back (page 135), plan on icing them the next day. Place the cooled cookies in an airtight container or zip-top bag and store them on the counter overnight.

DAY 3: DECORATE AND SERVE THE COOKIES!

Follow the recipe instructions to make any necessary frosting or icing. Decorate the cookies as you wish; if using Royal Icing (page 139), note that cookies usually require 4 to 6 hours at room temperature to dry completely. I usually ice cookies first thing in the morning and eat them in the afternoon.

freezing roll-out cookie dough to bake later

Alternatively, you can freeze unbaked cookie cutouts to bake later. Lay each cookie on a parchment paper–lined sheet pan; the cutouts can be fairly close to one another but not touching, or they might freeze together. Place a second sheet of parchment paper over the first layer of cookies, and arrange a second layer of cookies on top. If there's room in the pan, you can place another sheet of parchment paper over the second layer of cookies and arrange a third layer of cookies on top. Wrap the entire pan in plastic wrap and freeze. Frozen roll-out cookie dough will keep in the freezer for up to 6 months.

However, if you've shaped the dough into logs, there's no need to even slice the cookies before freezing the dough. Simply wrap each log of dough tightly in plastic wrap and then in a layer of aluminum foil. The day before you plan on baking the cookies, thaw the cookie dough logs by removing the foil layers (but keep them wrapped in plastic!) and placing them in the fridge overnight.

Regardless of which freezing method you chose, you'll need to add 3 to 5 minutes to the recipe's Bake Time when you bake the cookies.

a roll-out sugar cookie recipe
that actually has your back

Despite their time-consuming nature, I have a soft spot for making sugar cookies. I love that you can easily customize the dough into shapes fit for any occasion: I've made sugar cookie hearts for Valentine's Day, edible snowflakes for the winter holidays, and, my personal favorite, gingerDEAD men for Halloween.

My sugar cookie recipe yields a dough so sturdy that you can make sculptures from it. Not to mention that it's tasty as heck, too, with a crumb so buttery you could mistake it for shortbread. The trick is to use cold butter; cold butter will make a cool dough that is easier to roll out and cut. Make sure that the cookies are completely cooled before decorating them with royal icing; if the cookies are still warm from the oven, the residual heat will cause the icing to run and ruin your design.

🕐 **ACTIVE TIME**
20 minutes over 2 days

makes about 24
(3-inch) cookies

NOTE: The yield of this recipe will ultimately vary depending on the shape and size of your cookie cutter; however, I've provided an approximation based on a 3-inch round cookie cutter.

3⅓ cups (15 ounces) all-purpose flour

1½ teaspoons baking powder

¾ teaspoon kosher salt

1 cup (8 ounces) **very cold** unsalted butter, cut into 1-inch cubes

1 cup (7 ounces) granulated sugar

1 teaspoon pure vanilla extract

1 large egg

📅 **DAY 1**

prep time: **5 minutes**
work time: **10 minutes**

MAKE AND ROLL THE DOUGH

1. In a medium bowl, whisk together the flour, baking powder, and salt.

2. In the bowl of a stand mixer fitted with the paddle attachment, combine the butter, sugar, and vanilla. Beat on medium until light, fluffy, and doubled in volume, 3 to 5 minutes, using a rubber spatula to scrape down the bottom and sides of the bowl as necessary. Reduce the mixer to low, add the egg, and beat until just incorporated. Scrape down the bottom and sides of the bowl.

3. With the mixer on low, gradually add the dry ingredients and beat until combined. Increase the mixer to medium-low and beat until the dough clumps around the paddle and/or sides of the bowl, 2 to 3 minutes.

4. Tip the dough out onto a piece of parchment paper around the size of a half sheet pan and use your hands to shape it into a roughly 6-inch square. Place a second sheet of parchment over the dough, creating a parchment sandwich with the dough in the middle. Use a rolling pin to flatten the dough between the parchment sheets, working from left to right. Turn the dough 90 degrees and repeat every so often—doing so will help prevent the dough from cracking as you roll it. If the parchment starts to wrinkle and leave creases in the cookie dough, pull the sheet loose and smooth it before rolling the dough more. Continue rotating and rolling until you have a rough oval about 13 inches wide, 18 inches long, and between ⅛ and ¼ inch thick.

5. Transfer the slab of cookie dough, still in between the parchment, to a half sheet pan. Refrigerate for at least 1 hour, preferably overnight.

DAY 2

work time: **5 minutes**

bake time: **10 minutes for each batch**

STAMP OUT AND BAKE THE COOKIES

1. Position a rack in the center of the oven and preheat the oven to 350°F.

2. Remove the sheet pan of dough from the refrigerator. Use the overhanging parchment as handles to carefully lift the slab of dough off the sheet pan and onto the counter. Peel the top layer of parchment from the slab and use it to line the sheet pan once more. Line a second half sheet pan with parchment as well.

3. Use your favorite cookie cutters to cut out shapes, placing the cookies at least 1½ inches apart on the prepared sheet pans. The dough should still be cool and firm to the touch. If not, chill both sheet pans in the freezer for at least 10 minutes before baking.

4. Bake one pan at a time (keeping the other pan in the refrigerator) for 10 minutes, or until the cookies are golden brown around the edges. Cool the cookies on the pan on a wire rack for 20 minutes, or until the edges and bottoms of the cookies are set and feel firm to the touch. Repeat to bake the remaining cookies. Serve warm or at room temperature. If decorating the cookies, cool completely before frosting with Royal Icing (page 139). The cookies can be stored in an airtight container or zip-top bag at room temperature for up to 3 days.

make in one day

To expedite the process and make the cookies in 1 day, chill the rolled-out cookie dough in the freezer (as opposed to the refrigerator) for 5 to 10 minutes, until the dough is firm and doesn't indent when poked. Stamp out and bake the cookies as directed. If you find that the cookies are losing their shape in the oven, freeze the subsequent batches of cookie cutouts for an additional 5 to 10 minutes before baking.

bake later

Make the dough and stamp out the cookies as directed. Follow the instructions on page 134 to freeze the dough. When ready to bake, position a rack in the center of the oven and preheat the oven to 350°F. Line a half sheet pan (or two, depending on how many cookies you're making) with parchment paper. Place the cutout cookies at least 1½ inches apart on the prepared sheet pan(s). Bake one pan at a time (keeping the other in the refrigerator) for 12 minutes, or until the cookies are golden brown around the edges. Cool and serve as directed.

troubleshooting

If your refrigerator has limited space and does not fit a half sheet pan, you can divide the dough in two and roll out each piece between two sheets of parchment paper to make a slab that fits a quarter sheet pan. Layer and stack both slabs of cookie dough in the same pan with the instructions on page 134.

If you remove the cookie dough from the refrigerator and find that it is too solid for your cookie cutter to cut through, let it sit at room temperature for 5 to 10 minutes before trying again. As you're working, if you find that the dough has become too soft and your cutter is no longer able to cut clean shapes from the dough, the dough likely needs to be re-chilled. Carefully transfer the slab of dough back to the sheet pan and freeze for 5 to 10 minutes to allow the slab to firm up again.

royal icing

ACTIVE TIME

5 minutes

prep time: **<5 minutes**

work time: **5 minutes**

makes about 2 cups

NOTE: If you want to avoid using raw egg, substitute 1½ tablespoons meringue powder for the egg and reduce the water in the recipe to 3 tablespoons total.

Roll-out cookies are often decorated with royal icing, which hardens to a smooth, candy-like consistency. Most royal icings use confectioners' sugar and egg whites, but I've found that using the whole egg works just as well, and is less fussy and wasteful. You can divide the royal icing into many different batches and dye each with its own shade of food coloring; just be sure to transfer each immediately into a piping bag or cover the bowl with plastic wrap to prevent the royal icing from drying as you work.

2 cups (8 ounces) confectioners' sugar, sifted if lumpy

1 large egg

1 teaspoon pure vanilla extract

Pinch of kosher salt

¼ cup (2 ounces) water

1. In a medium bowl, whisk together the confectioners' sugar, egg, vanilla, and salt. Add the water 1 tablespoon at a time, whisking until the desired consistency is reached. For lining icing (the type of icing used for outlining shapes, borders, and lettering), the icing should hold a stiff peak. For flood icing (the type of icing used to fill in outlines), add additional water, a small splash at a time, until you reach a consistency similar to maple syrup; the icing should fall in ribbons when lifted with a spoon from the bowl. Pour into a piping bag fitted with a writing tip. Seal the bag as directed on page 109 and use immediately.

2. A cookie decorated with royal icing will take 4 to 6 hours to dry completely at room temperature. The decorated cookies can be stored in an airtight container or zip-top bag at room temperature overnight.

almost-no-mess shortbread cookies

ACTIVE TIME

20 minutes over 2 days

makes 16 cookies

NOTE: Because this recipe uses so few ingredients, each ingredient must be the very best quality you can find. This is one of the few recipes in the book where it's worth sourcing expensive, high-quality European butter (I'm partial to Vermont Creamery's European-style cultured butter).

 DAY 1

prep time: **<5 minutes**

work time: **10 minutes**

For many years, I led a kind of double life as I balanced my full-time job and my baking blog. Occasionally, my two lives would intersect. Upon discovering my baking hobby, my favorite boss (who happened to be Scottish) lovingly described his family's secret shortbread recipe, which consisted of a very generous amount of butter mixed with a handful of sugar and flour.

One of my biggest regrets was being too shy to ask him for his family recipe before he left the company. A good shortbread recipe is hard to find! Because shortbread cookies contain only a handful of ingredients, their ratios relative to each other must be *perfect*. This recipe makes what I consider an outstanding shortbread cookie, one that I hope would make my former boss proud. It is a pale golden brown shortbread with a super-buttery flavor and a tender crumb that melts in your mouth. The trick is to work the dough as little as possible, which is why I direct you to cut the cookies into squares instead of using cookie cutters. This prevents overhandling, as there is no need to gather the cookie dough scraps and reroll them repeatedly.

1 cup (8 ounces) **very cold** unsalted butter

2 cups (9 ounces) all-purpose flour

½ cup (3.5 ounces) plus 2 tablespoons granulated sugar

2 teaspoons kosher salt

MAKE AND ROLL THE DOUGH

1. Cut the butter into 1- to 1½-inch pieces and place them in a small bowl. Freeze while you prep the rest of the ingredients.

2. In the bowl of a stand mixer fitted with the paddle attachment, combine the flour, ½ cup (3.5 ounces) of the sugar, and the salt. Beat on low until just combined, about 15 seconds. Add the butter all at once and beat on low until the dough starts to resemble coarse meal, with pea-sized pieces of butter throughout, about 3 minutes. Increase the mixer to medium and beat until the dough clumps around the paddle and/or the sides of the bowl, 2 to 3 minutes. If necessary, use a mixer cover (or throw a towel over the mixer bowl) while beating to prevent any pieces of dough from shooting out of the bowl.

3. Tip the dough out onto a piece of parchment paper around the size of a half sheet pan and use your hands to shape it into a roughly 6-inch square. Place a second sheet of parchment over the dough, creating a parchment sandwich with the dough in the middle. Use a rolling pin to flatten the dough between the parchment sheets, working from left to right. Turn the dough 90 degrees and repeat every so often—doing so will help prevent the dough from cracking as you roll it. If the parchment starts to wrinkle and leave creases in the dough, pull the sheet loose and smooth it before rolling the dough more. Continue rotating and rolling until you have a 9-inch square of dough around ¼ inch thick.

4. Remove the top layer of parchment. Press a bench scraper against the sides of the dough to create straight edges. Transfer the slab of cookie dough, still on the bottom layer of parchment, to a half sheet pan. Cover with the top layer of parchment once more and refrigerate for at least 2 hours, preferably overnight.

DAY 2

work time: **5 minutes**

bake time: **15 minutes for each batch**

SLICE AND BAKE THE COOKIES

1. Position a rack in the center of the oven and preheat the oven to 350°F.

2. Remove the sheet pan of dough from the refrigerator. Use the overhanging parchment as handles to carefully lift the slab of dough off the sheet pan and onto a cutting board. Peel the top layer of parchment from the slab and use it to line the sheet pan once more. Line a second half sheet pan with parchment as well.

3. Use a paring knife to slice the slab of dough in half lengthwise, then slice each portion in half crosswise. You should have four smaller dough slabs of equal size. Repeat the process with each of the smaller dough slabs until you have sixteen 2-inch-square cookies. Place the cookies at least 2 inches apart on the prepared sheet pans. Sprinkle the remaining 2 tablespoons of sugar evenly over each cookie. The dough should still be cool and firm to the touch. If not, chill both sheet pans in the freezer for at least 10 minutes before baking.

4. Bake one pan at a time (keeping the other pan in the refrigerator) for 15 to 17 minutes, or until the edges of each cookie are pale golden brown with small hairline cracks visible on their surfaces. For straight cookie edges, gently press a bench scraper against the side of each cookie immediately after removing the cookies from the oven. Cool the cookies on the pan on a wire rack for 20 minutes, or until the edges and bottoms of the cookies are set and feel firm to the touch. Repeat to bake the remaining cookies. Serve warm or at room temperature. The cookies can be stored in an airtight container or zip-top bag at room temperature for up to 3 days.

make in one day

This recipe divides the work over 2 days; to expedite the process and make the cookies in 1 day, chill the rolled-out cookie dough in the freezer (as opposed to the refrigerator) for 15 minutes, until the dough is firm and doesn't indent when poked. Slice and bake the cookies as directed. If you find that the cookies are losing their shape in the oven, freeze the subsequent batches of cookie cutouts for an additional 5 to 10 minutes before baking.

bake later

Make the dough and cut out the cookies as directed. Follow the instructions on page 134 to freeze the dough. When ready to bake, position a rack in the center of the oven and preheat the oven to 350°F. Line a half sheet pan (or two, depending on how many cookies you're making) with parchment paper. Place the cookies at least 2 inches apart on the prepared sheet pan(s). Bake one pan at a time (keeping the other in the refrigerator) for 18 to 20 minutes, or until the cookies are golden brown around the edges. Cool and serve as directed.

black-and-white chocolate chunk shortbread cookies

Oreos are one of my favorite cookies; I love their dark chocolate color and the creamy vanilla filling sandwiched between each cookie. Over the years, I've tried to make my own at home, with varying success. Although I've come pretty close to the real thing, homemade Oreos require far more time and effort than what I like to reserve for my weeknight baking projects—it's much easier to go to the store and buy a package.

That being said, I knew I'd be sad if this cookbook didn't have at least one recipe honoring my favorite store-bought cookie. Which brings me to this recipe—these cookies have the midnight-black chocolate shortbread base that I love about Oreos. But instead of making a cream filling and creating cookie sandwiches (both of which require time and effort), I studded the shortbread with white chocolate chunks. The white chocolate tastes like the vanilla cream filling from my favorite cookie, but in solid, bite-size pieces throughout the shortbread. In a pinch, you can substitute whatever chocolate you prefer, but I personally love the contrast between the shortbread and the white chocolate chunks—it looks like a modern art homage to my favorite Oreo.

ACTIVE TIME

35 minutes over 2 days

makes 24 cookies

NOTE: Be sure to use Dutch-processed cocoa powder, which will result in the dark chocolate color of these cookies.

DAY 1

prep time: **10 minutes**

work time: **15 minutes**

2 cups (9 ounces) all-purpose flour

1 cup (3 ounces) Dutch-processed cocoa powder, sifted if lumpy

¼ teaspoon baking soda

1 teaspoon kosher salt

1 cup (8 ounces) unsalted butter, **at room temperature**

¾ cup plus 1 tablespoon (5.65 ounces) granulated sugar

8 ounces white chocolate, chopped into ¼- to ½-inch pieces

MAKE THE DOUGH

1. In a medium bowl, whisk together the flour, cocoa powder, baking soda, and salt.

2. In the bowl of a stand mixer fitted with the paddle attachment, combine the butter and sugar. Beat on medium-high until light, fluffy, and doubled in volume, 2 to 3 minutes, using a rubber spatula to scrape down the bottom and sides of the bowl as necessary.

3. With the mixer on low, gradually add the dry ingredients. Increase to medium-low and beat until the dough clumps around the paddle and/or the

sides of the bowl, 2 to 3 minutes. Add the white chocolate all at once and beat on medium-low until the chocolate is evenly distributed throughout, about 1 minute.

4. Tip the dough onto the counter and use your hands to shape it into a roughly 6-inch square. Use a bench scraper to divide the dough into four equal portions. Place one portion in the center of a piece of plastic wrap around the size of a quarter sheet pan and use your hands to shape it into a rough log. Fold the plastic over the log so it covers the dough completely and use your hands to roll the dough as you would clay or Play-Doh, rolling it back and forth in quick motions until it forms a circular log about 1½ inches wide and 5 inches long. Seal the plastic wrap tightly around the dough and refrigerate overnight. Repeat with the remaining dough portions.

🗓 DAY 2

work time: **10 minutes**
bake time: **15 minutes**

SLICE AND BAKE THE COOKIES

1. Position a rack in the center of the oven and preheat the oven to 325°F. Line two half sheet pans with parchment paper.

2. Unwrap each dough log and discard the plastic wrap. Use a serrated knife to slice each log crosswise into ½-inch-thick rounds, sawing the knife back and forth slowly to prevent the cookie dough from crumbling and the white chocolate pieces from falling out of the dough. Place the cookies about 2 inches apart on the prepared sheet pans. The dough should still be cool and firm to the touch. If not, chill both sheet pans in the freezer for at least 10 minutes before baking.

3. Bake one pan at a time (keeping the other pan in the refrigerator) for 15 to 18 minutes, or until small hairline cracks are visible on the surface of the cookies. Cool the cookies on the pan on a wire rack for 20 minutes, or until the edges and bottoms of the cookies are set and feel firm to the touch. Repeat to bake the remaining cookies. Serve warm, or at room temperature. The cookies can be stored in an airtight container or zip-top bag at room temperature for up to 3 days.

make in one day

This recipe divides the work over 2 days; to expedite the process and make the cookies in 1 day, refrigerate the cookie dough logs for at least 4 hours, until the dough is firm and doesn't indent when poked. Slice and bake the cookies as directed. If you find that the cookies are losing their shape in the oven, freeze the subsequent batches of cookie cutouts for an additional 5 to 10 minutes before baking.

bake later

Make the dough and shape it into logs as directed. Follow the instructions on page 134 to freeze the dough. The night before you plan to bake, transfer the dough logs to the refrigerator to thaw overnight. When ready to bake, position a rack in the center of the oven and preheat the oven to 325°F. Line a half sheet pan (or two, depending on how many cookies you're making) with parchment paper. Slice the logs into cookies as directed, placing the cookies at least 2 inches apart on the prepared sheet pan(s). Bake one pan at a time (keeping the other in the refrigerator) for 12 minutes, or until small hairline cracks are visible on the surface of the cookies. Cool and serve as directed.

BROWNIES, BLONDIES, AND LAYER BARS

Cookies have a reputation for being the fastest and easiest baked good to make, but I beg to differ—cookies may have the reputation, but brownies and blondies deserve the credit instead. Unlike cookie dough, which needs to be scooped and arranged on a sheet pan, brownie and blondie batter can be simply poured into a pan. That's it.

In addition to these fast-and-easy bar recipes, you'll also find recipes for layer bars like lime curd bars, cheesecake bars, and jammy pie bars. Don't be intimidated by these recipes—think of them as more approachable versions of classic desserts like key lime pie, New York cheesecake, and old-fashioned fruit pie. While the classics usually require special processes like garnishing with whipped cream and baking in water baths, their layer bar counterparts skip all those steps and are just as tasty. Because layer bars usually have multiple components, I like to break up the recipe over the course of a few days: each layer bar recipe instructs you to make and bake the crust on the first day, make and add the filling on the second day, and serve on the third day. The bars are best on their third day, anyway, after they've been refrigerated overnight and the filling has had a chance to set. Don't worry about the crust or filling getting soggy or stale—similar to cookie dough, this overnight rest makes everything taste better. If three days sounds like too long to wait for a dessert, you can ALWAYS expedite the recipe by making and baking all the recipe's components in one day—just know that your Work Time will be longer.

boxed-mix brownies, from scratch

In college, boxed-mix brownies made me popular. I would whip up a batch in our tiny communal kitchen, and as soon as the oven timer dinged, a crowd of my friends would appear to devour them. As a result, I have very fond memories of boxed-mix brownies. Maybe you do, too! A lot of us learned how to bake with mixes from Betty Crocker, Duncan Hines, and more. The flavor and texture of boxed-mix brownies often serve as the gold standard for the perfect brownie. Many of my blog readers lamented that they could never find a recipe to live up to their nostalgic flavor. Some even told me not to waste my time. But I had to try.

While this recipe comes pretty close to the real thing, it's not *exactly* the real thing. It's better! Many boxed mixes contain preservatives and chemical agents like soybean powder and/or soy lecithin, both of which act as emulsifiers to help oil and water mix more easily. Home bakers don't have access to these ingredients, and truthfully, we don't need them. Instead, I used confectioners' sugar (confectioners' sugar contains cornstarch, which helps thicken the batter in a similar way) and upped the amount of liquid and egg than what's traditionally used with a boxed mix. The resulting brownie has the beloved chew of boxed-mix brownies, but with a flavor that's 100 percent real.

ACTIVE TIME

10 minutes

prep time: **5 minutes**
work time: **5 minutes**
bake time: **40 minutes**

makes 16 brownies

NOTE: The key to the perfect brownie—even the boxed-mix brownie—is the chocolate. Hershey's Special Dark cocoa powder works best as its dark color yields a dry mix that looks identical to dry boxed mix. Ghirardelli's 60% Cacao Bittersweet Chocolate Premium Baking Chips work well here, since their chips are slightly larger than other brands' and leave you with more chocolate in every bite.

FOR THE DRY MIX

1½ cups (10.5 ounces) granulated sugar

¾ cup (3.35 ounces) all-purpose flour

⅔ cup (2 ounces) Dutch-processed cocoa powder, sifted if lumpy

½ cup (3 ounces) bittersweet chocolate chips

½ cup (2 ounces) confectioners' sugar, sifted if lumpy

¾ teaspoon kosher salt

FOR THE WET MIX

2 large eggs

½ cup (4 ounces) canola oil

2 tablespoons water

1. Position a rack in the center of the oven and preheat the oven to 325°F. Lightly spray an 8-inch square cake pan with cooking spray and line it with parchment paper, leaving a 2-inch overhang on two opposite sides of the pan. Spray the parchment, too.

2. In a medium bowl, combine all the ingredients for the dry mix.

3. In a large bowl, combine all the ingredients for the wet mix and stir with a rubber spatula to break up the egg yolks. Sprinkle the dry mix over the wet mix and stir until just combined.

4. Pour the batter into the prepared pan and use an offset spatula to smooth the top. Bake for 40 to 45 minutes, or until a skewer inserted into the center of the brownies comes out with a few crumbs attached. Cool completely on a wire rack before slicing.

5. Run a butter knife or offset spatula along the edges of the pan and use the overhanging parchment as handles to lift the brownies out of the pan and onto a cutting board. Slice into 2-inch squares and serve. The brownies can be stored in an airtight container or zip-top bag at room temperature for up to 3 days.

NOTE: It's better to pull the brownies out of the oven early than leave them in too long—if you overbake the brownies, they'll be tough. They might appear underbaked, but I promise that when they've cooled, they will be perfect.

better-than-supernatural fudge brownies

If you asked me the most valuable thing I learned while working in tech, my answer would surprise you. It wasn't how to code, or how to negotiate with vendors, or how to lead a team of engineers and analysts through a product launch. The most valuable thing I learned was the recipe for my favorite brownie, *ever*. A coworker discovered that I liked to bake and recommended I try a brownie recipe by Nick Malgieri, the director of the Institute of Culinary Education in New York City. Nick described these brownies as "supernatural"; after accidentally leaving out half the flour that the recipe called for, it still produced extremely fudgy brownies underneath a fragile, paper-thin sugar crust.

Throughout the years, I adapted the recipe to fit my needs as a weeknight baker, finding shortcuts to reduce its Work Time. As the chocolate and butter are melting, prep your pan and measure out the other ingredients you'll need for the recipe. I also found that there's no need to wait for the chocolate to cool; you can add the rest of the ingredients while the chocolate is still warm, saving yourself a significant amount of time. Just make sure to continually whisk as you do to prevent any eggs from accidentally cooking and scrambling.

ACTIVE TIME

15 minutes

prep time: **<5 minutes**
work time: **15 minutes**
bake time: **35 minutes**

makes 20 brownies

NOTE: The key to a perfect brownie is chocolate. Be sure to use a dark chocolate with between 63% and 73% cocoa.

1 cup (8 ounces) unsalted butter, chopped into 1- to 2-inch pieces

2 tablespoons Dutch-processed cocoa powder, sifted if lumpy

8 ounces dark chocolate (between 63% and 73% cocoa), from whole fèves or a high-quality chocolate bar, hand broken into pieces

1 cup (4.5 ounces) all-purpose flour

½ teaspoon kosher salt

4 large eggs

1 cup tightly packed (7.5 ounces) dark brown sugar

1 cup (7 ounces) granulated sugar

2 teaspoons pure vanilla extract

1. Position a rack in the center of the oven and preheat the oven to 350°F. Lightly spray a 9 x 13-inch cake pan with cooking spray and line with parchment paper, leaving a 2-inch overhang on the pan's two long sides. Spray the parchment, too.

2. Place the butter and cocoa powder in the top of a double boiler or in a heatproof bowl set over a medium, heavy-bottomed saucepan filled with a few inches of simmering water (be sure the bottom of the bowl does not touch the

water). Cook over medium heat to melt the butter. While the butter melts, in a food processor, pulse the chocolate for a few seconds at a time until roughly chopped. Add the chocolate to the butter and cook, using a heatproof rubber spatula to stir the mixture and scrape the sides of the bowl occasionally, until the butter and chocolate have melted and combined, about 10 minutes. Set the double boiler or bowl on a wire rack and let the chocolate mixture cool while you prep the other ingredients.

3. In a small bowl, whisk together the flour and salt.

4. In the bowl of a stand mixer fitted with the whisk attachment, combine the eggs, sugars, and vanilla. Whisk on low until combined, 1 to 2 minutes, using a rubber spatula to scrape down the bottom and sides of the bowl as necessary. Increase the mixer to medium and slowly pour in the chocolate mixture, aiming for the sides of the bowl as opposed to the whisk. Continue whisking on medium until the batter is smooth, about 1 minute.

5. Sprinkle the dry ingredients over the batter all at once and use a rubber spatula to mix until just combined.

NOTE: It's better to pull the brownies out of the oven early than leave them in too long—if you overbake the brownies, they'll be tough. They might appear underbaked, but I promise that when they've cooled, they will be perfect.

6. Pour the batter into the prepared pan and use an offset spatula to smooth the top. Bake for 35 to 40 minutes, or until a skewer inserted into the center of the brownies comes out with a few crumbs attached. Cool completely on a wire rack before slicing.

7. Run a butter knife or offset spatula along the edges of the pan and use the overhanging parchment as handles to lift the brownies out of the pan and onto a cutting board. Slice into 20 rectangles, each about 2¼ inches wide and 2½ inches long, and serve. The brownies can be stored in an airtight container or zip-top bag at room temperature for up to 3 days.

brown butter blondies

Brown butter is made by cooking butter until the water in it evaporates and you're left with an amber-colored liquid with a rich flavor and a wonderfully nutty aroma. When used in baking recipes, brown butter takes everything to the next level without too much extra work.

But real talk: It took me almost three years to figure out that I was browning butter wrong. I never cooked the butter long enough for its milk solids to caramelize. I was accidentally just melting the butter instead (what can I say, I was busy leading a double life!). But I've included a step-by-step guide on page 161 to help you through the process.

Once I started using brown butter in my baked goods, there was no looking back. It works especially well in these blondies, giving them an extra-rich toffee flavor. I like to add white chocolate, both mixing chunks in the batter and sprinkling a generous amount on top of the blondies before baking. In the oven, the sugars in the white chocolate caramelize, taking on a flavor similar to dulce de leche. In a pinch, use your favorite milk chocolate or dark chocolate for a blondie more reminiscent of a chocolate chip cookie.

1 cup (8 ounces) unsalted butter

8 ounces white chocolate, from whole fèves or a high-quality chocolate bar, hand broken into pieces

2 cups (9 ounces) all-purpose flour

1 teaspoon kosher salt

1¾ cups tightly packed (13.15 ounces) dark brown sugar

2 large eggs

1 tablespoon pure vanilla extract

ACTIVE TIME

20 minutes

prep time: **5 minutes**

work time: **15 minutes**

bake time: **25 minutes**

makes 20 blondies

NOTE: It takes about 10 minutes to brown butter. Watch it carefully—it takes only a few seconds for butter to go from browned to burnt. Once you're satisfied with the color of your brown butter, immediately pour it into a liquid measuring cup. Removing it from the hot pan will prevent it from burning and give the brown butter the time it needs to cool before using in this recipe.

1. In a light-colored saucepan, melt the butter over medium-low heat, swirling the pan occasionally, until it starts to foam. Use a heatproof rubber spatula to scrape the bottom and sides of the pan occasionally to prevent the milk solids in the butter from burning. Cook for 5 minutes, or until the butter smells nutty and is amber with dark flecks at the bottom of the pan. Remove from the heat and immediately pour the brown butter into a liquid measuring cup. Set it on a wire rack to cool while you prep the other ingredients.

2. Position a rack in the center of the oven and preheat the oven to 350°F. Lightly spray a 9 x 13-inch cake pan with cooking spray and line with parchment paper, leaving a 2-inch overhang on the pan's two long sides. Spray the parchment, too.

3. In a food processor, pulse the white chocolate a few seconds at a time until roughly chopped.

4. In a medium bowl, whisk together the flour and salt.

5. Place the sugar in the bowl of a stand mixer fitted with the paddle attachment. With the mixer on low, slowly pour in the brown butter and beat for 1 minute, until the mixture looks like wet sand. Add the eggs one at a time, adding the next egg only after the previous one has been fully incorporated, using a rubber spatula to scrape down the bottom and sides of the bowl after each addition. Add the vanilla and beat until just combined. With the mixer on low, gradually add the dry ingredients and beat until just combined. Scrape down the bottom and sides of the bowl once more, and beat on low for an additional 30 seconds. Add the white chocolate all at once, and beat on medium-low until the chocolate is evenly distributed throughout, about 1 minute.

6. Scrape the batter into the prepared pan and use an offset spatula to smooth the top. Bake for 25 to 30 minutes, or until a skewer inserted into the center of the blondies comes out with a few crumbs attached. Cool completely on a wire rack before slicing.

7. Run a butter knife or offset spatula along the edges of the pan and use the overhanging parchment as handles to lift the blondies out of the pan and onto a cutting board. Slice into 20 rectangles, each about 2¼ inches wide and 2½ inches long, and serve. The blondies can be stored in an airtight container or zip-top bag at room temperature for up to 3 days.

variations

birthday cake blondies

For my thirtieth birthday, I made a variation of this recipe with rainbow sprinkles to celebrate. It's one of the most popular recipes on my blog to date, and even got me a consulting job where I helped a small business owner develop his own recipe to be sold by grocery stores around the country!

Make the batter as directed, but replace the pure vanilla extract with 1 tablespoon clear artificial vanilla extract (it's what they use in Funfetti box mix to give it that extra birthday cake flavor). Add ⅓ heaping cup (2.15 ounces) rainbow sprinkles to the batter after mixing in the white chocolate. Mix until the sprinkles are evenly distributed throughout the batter. Continue with the recipe as directed. This variation does not significantly affect Prep, Work, or Bake Time.

halva blondies

When I lived in New York, I became obsessed with Seed + Mill, a specialty store that sold different varieties of halva. Halva is a Middle Eastern candy made from tahini, with a texture somewhere between that of fudge and meringue. This variation adds chunks of halva to the bars for unexpected bursts of chewy, nutty flavor.

Chop 4 ounces halva into 1- to 1½-inch pieces. Make the batter as directed, but add the halva pieces to the batter after mixing in the white chocolate and mix until the halva is evenly distributed throughout the batter. This variation does not significantly affect Prep, Work, or Bake Time.

chocolate hazelnut blondies

One of my favorite recipes on *Hummingbird High* is for chocolate hazelnut blondies. I used gianduja chocolate, which is made with a type of Italian milk chocolate that consists of 20% to 30% hazelnut paste. It's basically Nutella in chocolate bar form.

Proceed with the recipe as directed, but replace ½ cup (2.25 ounces) of the all-purpose flour with ½ cup (1.5 ounces) hazelnut meal and substitute gianduja chocolate for the white chocolate. Because gianduja chocolate is softer than regular chocolate, I recommend skipping the food processor and using a chef's knife to chop it into 1- to 2-inch pieces. This variation does not significantly affect Prep, Work, or Bake Time.

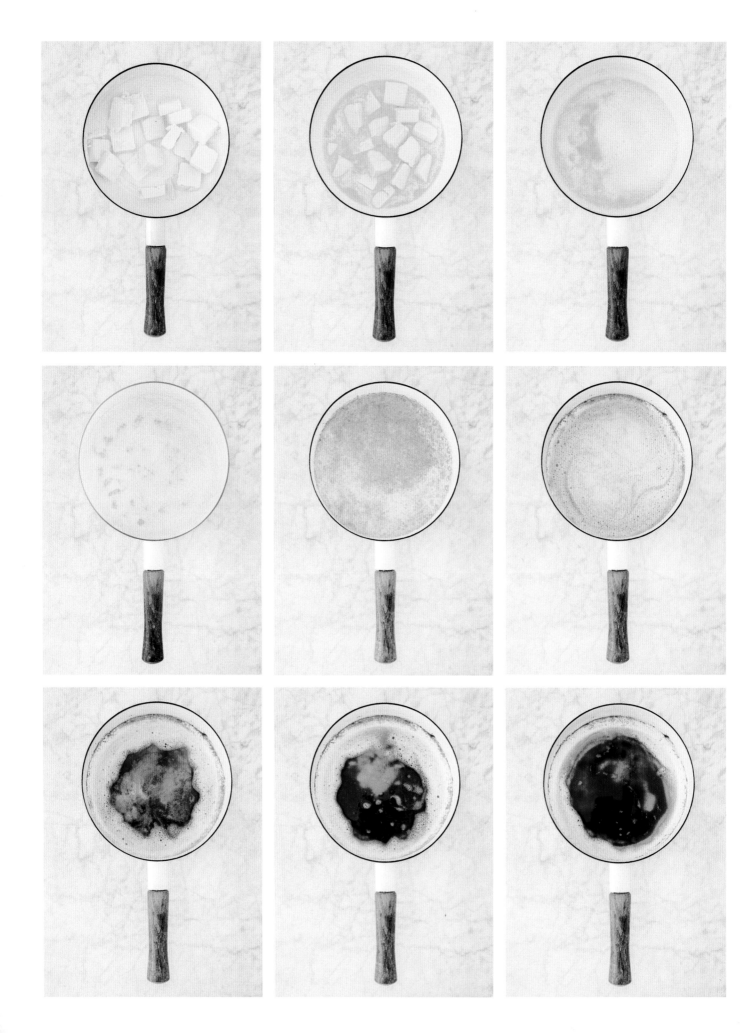

how to brown butter

To brown butter, melt the butter in a light-colored saucepan over medium heat, swirling the pan occasionally to help the butter melt evenly. Keep a heatproof rubber spatula nearby to scrape down the bottom and sides of the pan occasionally to help prevent the milk solids from sticking and burning. Depending on how high the heat is and how cold your butter was to begin with, browning butter can take anywhere between 5 and 15 minutes. To speed up the process, you can slice the butter into smaller pieces so it will melt faster.

As the butter melts, the mixture will begin to foam. It can be a little difficult to see what's going on at this point, so it's best to use the spatula to push the foam to the sides of the pan as best as you can to help you see the color underneath. If you're having trouble seeing the color of the butter, use a spoon to scoop a small amount of the butter onto a white plate to see its color more clearly. The color of the butter will progress from a bright lemon yellow to a golden tan and finally to a dark amber brown. The longer you cook the butter, the darker and more flavorful it will be, but note that there's a fine line between toasted and burnt. There's no salvaging butter once it's burnt, so be sure to watch it like a hawk as it browns.

Once you're satisfied with the color of the butter, immediately remove the pan from the heat and pour the brown butter into a clean bowl or liquid measuring cup to prevent it from cooking further. Set the bowl or measuring cup on a wire rack and let the brown butter cool to room temperature. The brown butter will be spotted with dark golden flecks; these are browned milk solids. Some folks pour brown butter through a fine-mesh strainer to discard these milk solids, but I like to keep them in for extra flavor. Once cooled, transfer the brown butter to an airtight container and store in the refrigerator for up to 1 week. You can use brown butter in any recipe that calls for melted butter, like Chocolate Chip Cookies (page 115) or Better-Than-Supernatural Fudge Brownies (page 153).

lime curd bars

A coworker of mine once lamented that there was no good key lime pie to be found in San Francisco. Determined to satisfy her craving, I baked and tested many key lime pie recipes until I finally found one I thought would impress her. I only had one problem: I commuted to work by bike, and, a key lime pie wasn't exactly the sort of thing I could pack into my pannier. So I decided to turn the key lime pie into a key lime *bar*. Genius, right? I rolled into the office, triumphantly holding up the bars, only to realize that I'd forgotten the cream I had whipped at home. Nevertheless, my coworkers devoured the bars. They liked them plenty without any whipped cream and I, ever the weeknight baker, was glad that I could skip another step in the future. And because key limes are seasonal, I began substituting regular limes in their place and found that their juice made the bars extra tangy. Eventually, I ditched the key limes completely and re-christened these bars "lime curd bars."

🕐 **ACTIVE TIME**

23 minutes over 2 days

makes 16 bars

NOTE: To make graham cracker crumbs, use a digital scale to weigh out as many crackers as needed to match the weight listed in the recipe. Use a food processor to pulse the crackers into fine crumbs.

FOR THE GRAHAM CRACKER CRUST

1½ cups (5.25 ounces) graham cracker crumbs

6 tablespoons (3 ounces) unsalted butter, melted

2 tablespoons granulated sugar

Pinch of kosher salt

FOR THE LIME FILLING

1 (14-ounce) can sweetened condensed milk

Zest of 1 medium lime

½ cup (4 ounces) strained freshly squeezed lime juice

3 large egg yolks

📅 **DAY 1**

prep time: **5 minutes**

work time: **5 minutes**

bake time: **10 minutes**

MAKE THE CRUST

1. Position a rack in the center of the oven and preheat the oven to 350°F. Line an 8-inch cake pan with a sheet of aluminum foil, leaving at least a 2-inch overhang on two opposite sides. Layer a second sheet of foil on top, perpendicular to the first, leaving a 2-inch overhang on the remaining sides.

2. In a medium bowl, combine the graham cracker crumbs, melted butter, sugar, and salt and toss with your fingers until the mixture looks like wet sand. Pour the mixture into the prepared pan and use a tart tamper or your hands

to press it evenly over the bottom of the pan, all the way to the edges. (You can use the bottom of a coffee mug or heavy glass to pound the crumbs in place—you want to apply some pressure here so the crust holds its shape.)

3. Bake for 10 minutes. The crust will look underbaked and feel soft to the touch when you remove it from the oven, but will firm up as it cools. Cool the crust completely on a wire rack, then cover loosely with plastic wrap and store on the counter overnight.

DAY 2

prep time: **8 minutes**

work time: **5 minutes**

bake time: **15 minutes**

NOTE: Use a glass or ceramic bowl to make the filling. A metal bowl will react with the lime juice, giving the filling a noticeable metallic taste.

MAKE THE FILLING AND BAKE THE BARS

1. Position a rack in the center of the oven and preheat the oven to 350°F.

2. In a large glass or ceramic bowl, whisk together the condensed milk, lime zest, lime juice, and egg yolks. Pour the filling over the crust and use an offset spatula to smooth the top.

3. Bake for 15 minutes, or until the sides of the bars are set but the center still wobbles slightly. Cool the bars completely on a wire rack. Cover loosely with plastic wrap and refrigerate until the filling is firm, at least 4 hours, preferably overnight.

4. Run a butter knife or offset spatula along the edges of the pan and use the overhanging foil as handles to lift the bars out of the pan and onto a cutting board. Use a hot knife (see page 165) to slice into 2-inch squares and serve. The lime bars can be stored in an airtight container in the refrigerator for up to 2 days.

make in one day

To expedite the process and make the bars in 1 day, make and bake the crust as directed. While the crust is in the oven, make the filling. Once the crust is done, keep the oven on and immediately pour the filling over the crust—there's no need to wait for the crust to cool to room temperature before filling! Bake, cool, and slice the bars as directed.

straight edges and smooth sides on cream bars

To get straight edges and smooth sides when slicing cream bars, you'll need to use a hot serrated knife. Fill a tall heatproof glass with VERY hot water (sometimes I even boil the water beforehand). Place a serrated knife in the water, blade down, for about 20 seconds. Use a kitchen towel to dry the knife. Slice the bars, dipping the knife in the hot water and drying it every so often, especially if the filling starts to stick to the blade.

When you're unmolding the bars from the pan, the foil will sometimes stick to the sides of the bars, ruining their smooth edges. You can fix this by slicing off any rough edges with the hot knife; just make sure you're cutting off very thin slices—you don't want to slice off any more filling than you need to.

cheesecake bars

⏱ **ACTIVE TIME**

18 minutes over 2 days

makes 16 bars

NOTE: It's especially important that your cream cheese, eggs, and sour cream are warmed to room temperature—the filling will be lumpy if the ingredients are cold. To ensure that my cream cheese has softened to the perfect temperature, I chop it into blocks and pop it in the microwave for 15 to 20 seconds. And be sure to check out my tips on how to bring eggs and sour cream to room temperature quickly on page 41!

NOTE: To make graham cracker crumbs, use a digital scale to weigh out as many crackers as needed to match the weight listed in the recipe. Use a food processor to pulse the crackers into fine crumbs.

The first showstopping dessert I ever tried to make from scratch was cheesecake. By then, I had mastered cupcakes, and I was confident I could manage a cheesecake. I committed to bringing a cheesecake to my boyfriend Erlend's family's Thanksgiving dinner. I didn't know then that I had made a grave mistake. Cheesecakes are notoriously difficult for beginners and first-time bakers: their tops tend to crack if the cake is overwhipped or cooled too quickly. Sure enough, my first cheesecake cracked. In fact, it looked like it had been hit by an earthquake. It took me several years to work up the confidence to try again.

In my many years of baking, I eventually mastered cheesecake. But no joke—they are NOT a weeknight baking project. Every step is time-consuming, from the minute you start, as you wait for ingredients to come to room temperature, to the minute you finish baking, as you make sure the cheesecake is cooling *verrryyy* slowly.

Which is why I present a recipe for cheesecake *bars*.

Cheesecake bars have none of cheesecake's pitfalls. Because the bars use less batter than a regular cheesecake, there are less opportunities for things to go wrong: there's no need to bake them in a water bath, and they don't crack as they cool. What's more, I'm confident that you'll find them to be just as tasty as the real thing.

FOR THE GRAHAM CRACKER CRUST

1½ cups (5.25 ounces) graham cracker crumbs

6 tablespoons (3 ounces) unsalted butter, melted

2 tablespoons granulated sugar

Pinch of kosher salt

FOR THE CHEESECAKE FILLING

1½ cups (12 ounces) cream cheese, **at room temperature**

½ cup (3.5 ounces) granulated sugar

2 large eggs, **at room temperature**

½ cup (4 ounces) sour cream, **at room temperature**

DAY 1

prep time: **5 minutes**
work time: **5 minutes**
bake time: **10 minutes**

MAKE THE CRUST

1. Position a rack in the center of the oven and preheat the oven to 350°F. Line an 8-inch cake pan with a sheet of aluminum foil, leaving at least a 2-inch overhang on two opposite sides. Layer a second sheet of foil on top, perpendicular to the first, leaving a 2-inch overhang on the remaining sides.

2. In a medium bowl, combine the graham cracker crumbs, melted butter, sugar, and salt and toss with your fingers until the mixture looks like wet sand. Pour the mixture into the prepared pan and use a tart tamper or your hands to press it evenly over the bottom of the pan, all the way to the edges. (You can use the bottom of a coffee mug or heavy glass to pound the crumbs in place— you want to apply some pressure here so the crust holds its shape.)

3. Bake for 10 minutes. The crust will look underbaked and feel soft to the touch when you remove it from the oven, but will firm up as it cools. Cool the crust completely on a wire rack, then cover loosely with plastic wrap and store on the counter overnight.

DAY 2

prep time: **<5 minutes**
work time: **8 minutes**
bake time: **30 minutes**

MAKE THE FILLING AND BAKE THE BARS

1. Position a rack in the center of the oven and preheat the oven to 325°F.

2. In the bowl of a stand mixer fitted with the paddle attachment, beat the cream cheese on medium-low until soft, about 1 minute. Add the sugar and beat until light and fluffy, about 1 minute, using a rubber spatula to scrape down the bottom and sides of the bowl as necessary. Reduce the mixer to low and add the eggs one at a time, adding the next egg only after the previous one has been fully incorporated, scraping down the bottom and sides of the bowl after each addition. With the mixer on low, add the sour cream all at once and beat until combined, about 1 minute. Scrape down the bottom and sides of the bowl once more, and beat on medium-high for an additional 30 seconds.

3. Pour the filling over the crust and use an offset spatula to smooth the top. Bake for 30 to 35 minutes, until the edges are set but the center still wobbles slightly. Cool the bars completely on a wire rack. Cover loosely with plastic wrap and refrigerate until the filling is firm, at least 4 hours, preferably overnight.

4. Run a butter knife or offset spatula along the edges of the pan and use the overhanging foil as handles to lift the bars out of the pan and onto a cutting board. Use a hot knife (see page 165) to slice into 2-inch squares and serve. The cheesecake bars can be stored in an airtight container in the refrigerator for up to 2 days.

make in one day

To expedite the process and make the bars in 1 day, make and bake the crust as directed. While the crust is baking, make the filling. Once the crust is done, reduce the oven temperature to 325°F and immediately pour the filling over the crust—there's no need to wait for the crust to cool to room temperature before filling! Bake, cool, and slice the bars as directed.

variations

citrus cheesecake bars

Before starting the recipe, in a small bowl, combine 2 tablespoons citrus zest (lemon, lime, grapefruit, orange, etc.) and the sugar required for the filling. Use your fingers to rub the zest into the sugar—this will infuse the sugar with oils from the zest. Proceed with the recipe as directed. This variation does not significantly affect Prep, Work, or Bake Time.

swirled cheesecake bars

After pouring the filling into the crust, dollop the filling with 2 tablespoons of your favorite jam or nut butter. Use a butter knife to swirl the dollops into the cheesecake filling. Bake as directed. This variation does not significantly affect Prep, Work, or Bake Time.

chocolate ganache cheesecake bars

Chill the bars as directed. Once the bars have chilled for at least 4 hours, make 1 recipe Dark Chocolate Ganache (page 280). While the ganache is still warm, pour it over the chilled cheesecake bars to cover. Refrigerate for at least 1 hour to set the ganache before slicing and serving. This variation adds about 10 minutes of Work Time.

jammy pie bars

I have a love-hate relationship with pie. While I love its buttery, flaky crust and its jammy fresh fruit filling, it takes time and effort to make: pie dough needs to chill repeatedly, fruit needs to be peeled and sliced.

So what if I told you you could bake a dessert that had the flavor and overall *spirit* of pie, but none of the work itself?

Behold these jammy pie bars. They're not *quite* pie. But the brown butter shortbread base is so buttery and flaky that it could pass as pie crust. The shortbread is then covered with jam, which, when baked, could pass as your favorite fruit pie filling. You can use any kind of fruit jam here to make a variety of pie bars like strawberry, cherry, and even marmalade. And finally, in place of more pie crust, we top the jam with cinnamon streusel (which I like to call "fancy cookie crumbs"). It's pie, minus the fuss.

 ACTIVE TIME

35 minutes over 2 days

makes 20 bars

FOR THE SHORTBREAD CRUST

2¼ cups (10.15 ounces) all-purpose flour

⅔ cup (2.65 ounces) confectioners' sugar, sifted if lumpy

Pinch of kosher salt

1 cup (8 ounces) unsalted butter, **at room temperature**

FOR THE STREUSEL

1 cup (4.5 ounces) all-purpose flour

½ cup (4 ounces) **very cold** unsalted butter, cut into 1-inch cubes

½ cup tightly packed (3.75 ounces) dark brown sugar

¼ teaspoon kosher salt

Pinch of ground cinnamon

1½ cups (18 ounces) seedless jam, for filling

NOTE: For this recipe, I recommend using a seedless jam (in particular, I love Stonewall Kitchen's seedless jam collection). Although you can use jams with seeds, a seedless jam is most reminiscent of traditional pie filling and won't distract from the crisp shortbread and streusel.

DAY 1

prep time: **5 minutes**

work time: **15 minutes**

bake time: **30 minutes**

MAKE THE CRUST

1. Position a rack in the center of the oven and preheat the oven to 350°F. Lightly spray a 9 x 13-inch cake pan with cooking spray and line it with parchment paper, leaving a 2-inch overhang on the pan's two long sides. Lightly spray the parchment, too.

2. In the bowl of a stand mixer fitted with the paddle attachment, combine the flour, sugar, and salt. Beat on low until combined. Add the butter and beat on low until the dough clumps around the paddle and/or the sides of the bowl, 2 to 3 minutes.

3. Transfer the dough to the prepared pan and use a tart tamper or your hands to press it evenly over the bottom of the pan, all the way to the edges. Place a sheet of parchment over the dough and fill it with pie weights. Bake for 30 to 35 minutes, until the crust is golden brown. Remove the pie weights and parchment. Cool the crust completely in the pan on a wire rack, then cover loosely with plastic wrap and store on the counter overnight.

DAY 2

prep time: **5 minutes**

work time: **10 minutes**

bake time: **30 minutes**

MAKE THE STREUSEL, ASSEMBLE, AND BAKE THE BARS

1. Position a rack in the center of the oven and preheat the oven to 350°F.

2. Make the streusel: In a medium bowl, combine the flour, butter, brown sugar, salt, and cinnamon and toss with your fingers to combine. Rub the dry ingredients into the butter cubes until the mixture looks like coarse meal, with pea-sized pieces of butter throughout. Refrigerate until ready to use.

3. Assemble the pie bars: Bake the crust for 5 minutes to reheat it. Place it on a wire rack (but keep the oven on!) and pour over the jam. Let sit for a minute or so to allow the jam to soften, then use an offset spatula to spread it evenly over the crust. Remove the streusel from the refrigerator and sprinkle it evenly over the jam, breaking up any large clumps with your hands.

4. Bake for 25 to 30 minutes, or until the jam is bubbling and the streusel is golden brown. Cool the bars on a wire rack for 20 minutes, or until the streusel topping feels firm to the touch.

5. Run a butter knife or offset spatula along the edges of the pan and use the overhanging parchment as handles to lift the bars out of the pan and onto a cutting board. Slice into 20 rectangles, each about 2¼ inches wide and 2½ inches long, and serve. The pie bars can be stored in a zip-top bag or airtight container at room temperature for up to 2 days.

make in one day

This recipe divides the work over 2 days; to expedite the process and make the bars in 1 day, make the crust first. While the crust is baking, prep the jam and make the streusel. Once the crust is done, keep the oven on and immediately pour the jam over the crust and top with the streusel—there's no need to wait for the crust to cool to room temperature before filling! Bake, cool, and slice the bars as directed.

TARTS

Tarts and pies are often mistaken for the same thing, but they have an important distinction between them. Tarts have shallow sides and no top crust over the filling; pies have deep sides and usually a top crust over the filling.

Many people assume that pies are made by home cooks and that, somehow, tarts are made by pastry chefs because they are more complicated to bake. But I think this is misguided: because tarts don't have a top crust, they're easier and faster to make than pies. Tart dough is also more forgiving than pie dough! My favorite tart dough recipe doesn't need to be rolled out and re-chilled like pie dough. So if you're intimidated by pies, I suggest you start with tarts instead. The secret to a successful tart on a weeknight, of course, is to break up the work over multiple days. Most recipes in this chapter instruct you to make and bake the crust on the first day, and make the filling and assemble the tart on the second day.

the easiest brown butter tart shell ever

ACTIVE TIME

10 to 15 minutes

prep time: **<5 minutes**

work time: **15 minutes**

bake time: **35 minutes**

makes one 8-inch round
tart shell or one 5 x 14-inch
rectangular tart shell

Traditional tart shells require lots of kneading, rolling, and chilling; they also involve tools like rolling pins and pie weights. But thanks to this recipe, you can skip all that.

This recipe is based on a brown butter tart shell recipe from Parisian pastry instructor Paule Caillat. Unlike other tart shell recipes that instruct you to roll out the dough with a rolling pin, you instead use your hands to press the dough into the pan. There are other steps within the recipe that make it perfect for weeknight baking, too: browning the butter in the oven, as opposed to on the stovetop, saves time and minimizes cleanup; piercing the tart shell with a fork allows steam to escape and prevents the dough from rising, eliminating the need to use pie weights.

Over the years, I've made tweaks to make this the tart shell of my dreams. The result is so buttery and flaky, it's almost as if my beloved Almost-No-Mess Shortbread Cookies (page 141) and pie crust had a love child. I've suggested a variety of creams and curds as fillings in this chapter, but I encourage you to pair this recipe with your own favorite fillings like Dark Chocolate Ganache (page 280) or Diplomat Cream (page 277)—this tart shell will shine no matter what.

NOTE: It takes some practice to bake this tart shell without any cracks, so don't be surprised if your first attempt has a crack or two. Reserve a pinch of raw dough and use it to spackle any cracks once the tart is out of the oven and cooling on a wire rack. There's no need to bake again; the residual heat from the freshly baked tart will cook the raw dough.

NOTE: For this recipe, it's important to use a tart pan with a removable bottom; the pastry is quite delicate, and you'll likely end up cracking the tart shell into pieces if you bake it in a traditional pie pan and try to remove it.

6 tablespoons (3 ounces) unsalted butter

3 tablespoons (1.5 ounces) water

1 tablespoon canola oil

1 tablespoon granulated sugar

Pinch of kosher salt

1⅓ cups (6 ounces) all-purpose flour

1. Position a rack in the center of the oven and preheat the oven to 400°F.

2. In a medium heatproof glass bowl, combine the butter, water, oil, sugar, and salt. Set the bowl directly on the oven rack and bake for 20 minutes, or until the mixture is boiling and the butter has started to brown.

3. Remove the bowl from the oven (but keep the oven on!), add flour all at once, and mix with a heatproof rubber spatula to combine. The dough is going to bubble and smoke—don't panic, this is what's supposed to happen! Mix until the dough pulls away from the sides of the bowl and looks a little bit like mashed potatoes, about 1 minute. Place the bowl on a wire rack and cool until the dough is still warm but can be handled, about 3 minutes.

4. Once cool, scoop 1 tablespoon of the dough into a small bowl. Place the remaining dough in an 8-inch round tart pan (or a 5 x 14-inch tart pan) with a removable bottom. Use a tart tamper or your hands to press the dough evenly over the bottom and up the sides of the pan. Use a fork to poke holes all over the bottom and sides of the dough.

5. Bake for 15 minutes, or until the tart shell is golden brown. Cool completely on a wire rack before filling. While the tart shell is still warm, use the reserved 1 tablespoon dough to "spackle" any cracks. The tart shell can be stored at room temperature, under a cake dome or a large bowl turned upside down, for up to 3 days.

coconut almond cream tart

When I lived in New York, I worked long hours to keep up with my West Coast–based team. In between meetings, I snuck out for snack breaks at the bodega around the corner from my office. If you're unfamiliar with New York bodega culture, you're in for a treat—most corners host tiny neighborhood grocery stores offering a wide range of snacks, sandwiches, and homestyle meals from their deli counter. These bodegas are often run by immigrants, who offer a variety of foods that reflect the city's diversity: tacos and burritos, doubles and rotis, bento boxes, curry bowls, and more.

My favorite snacks came from the candy aisle—at a bodega, you can often find candy and chocolate from all around the world. When work was particularly stressful, I'd treat myself to something sweet. One of my favorites was a coconut and almond truffle from Italy; it was sweet and creamy, and I loved how the nuttiness of the almond complemented the tropical flavor of the coconut.

Eventually, I drew inspiration for my baking from the flavors in those candy aisles. Like this coconut almond tart! To honor my favorite candy, I added almond extract and white chocolate to a coconut cream pie recipe I was developing. A bite of this tart immediately brought me back to my favorite bodega in New York City.

ACTIVE TIME
30 minutes over 3 days

makes one 8-inch tart

NOTE: This recipe divides the work over 3 days, but there's a lot of flexibility within its baking schedule. The coconut almond pastry cream will keep in the refrigerator for up to 1 week, allowing you to make it way in advance of the tart shell. Alternatively, you can shorten the timeline by making the filling first, then both the tart shell and the whipped cream on the next day. You can even fill the tart shell while it's still warm. If you do, serve the tart immediately, as the pastry cream will start to melt and the tart shell will soften faster.

FOR THE COCONUT ALMOND PASTRY CREAM

⅔ cup (4.65 ounces) granulated sugar

¼ cup (1 ounce) cornstarch

½ teaspoon kosher salt

1 (14-ounce) can full-fat coconut milk, shaken well

¼ cup (2 ounces) whole milk

2 large eggs

4 tablespoons (2 ounces) unsalted butter, cut into 1-inch cubes

1 tablespoon almond extract

1 cup (4 ounces) unsweetened shredded coconut

FOR THE TART SHELL AND ASSEMBLY

1 recipe The Easiest Brown Butter Tart Shell Ever (page 176), prebaked in an 8-inch tart pan with a removable bottom

2 ounces white chocolate from a high-quality chocolate bar, chopped into ¼- to ½-inch pieces

1 recipe Classic Whipped Cream (page 274), for serving

Sliced almonds, for garnish

Toasted coconut flakes, for garnish

📅 DAY 1

prep time: **<5 minutes**

work time: **10 minutes**

MAKE THE PASTRY CREAM

1. In a medium, heavy-bottomed saucepan, whisk together the sugar, cornstarch, and salt. Add the coconut milk and eggs and whisk until the yolks break. Bring to a boil over medium heat and cook, whisking continuously, until the mixture thickens enough to coat the back of a spoon, 5 to 8 minutes.

2. Remove from the heat, immediately add the butter and almond extract, and whisk until the butter is melted and combined. Place a fine-mesh sieve over a medium bowl and pour the pastry cream through the sieve to remove any lumps.

3. Add the shredded coconut to the pastry cream and whisk until evenly distributed throughout the cream. Pour the pastry cream into an airtight container and press a sheet of plastic wrap directly against the surface to prevent a skin from forming. Cover with a lid and refrigerate overnight.

📅 DAY 2

prep time: **<5 minutes**

work time: **10 minutes**

bake time: **35 minutes**

MAKE THE TART SHELL

Make the tart shell as directed and cool completely on a wire rack. Store, under a cake dome or a large bowl turned upside down, on the counter overnight.

📅 DAY 3

prep time: **<5 minutes**

work time: **10 minutes**

MAKE THE WHIPPED CREAM, ASSEMBLE THE TART, AND SERVE

1. Remove the pastry cream from fridge. Add the white chocolate to the pastry cream and stir until evenly distributed. Scoop the pastry cream into the tart shell and use an offset spatula to spread it evenly and smooth the top. Unmold the tart by setting the pan on top of a wide glass or mug and carefully pulling down the sides of the pan. Place the tart on a serving plate.

2. Make the whipped cream as directed and spoon it over the pastry cream. Top with sliced almonds and toasted coconut and serve immediately. This tart is best the day it's assembled.

magic dream lemon cream tart

Warning: The recipe you are about to read has a Work Time equivalent to what somebody would spend on a weeknight *dinner*. I'm sorry . . . but also, not really. Because once you try making this lemon cream, I'm 100 percent certain you'll never go back to making traditional lemon curd. It's so good that this tart remains one of the most popular recipes on my blog to date, despite the fact that it was one of the earliest recipes I ever published.

A quick glance at the recipe reveals nothing about its extraordinariness—it looks like any basic lemon curd with the same standard ingredients of lemon juice, sugar, eggs, and butter. But the magic comes from how you combine these ingredients. Traditional curds cook all these ingredients together until they thicken; butter is traditionally added last and whisked in by hand. In this recipe, however, you use a blender to *blend* in the butter. The result is the lightest, creamiest lemon curd you will ever taste.

NOTE: This recipe divides the work over 3 days, but there are plenty of opportunities to take shortcuts to make it even more weeknight baking-friendly. The majority of the Prep Time for the lemon cream involves juicing lemons; the lemon juice can be squeezed and strained up to a week ahead of time and stored in an airtight container in the fridge until ready to use. Similarly, the lemon cream itself will keep in the refrigerator for up to 1 week, allowing you to make it way in advance of the tart shell.

ACTIVE TIME

1 hour over 3 days

makes one 8-inch tart

NOTE: Pay attention to the equipment required for this recipe. Use a glass or ceramic bowl to make the lemon cream—a metal bowl will react with the lemon juice, giving the cream a noticeable metallic taste. An instant-read thermometer is also important, as the curd will need to be cooked to a specific temperature to set properly.

1 recipe The Easiest Brown Butter Tart Shell Ever (page 176), prebaked in an 8-inch tart pan with a removable bottom

FOR THE MAGIC DREAM LEMON CREAM

⅔ cup (5.35 ounces) strained freshly squeezed lemon juice

3 large eggs

1 large egg yolk

¾ cup (5.25 ounces) granulated sugar

Pinch of kosher salt

1 cup (8 ounces) **very cold** unsalted butter

⅓ cup fresh blueberries, for garnish

DAY 1

prep time: **<5 minutes**

work time: **10 minutes**

bake time: **35 minutes**

MAKE THE TART SHELL

Make the tart shell as directed and cool completely on a wire rack. Store, under a cake dome or a large bowl turned upside down, on the counter overnight.

 DAY 2

prep time: **10 minutes**

work time: **30 minutes**

MAKE THE LEMON CREAM

1. Pour 3 to 4 inches of water into a medium, heavy-bottomed saucepan. Bring to a simmer over medium heat while you prep the ingredients.

2. In a medium heatproof glass bowl, whisk together the lemon juice, eggs, egg yolk, sugar, and salt. Place the bowl over the saucepan of simmering water (be sure the bottom of the bowl does not touch the water). Cook, whisking constantly, until the mixture becomes very thick and registers 170°F on an instant-read thermometer, 15 to 20 minutes.

NOTE: In step 2, if you're having trouble bringing the lemon-egg mixture to the proper temperature, you can slow down your whisking to ensure that heat remains trapped in the mixture. I recommend whisking vigorously at the beginning of the cooking process to make sure the eggs don't accidentally scramble, then slowing your whisking significantly about 10 minutes into the process once the eggs have been emulsified.

3. Remove the bowl from the saucepan. Pour the mixture into a high-powered blender and let cool to 140°F before proceeding, 5 to 10 minutes. As you wait, chop the butter into 1- to 1½-inch pieces.

4. Blend the cooled lemon mixture on medium, adding the butter through the blender's feed tube one or two pieces at a time, adding more butter only once the previous pieces have been fully incorporated and the mixture is smooth. Once all the butter has been added, use a rubber spatula to scrape the sides of the blender pitcher. Blend on high until pale yellow and smooth, about 30 seconds more.

5. Immediately pour the cream into the tart shell and use an offset spatula to smooth the top. Press a sheet of plastic wrap directly against the surface of the cream to prevent a skin from forming. Refrigerate for at least 4 hours, preferably overnight.

 DAY 3

work time: **5 minutes**

ASSEMBLE AND SERVE

Remove the tart from the refrigerator and carefully peel off the plastic wrap. Use an offset spatula to smooth the surface of the lemon cream once more to remove any indentations left by the plastic wrap. Unmold the tart by setting the pan on top of a wide glass or mug and carefully pulling down the sides of the pan. Place the tart on a serving plate, garnish with the blueberries, and serve immediately. This tart is best the day it's assembled.

variations

blackberry lime tart

Substitute strained freshly squeezed lime juice for the lemon juice and fresh blackberries for the blueberries. This variation does not significantly affect Prep, Work, or Bake Time.

raspberry grapefruit tart

Substitute strained freshly squeezed grapefruit juice for the lemon juice and fresh raspberries for the blueberries. This variation does not significantly affect Prep, Work, or Bake Time.

choose-your-LOE berries and cream tart

ACTIVE TIME

**30 to 40 minutes
over 2 days**

makes one 5 x 14-inch tart

NOTE: Prep Time will vary depending on the type of berries you choose. To reduce Prep Time, choose blackberries, blueberries, or raspberries since these berries don't need to be hulled and sliced. Regardless of which topping you choose, I recommend making the tart shell the day before you plan to fill and serve the tart, since the tart shell needs to be cooled completely before filling.

NOTE: The weight of the fruit will vary significantly depending on the type of fruit you use, what season it is, and other factors (see page 49). As a result, this is one of the few recipes in this book where I encourage you to use a measuring cup (but only to portion out the fruit for the recipe—I still am an ardent believer in weight measures for everything else!).

In my day job, I spent a lot of time assessing "LOE": level of effort. My team and I would look at the upcoming projects for the quarter and prioritize them based on our available resources and the LOE needed to complete the task. The most successful quarters were the ones where we'd juggled projects that had a mix of high *and* low LOE rankings—you need a good balance of the two to keep the team feeling challenged but also satisfied with a sense of accomplishment. I found myself subconsciously applying this project management technique to baking, too: For as long as I've had my blog, I've maintained a list of recipes and recipe ideas I want to try. I end up tackling the recipes with a higher LOE on the weeks I don't have a whole lot going on, and the ones with a lower LOE on more stressful weeks where I just need a quick dessert.

When developing this berries and cream tart for this book, I was torn. A fruit tart is one of the most ubiquitous pastry desserts, and I've baked many variations that each had their own merits: topped with fresh fruit in all their summertime glory; or tossed in a small amount of sugar and liqueur to encourage the fruits to release their juices; or roasted with a hint of balsamic vinegar for extra flavor. I wanted all the recipes in this book to be the very best, but how could I choose between these?

Then I realized I didn't have to. I've included three different ways to prepare the fruit topping. Some take a bit longer than others, and it's up to *you* to decide what you have time to accomplish. There's no right or wrong answer here! All three options are delicious, especially with the mascarpone cream filling. Just be sure to read the recipes in full beforehand, because each has different cues that require you to prep the fruit at different points in the baking process.

FOR THE TART SHELL AND ASSEMBLY

1 recipe The Easiest Brown Butter Tart Shell Ever (page 176), prebaked in a 5 x 14-inch tart pan with a removable bottom

1 recipe Fresh, Macerated, or Roasted Berry Topping (page 188)

FOR THE MASCARPONE CREAM

1 cup (8 ounces) **very cold** mascarpone cheese

⅓ cup (2.65 ounces) **very cold** heavy cream

¼ cup (1 ounce) confectioners' sugar, sifted if lumpy

2 teaspoons pure vanilla extract

Pinch of kosher salt

DAY 1

prep time: **<5 minutes**

work time: **15 minutes**

bake time: **35 minutes**

DAY 2

prep time: **<5 minutes**

work time: **5 minutes for assembly, plus more to make the topping**

MAKE THE TART SHELL

Make the tart shell as directed and cool completely on a wire rack. Store, under a cake dome or large bowl turned upside down, on the counter overnight.

MAKE THE BERRY TOPPING AND THE MASCARPONE CREAM, ASSEMBLE THE TART, AND SERVE

1. Make the berry topping of your choice.

2. Make the mascarpone cream: In the bowl of a stand mixer fitted with the whisk attachment, combine the mascarpone, cream, confectioners' sugar, vanilla, and salt. Whisk on medium-high until the cream is glossy and holds stiff peaks, 1 to 2 minutes.

3. Scoop the cream into the tart shell and use an offset spatula to spread it evenly and smooth the top. Garnish with the fruit topping and serve immediately. This tart is best the day it's assembled.

prep time: **5 to 10 minutes**

work time: **<5 minutes**

makes 2½ cups

FRESH BERRY TOPPING

2½ cups fresh berries

Once the tart shell has been filled with the mascarpone cream, rinse the berries in a colander and pat them dry. If using strawberries, hull and slice them to the desired size (halves or quarters work well in this recipe). Scoop the berries evenly over the tart and serve immediately.

prep time: **5 to 10 minutes**

work time: **<5 minutes, but allow to soak overnight**

makes 2½ cups

MACERATED BERRY TOPPING

2½ cups berries

1 tablespoon granulated sugar

1 teaspoon Grand Marnier, red wine, or freshly squeezed lemon juice

1. If making the tart over 2 days, make the topping after baking the tart shell on the first day. In a medium bowl, combine the berries, sugar, and liquid of your choice and toss to combine. Cover with plastic wrap. The berries are ready when there's a small amount of liquid at the bottom of the bowl. This can take as little as 30 minutes or up to 2 hours at room temperature, depending on the berries and how ripe they are. I recommend refrigerating the berries overnight.

2. Scoop the berries and juices evenly over the tart and serve immediately.

prep time: **<5 minutes**

work time: **<5 minutes**

bake time: **20 minutes**

makes 2½ cups

ROASTED BERRY TOPPING

2½ cups berries

1 tablespoon granulated sugar

1 teaspoon balsamic vinegar

Pinch of kosher salt

1. If making the tart over 2 days, make the topping before making the mascarpone cream on the second day. Position a rack in the center of the oven and preheat the oven to 375°F. Line a half sheet pan with parchment paper.

2. In a medium bowl, combine the berries, sugar, vinegar, and salt. Toss until the berries are evenly coated. Spread over the prepared sheet pan and roast for 20 to 25 minutes, until the berries have darkened and released some of their juices. Cool slightly on a wire rack while making mascarpone cream.

3. Fill the tart with the mascarpone cream. Scoop the roasted berries and juices evenly over the tart and serve immediately. The warm fruit will cause the cream to soften, so wait until right before serving to add the berry topping.

PIES

I have a love-hate relationship with pie.

For a long time, pie was my least favorite dessert to make. My early pie doughs stuck to the counter or cracked once I rolled them out. A lattice top or pie design I'd worked so hard on would often be unrecognizable when I pulled the pie out of the oven.

But in case you haven't figured it out by now, I love a challenge. One evening, after pulling another hot mess of a pie from the oven, I said, *"No more."* I vowed to teach myself how to make a good pie. I committed to baking and perfecting a new pie every month for a full year. Each month, I chose a recipe that would teach me something new. I made fruit pies and custard pies, and pie crusts with different fats like butter, shortening, coconut oil, cheese, and lard. I taught myself how to crimp, lattice, parbake, and more. During that year, I learned some nifty tricks to make a better pie, including some things that might surprise you. A few go directly against conventional wisdom.

TRICK 1: USE A SHALLOW METAL PAN.

Pie pans come in a variety of materials: glass, ceramic, and metal. The best pie pans are thin metal pans that conduct heat quickly and will brown and crisp the crust. Look for a pan that isn't too deep—a shallower pan means that you won't need to handle the dough as much since the pan requires smaller dough circles for its top and bottom crusts. All the pie recipes in this chapter were developed using a shallow 9-inch aluminum pie pan. If you prefer to use a deep-dish pie pan, you'll need to account for the extra volume and use ½ cup more fruit to fill the pan completely.

TRICK 2: DON'T OVERFILL YOUR PIE PAN.

I've found that it's easiest to work with pies that aren't stuffed to the brim with filling. I like to fill my fruit pies until they're level with the pan, then top them with a lattice or lid. This method results in more consistent slices, with a crust-to-filling ratio that's about 50:50. A pie pan piled high with fruit means you'll need to roll out your lattice or lid slightly larger. More fruit also means more liquid is released into the pie as it bakes, potentially leading to soggy-bottomed pies.

TRICK 3: BAKE YOUR PIES AT A LOWER TEMPERATURE CONSISTENTLY THROUGHOUT ITS BAKE TIME.

Most modern pie recipes instruct you to bake the pie at a high temperature like 425° or 450°F, and then lower the oven temperature to 350°F halfway through its Bake Time to finish. According to some pastry chefs, baking at a high temperature encourages the butter in the dough to melt quickly, which causes the water in the butter to evaporate and release steam, creating flaky layers within the crust. However, when I experimented with this method, my crusts always shrank and my designed pie lids came out unrecognizable.

I turned to the internet to figure out where and how I was going wrong, and discovered that there was an entire school of older pastry chefs who advocated against this method. They instead preferred to bake their pies at a lower temperature. When I tried their way, it was a resounding success. After an hour in the oven, the fully baked pie looked exactly like it had when I'd placed it in the oven (only beautifully browned, of course). No shrinkage! I nearly wept tears of joy. And then I tasted it. A forkful of pie yielded even better results; the crust was as crispy, flaky, and tender as all the delicious pies I'd ever eaten. I was converted.

TRICK 4: RESTING THE PIE DOUGH IS IMPORTANT; THERE IS REALLY NO WAY AROUND IT.

Making a pie feels like completing a marathon: the constant rolling and re-rolling of the dough, the chilling and re-chilling of the pie, the crimping, the lattice-weaving, the filling. Unfortunately, you can't skip any of these steps. You have to run the race.

It's important that pie dough rests, because it contains gluten, a protein found in wheat and other grains that's responsible for the shape and texture of many baked goods. When wheat flour is "worked" by being mixed or kneaded with water and/or other liquids, gluten strands start to form. Because gluten tends to be very elastic, those strands will rebound after you roll out and work the dough. Resting the rolled dough allows the gluten strands to relax and adjust to their new shape. Without resting, the gluten strands will fight their way back to their original shape and your crust will end up misshapen and shrunken.

TRICK 5: YOU CANNOT SKIP THE CHILLING (AND RE-CHILLING) OF THE PIE DOUGH.

Similarly, it's important to chill pie dough. Room-temperature pie dough will stick to your counter and rolling pin, and if you do manage to wrestle it into the pan, it will likely melt during the baking process and lose its shape. After putting my pie together, I usually freeze the pie (the whole thing—filling and top crust, too!) for a few hours, preferably overnight.

Because of this constant resting and chilling, it's rare that I make a pie from start to finish in one day. All the recipes in this chapter are broken up over multiple days, in true weeknight baking fashion.

stand mixer all-butter pie dough

On my epic quest to learn the secrets of pie crust, I tried a multitude of pie dough recipes that used different kinds of flours and fats. I also made these pie doughs in different ways: by rubbing the fat into the flour with just my hands, with a pastry cutter, with a food processor, and more. But the way I liked the best was the most unusual method of them all—making the dough with my stand mixer (a tool rarely used in traditional pie recipes). A stand mixer saves you from making a mess with your hands or a pastry cutter, and prevents you from accidentally overworking the dough, which can be easy to do in a food processor.

Similarly, the ingredients list for my favorite pie crust reflects this tried-and-tested process. A touch of apple cider vinegar gives the crust a tangy flavor that complements fruit fillings. Using all butter for the dough makes for the most flavorful crust. For the prettiest pies, keep your ingredients as cold as possible—again, it will make the pie dough easier to work with and ensure the crust keeps its shape in the oven.

ACTIVE TIME

13 minutes

prep time: **5 minutes**
work time: **8 minutes**

makes enough for
one 9-inch pie

SINGLE-CRUST STAND MIXER ALL-BUTTER PIE DOUGH

3 tablespoons (1.5 ounces) **very cold** water

1½ teaspoons apple cider vinegar

½ cup ice

½ cup (4 ounces) **very cold** unsalted butter

1¼ cups (5.65 ounces) all-purpose flour

1½ teaspoons granulated sugar

½ teaspoon kosher salt

DOUBLE-CRUST STAND MIXER ALL-BUTTER PIE DOUGH

6 tablespoons (3 ounces) **very cold** water

1 tablespoon apple cider vinegar

1 cup ice

1 cup (8 ounces) **very cold** unsalted butter

2½ cups (11.25 ounces) all-purpose flour

1 tablespoon granulated sugar

1 teaspoon kosher salt

1. In a large liquid measuring cup, whisk together the water and vinegar. Add the ice and whisk. Refrigerate while you prep the rest of the ingredients.

2. Cut the butter into 1-inch cubes and place them in a small bowl. Freeze while you prep the rest of the ingredients.

3. In the bowl of a stand mixer fitted with the paddle attachment, combine the flour, sugar, and salt. Beat on low until just combined, about 15 seconds. Add the butter all at once and beat on low until the mixture has the texture of coarse meal, with pea-sized pieces of butter throughout, about 3 minutes.

4. Remove the ice water mixture from the refrigerator. With the mixer on low, add liquid from the ice water mixture (use 4 tablespoons for a single crust, 6 tablespoons for a double crust). Beat on low for 2 to 3 minutes, or until the dough clumps around the paddle and/or the sides of the bowl. If the dough seems too dry, add more liquid from the ice water mixture 1 teaspoon at a time.

5. Tip the dough out onto a lightly floured counter with the spatula. Quickly knead the dough into a rough ball. If making a double-crust pie, divide the dough in half with a bench scraper and shape each half into a rough ball (each should weigh about 11 ounces). Wrap each portion tightly in plastic wrap and flatten into a small disc. Refrigerate for at least 1 hour, preferably overnight before using. The dough will keep in the refrigerator for up to 3 days or frozen for longer storage. To freeze the dough, tightly wrap each portion in a second layer of plastic wrap and then a layer of aluminum foil to prevent the dough from absorbing any flavors or odors in the freezer. Freeze for up to 3 months. When ready to use, transfer to the refrigerator to thaw overnight.

how to form the bottom crust

Rolling out pie dough is a very personal experience and depends on various factors like how cold the dough is, how forgiving the temperature in your kitchen is, and how much practice you have working with pie dough to begin with. Because of these factors, it can take as little as 5 minutes to roll out the dough for a single-crust pie, or up to a full hour for a double-crust pie with an elaborate top crust. That's quite a range, so I've left out specific time estimates for rolling out pie dough (but between you and me, it usually takes me about 15 minutes to roll out the dough for a single-crust pie and shape it to the pan).

Start with a chilled disc of dough that has rested in the refrigerator for at least 1 hour, preferably overnight. Keep a bag of flour nearby; it's difficult to know how much you'll need in advance since it will depend on a variety of factors like the temperature of your dough, your hands, and your kitchen. Generously dust your counter with flour, unwrap the disc of dough, and place it on the counter. Sprinkle flour on top of the dough, too.

Give the dough a feel. Workable pie dough in disc form feels like slightly-colder-than-room-temperature butter—it's still pretty solid but gives a little when poked. If you find your dough feels like a rock, it's too cold. But we can fix this! Give it a few whacks with your rolling pin, rotating the disc after every whack to ensure it's flattening evenly. Let it sit for a minute or two, then test it again. If it's still too solid, keep whacking it until you're able to roll it out with *some* resistance against your rolling pin (you want the dough to feel a little bit like saltwater taffy when you roll it out). If it's too warm, the dough will start sticking to the counter—if this happens, try dusting the dough and counter with more flour. If that doesn't help, refrigerate the dough for 15 minutes, then try again.

Roll out the dough, starting with your rolling pin in the center of the disc and moving outward. Rotate the dough with every other roll until you have an even circle 1 to 1½ inches larger than your pie pan (most recipes in this book are written for a 9-inch pie pan, so you're aiming for a 10- to 11-inch circle here). As you roll out the dough, check its consistency: If it's starting to stick to the counter, run a long offset spatula underneath the dough and throw a handful of flour onto the counter and over your rolling pin. If the dough is starting to melt, scoot it onto a parchment paper–lined sheet pan and freeze it for 5 minutes. Repeat either of these steps as necessary. If it's a cold day and your kitchen is cool, you might not need to do this at all. But if you've decided to make pie on a 100°F day, you might find yourself doing this often. Check the size of the dough circle by inverting your pie pan and holding it over the dough. There should be about an inch-wide border of dough around the pan. If you're using a deep-dish pie pan, keep rolling until the circle is an inch or so wider to account for the pan's extra depth.

Once you're satisfied with your circle, it's time to move it into a pie pan. There are many ways to transfer the pie dough to its pan, but my favorite way is the Fold Method: Fold the rolled-out dough round in half vertically, then in half again horizontally. You'll end up with a triangular pizza slice. Pick it up carefully with your hands and place the tip of the triangle in the center of the pie pan. Carefully unfold the dough—it should be perfectly centered in the pan, but you can adjust as needed.

At this point, depending on how deep your pan is, you'll find that you have extra dough hanging over the rim. This is ideal—you'll need about 1 inch of overhanging dough to roll and crimp into a border. If you were a little too enthusiastic and rolled out the circle a few inches larger than necessary, use kitchen shears to trim off any excess. Similarly, if some parts of your circle are longer than others, use kitchen shears to trim any extra overhanging dough so that it's an even 1-inch overhang all around the pie pan. This step is important—if the overhang is uneven, the border will be uneven, too.

To make the pie crust's border, fold the overhanging dough onto itself, aligning the edge of the dough to the inner edge of the pie pan. Pinch along the fold all the way around to create a firm edge. Don't worry if it looks big; the crust will shrink a little bit in the oven, so bigger is better in this case. Dust your fingers with flour. Take your thumb and press it into the folded overhang, using your thumb and index finger on the opposite hand to pinch around your thumb to create your first crimp. Repeat, crimping the dough around the entire pan, flouring your hands as necessary to prevent the dough from sticking.

Once the border is crimped, it's time for the pie dough's second rest. Cover the pie dough loosely with plastic wrap and freeze for at least 1 hour, preferably overnight, before using in any of the pie recipes in this chapter.

weeknight baking pie lid designs

Think of a pie's top crust (or "lid") as similar to the frosting on a cake—it's a canvas for you to customize. Although Instagram is teeming with pie lids that have been elaborately woven (which takes hours to do—I'll save those patterns for my next book, *WeekEND Baking*), I rely on four simple, fast designs when I'm weeknight baking. After rolling out and shaping any of the following pie lids, cover the assembled pie loosely with plastic wrap and freeze for at least 1 hour (but preferably overnight) before baking.

simple top crust or patterned lid

Line a pie pan with dough as directed on page 197, but don't crimp the edge—you'll use the overhanging dough to seal the lid onto the pie. Fill the pie with the filling of your choice. Roll out a second disc of chilled pie dough into a circle about ½ inch wider than your pie pan; if you're using a 9-inch pie pan, you'll need to roll out a circle around 10 inches wide. Use the Fold Method (page 197) to transfer the dough to the center of a parchment paper-lined sheet pan.

For a simple top crust: Use a floured cookie cutter to stamp out a shape in the middle of the lid—this will allow steam from the fruit filling to escape as it bakes, preventing a soggy-bottomed pie. Alternatively, you can use a sharp knife to cut three slits into the pie lid, like the old-fashioned pies of yesteryear. Freeze the dough on the sheet pan for 5 minutes—it should then be firm enough to lift by its edges.

Place the pie lid carefully on top of the filled pie pan. Center the lid if necessary. You may need to trim off any excess overhang from both the top and the bottom crust of the pie lid so it fits the pie pan perfectly. Dust a fork with flour and press its tines into the dough all around the edge of the pan to seal the top and bottom crusts together and create a pattern.

For a patterned lid: Use a floured cookie cutter (or two!) to stamp out several shapes in the lid. Be careful not to stamp the shapes too close to each other; doing so will make it difficult to arrange the lid on top of the pie filling. If the dough gets too soft, freeze the dough on the sheet pan for 5 minutes. It should then be firm enough to continue your work. Once you're done with your pattern, freeze the dough again for 5 minutes. It should then be firm enough to lift by its edges.

Place the pie lid carefully on top of the filled pie pan. Center the lid if necessary. You may need to trim off any excess overhang from the pie lid so it fits the pie pan perfectly. Fold the overhanging dough from the bottom crust over the edge of the lid to seal. At this point, you can follow the instructions on page 198 to crimp the edges.

cookie cutter shapes

Line a pie pan with dough as directed on page 197. For this design, you can use a traditional crimped edge or a more minimalist look with no edge. For the latter, trim off any overhanging dough so the edge of the bottom crust perfectly aligns with the edge of the pan. Fill the pie with the filling of your choice. Roll out a second disc of chilled pie dough to a slab about ¼ inch thick—the shape and size of the slab doesn't need to be precise. Use a floured cookie cutter (or two!) to stamp out shapes from the dough and arrange them on top of the pie. Gather the dough scraps into a ball and repeat, stamping out more shapes and arranging them on the pie as you like.

If layering shapes on top of each other, I recommend using egg wash (see page 207) to "glue" it into position. Use a pastry brush to brush the bottom of the smaller shape with the egg wash; position it accordingly on top of a larger shape.

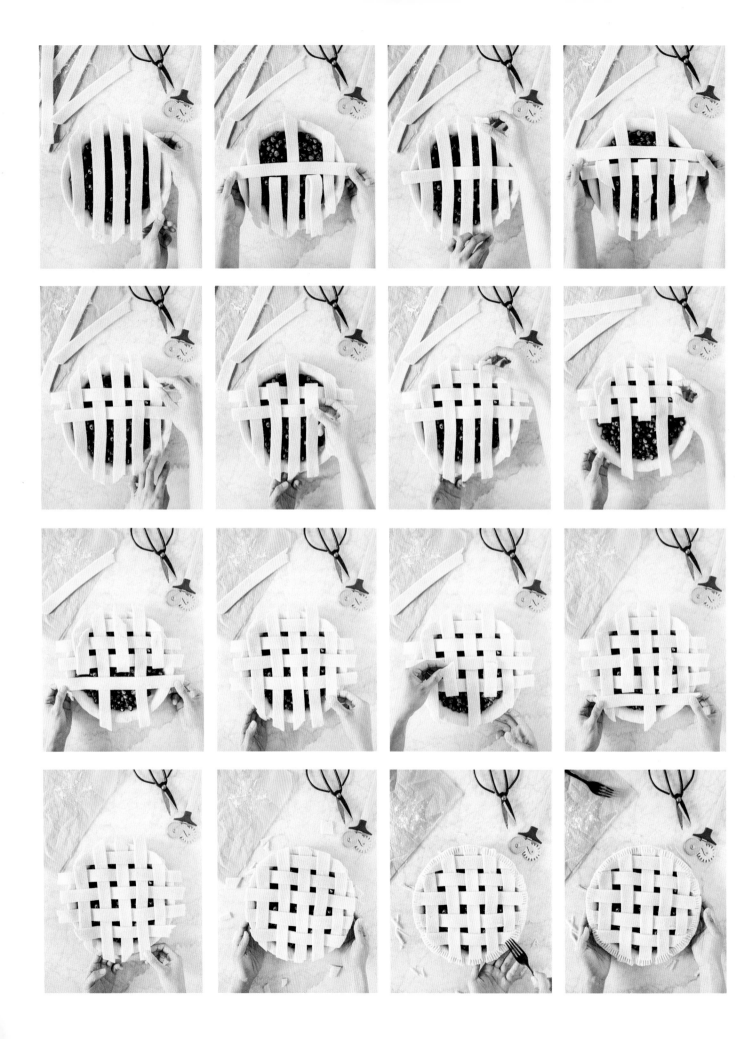

traditional lattice top

Line a pie pan with dough as directed on page 197, but don't crimp the edge—you'll use the overhanging dough to seal the lattice onto the pie. Fill the pie with the filling of your choice. Roll out a second disc of chilled pie dough into a circle about 12 inches wide. Use a sharp knife to cut the circle into 10 strips, each about 1 inch wide. You'll have some dough leftover, and although the strips will all be the same width, they'll have varying lengths—this is okay! Place 5 of the strips on top of the pie filling, arranging them so they're parallel to and evenly spaced from one another. Make sure to use the longer strips toward the center of the pie, and the shorter ones on the edges. If necessary, turn the pie so that the strips are vertical.

Fold the 2nd and 4th vertical strips in half toward yourself. Place one of the 5 remaining strips horizontally across the pie (so it runs perpendicular to the vertical strips), close to the fold in the 2nd and 4th vertical strips. Unfold the 2nd and 4th vertical strips so they fall over the 1st horizontal strip.

Fold the 1st, 3rd, and 5th vertical strips over the horizontal strip in the center of the pie. Lay another strip horizontally across the pie, close to the fold in the 1st, 3rd, and 5th vertical strips. Unfold the 1st, 3rd, and 5th vertical strips so they fall over the 2nd horizontal strip.

Fold the 2nd and 4th vertical strips down over the 2nd horizontal strip you just laid across the pie. Lay another strip horizontally across the pie, close to the fold in the 2nd and 4th vertical strips. Unfold the strips so that the 3rd horizontal strip is running underneath the 2nd and 4th vertical strips.

At this point, you've successfully woven the top half of your pie into a lattice. You'll need to do the bottom half of the pie. It's the same process as the one you just completed, except this time, you'll fold the vertical strips up. Start by folding the 1st, 3rd, and 5th vertical strips up over the horizontal strip that is running across the center of the pie. Lay another horizontal strip parallel about ½ inch underneath it. Fold the 1st, 3rd, and 5th strips back down so that they are now running over the horizontal strip.

Finally, fold the 2nd and 4th vertical strips up over the horizontal strip you just placed across the pie. Lay the final strip horizontally across the pie, then fold the 2nd and 4th vertical strips back down. Now step back—congratulations, you've woven a lattice! Trim any excess dough hanging over the edge of the pan and use a fork to seal the lattice strips to the bottom crust. Alternatively, you can roll the excess overhanging dough up onto the pan and shape it into a more traditional crimp with the instructions on page 198.

any kind of fruit pie

The numbers-driven, analytical engineer in me hates to admit this, but there's no standard, one-size-fits-all recipe for fruit pie. Fruit can be incredibly variable: the same fruits that burst with juice in the summertime are dry and hard in the winter. So instead of taking this recipe as the final word, I'd like to encourage you to think of it as more of an outline to making your favorite fruit pie.

What does it mean? It means lots of flexibility, which is perfect for us weeknight bakers. Prep Time will vary depending on the type of fruit you choose. Strawberries need to be hulled and sliced, rhubarb needs to be sliced, and stone fruit like cherries, nectarines, and peaches need to be pitted and sliced. Apples and pears need to be peeled, cored, and sliced. To reduce Prep Time, choose fruit like blackberries, blueberries, or raspberries, since these berries don't require any preparation beyond washing.

The most important thing is to taste the fruit so you know what you're working with. Is your fruit in season and ripe? That means it will release more juice as it bakes, so you'll need to use more cornstarch to thicken the filling. Is your fruit out of season and firm? Be sure to use more sugar for a more flavorful pie; you probably also won't need as much cornstarch since the fruit won't release as much juice as its in-season counterparts. Taste your fruit. Then trust your gut. Don't overthink it!

NOTE: This recipe divides the work over 3 days; to expedite the process and make the pie in 2 days, freeze the fully assembled, unbaked pie for at least 2 hours. Bake and cool as directed.

NOTE: The weight of the fruit will vary significantly depending on the type of fruit you use, what season it is, and other factors (see page 49). As a result, this is one of the few recipes in this book where I encourage you to use a measuring cup (but only to portion out the fruit for the recipe—I still am an ardent believer in weight measures for everything else!).

🕐 ACTIVE TIME

18 to 28 minutes over 3 days

makes one 9-inch double-crust pie

1 recipe Double-Crust Stand Mixer All-Butter Pie Dough (page 194)

FOR THE FRUIT FILLING

4½ cups fresh fruit, peeled, cored/pitted/hulled, and chopped into 1½- to 2-inch chunks as necessary

¼ cup (1.75 ounces) to ½ cup (3.5 ounces) granulated sugar

¼ cup (1 ounce) to ⅓ cup (1.35 ounces) cornstarch

1 tablespoon strained freshly squeezed lemon juice

Pinch of kosher salt

NOTE: Pie Dust is a mixture of flour and sugar that you sprinkle over the bottom crust to prevent it from absorbing fruit juices and getting soggy.

FOR THE PIE DUST

½ teaspoon all-purpose flour

½ teaspoon granulated sugar

FOR FINISHING

1 large egg

1 teaspoon water

Pinch of kosher salt

2 tablespoons Demerara, sanding, or other coarse sugar

🗓 **DAY 1**

prep time: **5 minutes**

work time: **8 minutes**

MAKE THE PIE DOUGH

Make the pie dough. Form it into two discs, tightly wrap each in plastic wrap, and refrigerate overnight.

🗓 **DAY 2**

prep time: **5 to 15 minutes**

work time: **<5 minutes for the filling, plus more for rolling out the dough**

MAKE THE FILLING AND PIE DUST AND ASSEMBLE THE PIES

1. Make the filling: In a medium bowl, combine the fruit, sugar, cornstarch, lemon juice, and salt and toss to coat.

2. Make the pie dust: In a small bowl, whisk together the flour and sugar.

3. Roll out one disc of chilled dough on a lightly floured counter and use the Fold Method (page 197) to transfer it to a 9-inch pie pan. Sprinkle the pie dust over the dough. Scoop the filling into the pie crust and use a rubber spatula to spread it into an even layer. Refrigerate while you work on the top crust.

4. Following the instructions on page 199, roll out and shape the second disc of chilled dough into the pie lid style of your choice. Remove the pie from the refrigerator and arrange the lid on top of the filling. If necessary, crimp the edges as directed on page 198.

5. Cover loosely with plastic wrap and freeze overnight. The assembled pie can stay in the freezer for up to 3 months. To store for longer, freeze the pie overnight. The next day, when it's frozen solid, tightly wrap the entire pie in two layers of plastic wrap and then a layer of aluminum foil to prevent it from absorbing any flavors or odors in the freezer.

🗓 **DAY 3**

work time: **<5 minutes**

bake time: **60 minutes**

BAKE AND SERVE

1. Position a rack in the lower third of the oven and preheat the oven to 375°F. Line a sheet pan with parchment paper.

2. In a small bowl, whisk together the egg, water, and salt to make an egg wash. Remove the frozen pie from the freezer, discard the plastic wrap, and place the pie in the center of the prepared sheet pan. Working quickly, use a pastry brush to coat the entire surface of the pie with a thin layer of egg wash, then sprinkle with the coarse sugar. Bake for 60 minutes, or until the crust is golden brown and the fruit juices are bubbling slowly in the center of the pie. Check the pie 45 minutes into the Bake Time—if the crust is browning too quickly, loosely cover the top of the pie with a sheet of foil.

3. Cool completely on a wire rack before slicing. Serve warm or at room temperature. The pie can be stored at room temperature, under a cake dome or a large bowl turned upside down, for up to 1 day. After that, cover loosely with plastic wrap and refrigerate for up to 2 days.

troubleshooting underbaked pies

An underbaked pie will have a runny filling, and the dough will be pale on the bottom crust and underneath the lid. Unfortunately, it's hard to know when fruit pies are done baking since these signs are visible only when you slice into the pie! So how do you prevent underbaking your pie in the first place? Here are some tips to help:

Don't be afraid to bake your fruit pie beyond the recipe's Bake Time. It's actually pretty difficult to overbake fruit pies, especially when baking them at a lower temperature. Some fruit pies will need to be baked for an additional 30 to 60 minutes (yes, 60 minutes!) depending on how ripe and juicy the fruit you used for the filling was. Additionally, egg wash can trick you into thinking that the pie is done since it browns the top of the pie quickly. If you suspect that the filling isn't done but the top crust is already golden brown, don't worry! Cover the top and edges of the pie loosely with a sheet of aluminum foil to prevent the crust from browning further. Return the pie to the oven, placing it on the middle rack instead of the bottom rack, and continue baking.

Make a pie lid that allows you to see if the filling is bubbling. Most recipes instruct you to create some sort of vent in the top lid when making a double-crust pie. The vents allow steam to escape, which prevents the bottom and the inside of the pastry from getting soggy. But these vents can also provide some insight into the filling—you should see the fruit filling bubbling through the vents in the crust. When the pie is close to done, its juices will be thick, complete with bubbles that pop slowly. Note that the juices will usually start

to bubble at the edges of the pie; it can be easy to spot this and think that the pie is ready, but wait until the juices bubble at the center. At this point, wait 10 minutes more—your pie will be perfectly done then.

If you can't see the center of your lidded pie, use a skewer to test the filling. This method is very similar to how you would test cakes and bars for doneness. A skewer inserted into the center of the pie should meet little to no resistance; this means that the fruit is cooked, and your pie is done baking. That said, this method isn't always the most accurate, especially if the fruit was incredibly ripe to begin with. Always try to leave a large vent in the center of your pie so you can peek inside.

When all else fails, don't be afraid to cook your fruit filling beforehand. All right, you've tried all my tricks and your fruit pies are still runny. No worries! That just means you are using incredibly juicy fruit. To prevent runny pies, you can cook half the fruit beforehand to the perfect consistency for pie filling. I don't generally recommend this method because it's more time-consuming; however, you can break up the work over multiple days. In a medium, heavy-bottomed saucepan, combine half the fruit in the recipe with the entire quantity of sugar called for and cook over medium heat, stirring frequently, until the fruit is thick and jammy, about 15 minutes. Remove from the heat, add the remaining fruit and the cornstarch and lemon juice called for in the recipe. Mix until combined. Cool completely before filling the pie. The cooked filling will keep in an airtight container in the refrigerator for up to 3 days.

key lime pie

I met two of my closest friends, Sze Wa Cheung and Michelle Carroll, when we were in our early twenties and working for a tech start-up in Portland. We bonded by exploring the lunch options near our office. Eventually, our favorite places turned into routine: we'd go out for a quick ice cream break if one of us was having a bad day, and we'd splurge at the diner with massive fried chicken sandwiches and slices of key lime pie when someone was having a bad *week*. Later, as we got older, we realized that our metabolisms couldn't keep up with our appetites. We begrudgingly started bringing healthier packed lunches, trading in the fried chicken sandwiches for salads (though we still went out for ice cream when somebody was having a bad day, of course). And although we still ate almost every lunch together, a part of me missed the decadence of our previous excursions. To me, key lime pie will always be a reminder of those weekday lunches that cemented our friendship. This recipe is modeled after our favorite diner's creamy and delicious version.

ACTIVE TIME

23 minutes over 3 days

makes one 9-inch single-crust pie

NOTE: This recipe divides the work over 3 days; to expedite the process and make the pie in 2 days, make and bake the crust as directed. While the crust is in the oven, make the filling. Once the crust is done, keep the oven on and immediately pour the filling over the crust—there's no need to wait for the crust to cool to room temperature before filling! Bake, cool, and chill the pie overnight as directed. On the following day, make the whipped cream, assemble the pie, and serve as directed.

NOTE: To make graham cracker crumbs, use a digital scale to weigh out as many crackers as needed to match the weight listed in the recipe. Use a food processor to pulse the crackers into fine crumbs.

NOTE: You can substitute regular lime juice and the zest from 2 medium limes for the key lime juice and zest.

NOTE: Use a glass or ceramic bowl to make the filling—a metal bowl will react with the lime juice, giving the filling a noticeable metallic taste.

FOR THE GRAHAM CRACKER CRUST

1½ cups (5.25 ounces) graham cracker crumbs

6 tablespoons (3 ounces) unsalted butter, melted

2 tablespoons granulated sugar

Pinch of kosher salt

FOR THE KEY LIME FILLING

1 (14-ounce) can sweetened condensed milk

4 large egg yolks

Zest of 6 key limes

Pinch of kosher salt

⅔ cup (5.35 ounces) strained freshly squeezed key lime juice

1 recipe Crème Fraîche Whipped Cream (page 275), for serving

MAKE THE CRUST

1. Position a rack in the center of the oven and preheat the oven to 350°F.

2. In a medium bowl, combine the crumbs, melted butter, sugar, and salt and toss with your fingers until the mixture looks like wet sand. Pour the mixture into a 9-inch pie pan and use a tart tamper or your hands to press it evenly over the bottom of the pan, all the way to the edges. (You can use the bottom of a coffee mug or heavy glass to pound the crumbs in place—you want to apply some pressure here so the crust holds its shape.)

4. Bake for 10 minutes. The crust will look underbaked and feel soft to the touch when you remove it from the oven, but will firm up as it cools. If you find that the crust has slumped down the sides of the pan, use the back of a spoon to gently ease it back into place while it's still warm. Cool the crust completely on a wire rack. Store, under a cake dome or a large bowl turned upside down, on the counter overnight.

MAKE THE FILLING AND BAKE THE PIE

1. Position a rack in the center of the oven and preheat the oven to 350°F.

2. In a medium glass bowl, combine the condensed milk, egg yolks, lime zest, and salt. Mix with a rubber spatula. Add the lime juice and mix until smooth. Pour the filling over the crust and use an offset spatula to smooth the top.

3. Bake for 18 minutes, or until the edges of the pie are set but the center still wobbles slightly. Cool completely on a wire rack. Cover loosely with plastic wrap and refrigerate for at least 4 hours, preferably overnight.

ASSEMBLE AND SERVE

Make the whipped cream and spoon it over the filling. Serve immediately. The key lime pie can be stored in the refrigerator, covered loosely with plastic wrap, for up to 3 days.

banana cream pie

makes one 9-inch
single-crust pie

NOTE: This recipe works best if you use incredibly ripe, spotted, and *almost* black bananas. If you bought bananas specifically for this recipe, check out Bananas About Bananas on page 61 for neat tricks on how to ripen them quickly and store any extras for future baking projects. You **need** yellow food coloring for this recipe, because super-ripe bananas turn an unsightly grayish brown when cooked. There's no way around it.

NOTE: Bananas are listed in the recipe by weight, not volume or size—learn why on page 57. For best results, first peel the bananas, then use a digital scale to weigh the naked fruit. For those of you who need volume measurements, that's 1 cup mashed bananas, from around 2 large bananas.

In 2016, my boyfriend Erlend and I moved to New York City for his graduate program at Columbia University. I was thrilled for him and excited for the opportunity to live in one of my favorite cities. Every week, I hit up renowned bakeries in an attempt to try every dessert and sweet available only in New York. My mission knew no bounds—I tried classics like Junior's Cheesecake, Levain Bakery's chocolate chip cookies, and Dominique Ansel's Cronuts.

One of my stops was Magnolia Bakery. Although a popular TV show put the bakery's cupcakes on the map, their banana pudding—made with Nilla wafers and instant pudding mix, to boot—is the real star of their menu. I drew inspiration from those flavors for my banana cream pie recipe, using Nilla wafers in the pie crust. Make Nilla wafer crumbs by using a digital scale to weigh out as many wafers as needed to match the weight in the recipe. Use a food processor to pulse the wafers into fine crumbs.

This recipe is straightforward yet flexible, perfect for weeknight baking. The cookie crust comes together quickly; there's no need to roll, shape, and chill the pie repeatedly as you would if using pie dough. The banana pastry cream can be made up to 3 days in advance and stored in the refrigerator in an airtight container until ready to use. My only hard rule is that you serve the pie the day you assemble it; its fresh bananas will turn brown the longer it sits in the refrigerator.

NOTE: This recipe divides the work over 3 days; to expedite the process and make the pie in 2 days, make and bake the crust as directed. While the crust is in the oven, make the filling. Store both the crust and filling overnight as directed. On the following day, make the whipped cream, assemble the pie, and serve as directed.

FOR THE PIE CRUST

1½ cups (5.25 ounces) Nilla wafer crumbs

6 tablespoons (3 ounces) unsalted butter, melted

2 tablespoons granulated sugar

Pinch of kosher salt

FOR THE BANANA CREAM FILLING

8 ounces very ripe peeled bananas

1 cup (8 ounces) whole milk

1 large egg

5 tablespoons (2.15 ounces) granulated sugar

2 tablespoons cornstarch

¼ teaspoon kosher salt

2 tablespoons (1 ounce) unsalted butter

5 drops yellow food coloring

FOR ASSEMBLY

1 very ripe banana

1 recipe Classic Whipped Cream (page 274), for serving

DAY 1

prep time: **5 minutes**

work time: **5 minutes**

bake time: **10 minutes**

MAKE THE CRUST

1. Position a rack in the center of the oven and preheat the oven to 350°F.

2. In a medium bowl, combine the crumbs, melted butter, sugar, and salt and toss with your fingers until the mixture looks like wet sand. Pour the mixture into a 9-inch pie pan and use a tart tamper or your hands to press it evenly over the bottom of the pan, all the way to the edges. (You can use the bottom of a coffee mug or heavy glass to pound the crumbs in place—you want to apply some pressure here so the crust holds its shape.)

3. Bake for 10 minutes. The crust will look underbaked and feel soft to the touch when you remove it from the oven, but will firm up as it cools. If you find that the crust has slumped down the sides of the pan, use the back of a spoon to gently ease it back into place while it's still warm. Cool the crust completely on a wire rack. Store, under a cake dome or a large bowl turned upside down, on the counter overnight.

DAY 2

prep time: **8 minutes**

work time: **10 minutes**

MAKE THE FILLING AND BAKE THE PIE

1. Combine the bananas and milk in a high-powered blender. Blend on high until completely smooth, about 20 seconds. Scrape down the sides of the blender with a rubber spatula and add the egg, sugar, cornstarch, and salt. Blend on high until smooth, about 10 seconds.

2. Pour the mixture into a medium, heavy-bottomed saucepan. Bring to a boil over medium heat and cook, whisking continuously, until the mixture thickens enough to coat the back of a spoon, 5 to 8 minutes.

3. Remove from the heat, immediately add the butter, and whisk until the butter is melted and combined. Add the food coloring and whisk until the custard turns yellow. Place a fine-mesh sieve over a medium bowl and pour the custard through the sieve to remove any lumps. Pour the custard into an airtight container and press a sheet of plastic wrap directly against the surface of the custard to prevent a skin from forming. Cover with a lid and refrigerate overnight.

🗓 DAY 3

prep time: **<5 minutes**
work time: **5 minutes**

ASSEMBLE AND SERVE

1. Peel the banana and slice it into ½- to 1-inch-thick coins. Arrange them in an even layer over the bottom of the prepared pie crust. Scoop the filling over the banana slices and use an offset spatula to smooth the top.

2. Make the whipped cream and spoon it over the filling. Serve immediately. This pie is best the day it's assembled.

the silkiest pumpkin pie

ACTIVE TIME

38 minutes over 4 days

makes one 9-inch
single-crust pie

NOTE: This recipe divides the work over 4 days; to expedite the process and make it in 2 days, make the dough and form the bottom crust all in one day; freeze overnight. The next day, parbake the crust as directed. While the crust is in the oven, make the filling. Once the crust is done, keep the oven on and immediately pour the filling over the crust–there's no need to wait for the crust to cool to room temperature before filling! Bake and cool the pie as directed.

NOTE: This recipe instructs you to parbake the bottom crust before filling it with the pumpkin filling. Parbaking, also known as blind-baking, refers to the process of baking a pie crust before filling it. There are two main reasons to parbake a pie crust: (1) parbaking helps keep the crust crisp, preventing soggy bottoms, and (2) some fillings cook much faster than the crust itself, so the crust needs extra time in the oven.

Here's some background information about me, your friend who has been guiding you through all these weeknight baking adventures: I wasn't born in the United States. My parents temporarily emigrated here from the Philippines and the Netherlands when I was in high school. As a result, I experienced a lot of American traditions like Thanksgiving later in life. Because neither of my parents celebrated the holiday, I found myself at friends' family dinners and Friendsgivings, shuffling to a different Thanksgiving celebration every year.

And although I loved the turkey, stuffing, and mashed potatoes, I always thought—and this is a hot take!—that Thanksgiving desserts were *kinda* lame. Specifically, I was disappointed in pumpkin pie. Most of the pumpkin pies I'd eaten had soggy crusts filled with dense, heavy custards. I dreamed of a light and silky pumpkin custard set in a crispy, flaky crust, so I set out to make my own.

There are two tricks that make my pumpkin pie stand out from the disappointing pies of my past: cooking down the pumpkin puree caramelizes the pumpkin and gives it deeper flavor, while sweetened condensed milk makes it incredibly creamy. The result is the pumpkin pie I've always wanted.

Now, at first glance, the recipe is daunting. I've broken the work up over 4 days. Fear not—you're doing only 15 minutes or less of Work Time each day. This is perfect for Thanksgiving: you can prep this pie far ahead to save yourself time for the mains and appetizers on the big day itself. If 4 days still seems excessive (I get it!), check out the notes to see how to cut it down to 2.

1 recipe Single-Crust Stand Mixer All-Butter Pie Dough (page 194)

FOR THE EGG WASH

1 large egg

1 teaspoon water

Pinch of kosher salt

FOR THE FILLING

1 (15-ounce) can pumpkin puree

¾ cup tightly packed (5.65 ounces) dark brown sugar

1 recipe Classic Pumpkin Spice, Vanilla Pumpkin Spice, Chai Pumpkin Spice, or Actually Spicy Pumpkin Spice (page 67)

½ teaspoon kosher salt

1 (14-ounce) can sweetened condensed milk

2 large eggs

1 large egg yolk

 DAY 1

prep time: **5 minutes**

work time: **8 minutes**

MAKE THE PIE DOUGH

Make the pie dough, wrap tightly in plastic wrap, and refrigerate overnight.

 DAY 2

work time: **about 15 minutes**

FORM THE BOTTOM CRUST

1. Roll out the disc of chilled dough on a lightly floured counter and transfer it to a 9-inch pie pan using the Fold Method (page 197). Crimp the edge following the instructions on page 198. Use a fork to poke holes all over the bottom and sides of the dough.

2. Cover loosely with plastic wrap and freeze overnight.

 DAY 3

bake time: **40 minutes**

PARBAKE THE CRUST

1. Position a rack in the center of the oven and preheat the oven to 350°F. Line a sheet pan with parchment paper and place the frozen crust in the center of the pan. Cover the crust with foil, making sure the crimped edges are completely covered and that there are no gaps between the foil and the crust. Fill with pie weights and spread them out so they are more concentrated around the edges of the crust.

2. Bake for 35 minutes. While the crust is in the oven, make the egg wash: In a small bowl, whisk together the egg, water, and salt.

3. Remove the sheet pan from the oven, keeping the oven on. Carefully lift out the pie weights and foil. Use a pastry brush to coat the bottom and sides of the pie crust (but not the crimped border) with a thin layer of egg wash. Bake, uncovered, for an additional 5 minutes. Cool completely on a wire rack. Store, under a cake dome or a large bowl turned upside down over the pie, on the counter overnight.

 DAY 4

prep time: **5 minutes**

work time: **10 minutes**

bake time: **45 minutes**

MAKE THE FILLING AND BAKE THE PIE (FINALLY!)

1. Position a rack in the center of the oven and preheat the oven to 350°F. Line a sheet pan with parchment paper and place the parbaked crust in the center of the pan. Cover the crimped edges of the crust with foil, leaving the center of the pie exposed.

2. In a medium, heavy-bottomed saucepan, whisk together the pumpkin, sugar, pumpkin spice, and salt. Cook over medium heat, whisking continuously, until the mixture starts to bubble and becomes fragrant, about 5 minutes. Remove from the heat, immediately pour in the condensed milk, and whisk to combine. Add the eggs and egg yolk one at a time, adding the next egg only after the previous one has been fully incorporated, and whisk to combine. Pour the filling into the prepared crust.

3. Bake for 45 to 50 minutes, or until the edges of the filling are set but the center still wobbles slightly. Cool on a wire rack. Serve warm or at room temperature. The pie can be stored at room temperature, under a cake dome or a large bowl turned upside down, for up to 1 day. After that, cover loosely with plastic wrap and refrigerate for up to 2 days.

pie crust cookies

Pumpkin pies can look a little bland without a topping; I like to save extra scraps of pie dough to shape into cookies that I then decorate the pie with.

To make pie crust cookies, gather any scraps of pie dough into a ball, form it into a small disc, and roll it out on a lightly floured counter to ¼ inch thick—the shape and size of the slab doesn't need to be precise. Use a floured cookie counter to stamp out cookie cutouts, placing them 2 inches apart on a parchment paper–lined sheet pan as you go. Freeze for at least 1 hour, preferably overnight. Because pie crust cookies bake faster than a pie crust, you'll need to bake them separately. Preheat the oven to 350°F. Bake for 20 to 25 minutes, or until golden brown. Cool on the pan on a wire rack for 20 minutes, then arrange them on top of the finished pie. Alternatively, just eat the cookies on their own, because pie crust cookies are delicious.

MUFFINS AND SCONES

When I graduated from college and started my first job, I struggled to get up early to make breakfast. I never had enough time to make a meal from scratch, so instead I would pick up a pastry from the coffee shop near my office. Every morning, I would run on sugar until I crashed hard a short while later.

I soon started experimenting with pastry recipes at home to see if I could solve my breakfast problem. I had two rules: (1) the recipes had to produce pastries that were easy to eat on my commute (no cutlery required!), and (2) they needed to keep me full until noon. I quickly found that muffins and scones made with whole-grain flours full of fiber and protein kept me going much longer than traditional coffee shop pastries. As a result, all the recipes in this chapter use a variety of whole-grain flours, nuts, and seeds to give you a strong start in your day.

During these experiments, I also discovered that, just like cookie dough (see page 121), most breakfast pastry batters and doughs could be saved and baked later. Muffin batter keeps for up to 36 hours in the fridge; that means you can bake a muffin or two for your breakfast immediately, and refrigerate the rest of the batter for baking later in the week. Simply scoop an individual portion of batter into a muffin tin and put it in the oven as you go about your routine. Similarly, scone dough freezes wonderfully; make and freeze a batch, then bake a few straight from frozen on weekday mornings. Most of the recipes in this chapter have a Bake Time between 15 to 30 minutes, which is usually how long it takes to get ready in the morning. At the end, you'll be rewarded with a freshly baked good with little to no effort. It's the weekday-morning routine you deserve.

matcha pistachio nut muffins

ACTIVE TIME

20 minutes

prep time: **5 minutes**
work time: **15 minutes**
bake time: **18 minutes**

makes 12 muffins

NOTE: To save on Prep Time, be sure to buy shelled pistachios. Most shelled pistachio nuts come roasted and salted; I've accounted for this by decreasing the recipe's salt quantity. However, if you're using unsalted pistachios, increase the recipe's salt to ½ teaspoon.

NOTE: For this recipe, you'll need to buy pistachio extract (see Resources on page 287). In a pinch, you can substitute vanilla extract, but your pistachio muffin won't taste that much like pistachio. Pistachio extract is the key to that signature pistachio flavor (that, or Jell-O powder, which I don't use in this recipe).

While my boyfriend Erlend and I lived in New York City, in addition to exploring all the desserts and sweets the city had to offer (see page 213), I made it my mission to find the city's best bagel. My friend Julie would often accompany me on my explorations; we'd get two bagels (a bacon-and-egg bagel sandwich for her, and a simple bagel-with-schmear for me), along with a pastry to share. One day, she texted me excitedly: she had discovered that a bagel place in the East Village made the best pistachio nut muffins. We made a date and met there the following weekend, ordering our usual order of two bagels and a pistachio muffin to share.

When I pulled the muffin out of the bag, I was skeptical—it was NEON green. But a quick bite confirmed that Julie was right; the muffin was incredibly moist, with a wonderful flavor that reminded me of pistachio ice cream. I turned to the baker behind the counter to compliment him on the muffin and asked how it was so green. He grinned at me and whispered the secret ingredient: Jell-O powder. I reported my findings back to Julie, and we were both less enthused about the muffin after that.

I've since created my own pistachio nut muffin recipe that's just as tasty. My recipe, however, skips the Jell-O powder in favor of using real pistachio nuts and matcha powder to achieve the muffin's signature green color. The matcha in the recipe is also a wonderful addition to my morning routine, giving me a caffeine buzz without coffee's harshness.

1 cup (5 ounces) shelled pistachios

1⅓ cups (6 ounces) all-purpose flour

1½ tablespoons matcha green tea powder

2 teaspoons baking powder

¼ teaspoon kosher salt

½ cup (4 ounces) unsalted butter, **at room temperature**

⅔ cup (4.65 ounces) granulated sugar

2 large eggs

½ cup (4 ounces) plain full-fat Greek yogurt

1 tablespoon pistachio extract

Roughly chopped pistachios, for garnish

1. Position a rack in the center of the oven and preheat the oven to 400°F. Line a muffin tin with paper liners.

2. In a food processor, pulse the pistachios for a few seconds at a time until the nuts are broken down into a fine meal, 15 to 20 seconds.

3. Pour the pistachio meal into a medium bowl and add the flour, matcha, baking powder, and salt. Whisk to combine.

4. In the bowl of a stand mixer fitted with the paddle attachment, combine the butter and sugar. Beat on medium until light, fluffy, and doubled in volume, 2 to 3 minutes, using a rubber spatula to scrape down the bottom and sides of the bowl as necessary. Reduce the mixer to low and add the eggs one at a time, adding the next egg only after the previous one has been fully incorporated, scraping down the bottom and sides of the bowl after each addition. Add the yogurt and pistachio extract all at once and beat until combined. Gradually add the dry ingredients and beat on low until just combined. Scrape down the bottom and sides of the bowl once more, and beat on low for an additional 30 seconds.

5. Use a 3-tablespoon cookie dough scoop to fill each paper liner with 3 tablespoons of the batter. Sprinkle the roughly chopped pistachios over each muffin.

6. Bake for 18 minutes, or until the muffins are domed and golden brown around the edges and a skewer inserted into the center of a muffin comes out with a few crumbs attached. Cool in the muffin tin on a wire rack for 10 minutes, then turn the muffins out onto the rack. Serve warm or at room temperature. The muffins can be wrapped individually in plastic wrap and stored at room temperature for up to 2 days.

berry almond muffins

ACTIVE TIME

20 minutes

prep time: **5 minutes**
work time: **15 minutes**
bake time: **30 minutes**

makes 12 muffins

NOTE: This recipe does not contain weight measures for the berries since the weight will vary significantly depending on the type of berry you use. The variations, however, include exact weights for the specific berries used.

When I worked in San Francisco, a lot of the engineers on my team kept odd office hours; although we worked long into the night, it was rare for most of us to arrive at the office before 10 a.m. From time to time, my boss took to bribing our team with boxes of breakfast pastries from the bakery downstairs, using danishes and muffins to incentivize us to arrive earlier. The most popular pastry in the box was the blueberry muffin—I'd jockey for the lone one in the box with the rest of my team.

Tired of competing for the muffin, I decided to develop my own recipe. This recipe makes what I consider to be the perfect blueberry muffin: a moist, fluffy cake base with bursts of tartness from the blueberries, topped with a sky-high crispy top. I've also added some almond flour to the recipe, which not only tastes delicious but also provides some protein to keep you going until lunchtime. You can also substitute different berries and citrus zest to use whatever fruit is in season. I've included some variations to get you started.

2 cups (9 ounces) all-purpose flour

½ cup (1.75 ounces) almond meal

1½ teaspoons baking powder

½ teaspoon kosher salt

2 cups fresh or frozen berries

½ cup (4 ounces) unsalted butter, **at room temperature**

1 cup (7 ounces) granulated sugar

2 teaspoons zest from your favorite citrus fruit

2 large eggs

½ cup (4 ounces) whole milk

1. Position a rack in the center of the oven and preheat the oven to 375°F. Line a muffin tin with paper liners.

2. In a medium bowl, whisk together the flour, almond meal, baking powder, and salt.

3. Place the berries in a deep bowl. Sprinkle 1 teaspoon of the dry ingredients over the berries and use your hands to gently toss the berries until completely coated.

4. In the bowl of a stand mixer fitted with the paddle attachment, combine the butter, sugar, and citrus zest. Beat on medium-high until light, fluffy, and doubled in volume, 2 to 3 minutes, using a rubber spatula to scrape down the

bottom and sides of the bowl as necessary. Reduce the mixer to low and add the eggs one at a time, adding the next egg only after the previous one has been fully incorporated, scraping down the bottom and sides of the bowl after each addition. With the mixer still on low, add the dry ingredients in two equal parts, adding the second half only when the first has been just combined. Slowly pour in the milk in a steady stream down the side of the bowl and beat until just combined, 30 to 45 seconds. Scrape down the bottom and sides of the bowl once more, then beat on low for an additional 30 seconds. Gently fold the berries into the batter with the spatula.

5. Use a 3-tablespoon cookie dough scoop to fill each paper liner with 6 tablespoons of the batter.

6. Bake for 30 minutes, or until the muffins are domed and golden brown around the edges and a skewer inserted into the center of a muffin comes out with a few crumbs attached. Cool in the muffin tin on a wire rack for 10 minutes, then turn the muffins out onto the rack. Serve warm or at room temperature. The muffins can be wrapped individually in plastic wrap and stored at room temperature for up to 2 days.

NOTE: The recipe instructs you to fill your muffin tin with a generous portion of batter (6 tablespoons per cavity). The batter is fairly thick, so it will hold its shape before and during baking, resulting in sky-high domes. Use a 3-tablespoon cookie dough scoop to fill each cavity evenly and efficiently with the right amount of batter.

variations

blueberry lemon muffins
Use 2 cups (12 ounces) fresh or frozen blueberries for the fruit and 2 teaspoons lemon or Meyer lemon zest.

cranberry orange muffins
Use 2 cups (7 ounces) fresh or frozen cranberries for the fruit and 2 teaspoons orange zest.

blackberry lime muffins
Use 2 cups (8 ounces) fresh or frozen blackberries for the fruit and 2 teaspoons lime zest.

banana yogurt muffins

ACTIVE TIME

23 minutes

prep time: **8 minutes**

work time: **15 minutes**

bake time: **22 minutes**

makes 12 muffins

NOTE: This recipe works best if you use incredibly ripe, spotted, and *almost* black bananas. If you bought bananas specifically for this recipe, check out Bananas About Bananas on page 61 for neat tricks on how to ripen them quickly and store any extras for future baking projects.

NOTE: Bananas are listed in the recipe by weight, not volume or size—learn why on page 57. For best results, first peel the bananas, then use a digital scale to weigh the naked fruit. For those of you who need volume measurements, that's 1¼ cups mashed bananas, from around 2½ large bananas.

In order to graduate from the college I attended, all students were required to write a thesis in their senior year. Students then had to orally defend their theses in front of a panel of professors. Because these oral defenses were two hours long and ran back-to-back for professors, we were instructed to ~~bribe~~ incentivize our panel for their attention by bringing snacks and treats.

The night before my orals, I tossed and turned in bed, unable to sleep from nerves. I suddenly remembered that my thesis advisor once expressed a fondness for banana nut muffins. I decided right then to make some from scratch, jumping out of bed and trying the first recipe I found online. Needless to say, it was a disaster—the muffins were hard, dry, and shaped like hockey pucks. Though I passed my orals, none of my professors seemed particularly excited by my muffins.

I wish I had a time machine so I could travel back in time, pat my younger self on the back, and give her this recipe for banana yogurt muffins. Not only do these muffins come together quickly (the Work Time is just 15 minutes, perfect for a panicked 2 a.m. baking session), they have a flavor similar to banana bread but are much lighter. This is thanks to the Greek yogurt, a breakfast staple that most folks already have in their fridge. For extra protein, toss in up to 1 cup of your favorite nuts, chopped and toasted—I recommend almonds, pecans, or walnuts.

10 ounces very ripe peeled bananas

¼ cup (2 ounces) plain full-fat Greek yogurt

1 teaspoon pure vanilla extract

1 cup (4.5 ounces) all-purpose flour

1 cup (4.5 ounces) whole wheat flour

1 teaspoon baking soda

¾ teaspoon baking powder

1½ teaspoons kosher salt

¾ cup (6 ounces) unsalted butter, **at room temperature**

1 cup tightly packed (7.5 ounces) dark brown sugar

2 large eggs

1. Position a rack in the center of the oven and preheat the oven to 400°F. Line a muffin tin with paper liners.

2. In a medium bowl, use a fork to mash the bananas, adding the yogurt and vanilla and stirring them into the mixture as you do. The mixture will be thick and chunky, but that's totally okay, I promise!

3. In another medium bowl, whisk together the flours, baking soda, baking powder, and salt.

4. In the bowl of a stand mixer fitted with the paddle attachment, combine the butter and sugar. Beat on medium until light, fluffy, and doubled in volume, 2 to 3 minutes, using a rubber spatula to scrape down the bottom and sides of the bowl as necessary. Reduce the mixer to low and add the eggs one at a time, adding the next egg only after the previous one has been fully incorporated, scraping down the bottom and sides of the bowl after each addition. With the mixer on low, add the dry ingredients in two equal parts, adding the second half only when the first half has been just combined. Add the banana mixture all at once and beat on low until just combined. Scrape down the bottom and sides of the bowl once more, and beat on low for an additional 30 seconds.

5. Use a 3-tablespoon cookie dough scoop to fill each paper liner with 6 tablespoons of the batter.

6. Bake for 22 minutes, or until the muffins are domed and golden brown around the edges and a skewer inserted into the center of a muffin comes out with a few crumbs attached. Cool in the muffin tin on a wire rack for 10 minutes, then turn the muffins out onto the rack. Serve warm or at room temperature. The muffins can be wrapped individually in plastic wrap and stored at room temperature for up to 2 days.

NOTE: This recipe instructs you to fill your muffin tin with a generous portion of batter (6 tablespoons per cavity). The batter is fairly thick, so it will hold its shape before and during baking, resulting in sky-high domes. Use a 3-tablespoon cookie dough scoop to fill each cavity evenly and efficiently with the right amount of batter.

sweet crème fraîche scones

The pastry that nobody ever wanted from my boss's box of breakfast pastries (see page 225) was a simple vanilla scone. I never gave the scone much thought, either. But one morning, after a punctured bike tire made me 30 minutes late to our team meeting, I found myself face-to-face with the scone nobody wanted. I took a bite: it was hard, dry, and solid as a rock.

That was when I realized a good scone is hard to find. A good scone has edges that are crisp and crumbly, but with a center that is soft and almost cakelike. But not *too* soft, of course—its crumb should withstand a generous smear of butter or jam without falling into pieces. This recipe ticks all those boxes and more. The addition of crème fraîche gives these scones a wonderful tangy flavor that works well on its own or with butter and jam.

In many ways, scones are ideal for weeknight baking. For the best scones, all ingredients used in the recipe must be super cold, allowing you to use them straight from the fridge—there's no need to wait around for anything to come to room temperature. And similar to cookie dough, scone dough keeps wonderfully; be sure to check out the Bake Later instructions so you can freeze the dough and bake as needed.

ACTIVE TIME

15 minutes

prep time: **5 minutes**
work time: **10 minutes**
bake time: **15 minutes**

makes 8 scones

FOR THE SCONES

2 cups (9 ounces) all-purpose flour, plus more for dusting

⅓ cup (2.35 ounces) granulated sugar

2 teaspoons baking powder

½ teaspoon kosher salt

4 tablespoons (2 ounces) **very cold** unsalted butter, cut into 1-inch cubes

1 cup (8 ounces) **very cold** crème fraîche

1 **very cold** large egg

FOR ASSEMBLY

1 tablespoon all-purpose flour

2 tablespoons sanding sugar (or other coarse sugar like Demerara or raw)

1. Position a rack in the center of the oven and preheat the oven to 375°F. Line a half sheet pan with parchment paper. Line an 8-inch round cake pan with plastic wrap and lightly dust with flour.

2. In the bowl of a stand mixer fitted with the paddle attachment, combine the flour, sugar, baking powder, and salt. Beat on low until just combined, about

15 seconds. Add the butter all at once and beat on low until the mixture has the texture of coarse meal, with pea-sized pieces of butter throughout, about 3 minutes.

3. In a large liquid measuring cup, whisk together the crème fraîche and egg. With the mixer on low, slowly pour the crème fraîche mixture into the dry ingredients. Beat until the dough clumps around the paddle and/or sides of the bowl, about 1 minute. Scrape down the bottom and sides of the bowl with a rubber spatula.

NOTE: The key to a good scone is to handle the dough as little as possible; this results in that soft-but-not-too-soft crumb. This recipe instructs you to pat the dough in a cake pan, which helps prevent overhandling *and* results in perfectly shaped scones each time. Just be sure to line your pan with plastic wrap to prevent the dough from sticking!

4. Dust your hands and sprinkle your counter with the remaining 1 tablespoon of flour. Knead the dough once or twice into a rough ball, incorporating all the flour on the counter into the dough. Place the dough in the center of the prepared cake pan. Dust your hands with flour again, and, working quickly, lightly pat out the dough so it fills the pan.

5. Use the plastic wrap to carefully lift the dough out of the pan and onto a counter. Flour the edge of a bench scraper and use it to quarter the dough into 4 even wedges. Cut each wedge in half so you have 8 wedges total. Place the wedges at least 3 inches apart on the prepared sheet pan. Sprinkle the top of each wedge with about 1 teaspoon of the sanding sugar.

6. Bake for 15 minutes, or until the scones have almost doubled in size and lightly browned. Cool the scones on the pan on a wire rack for 10 minutes, or until the edges and bottoms of the scones have set and feel firm to the touch. Serve the scones warm or at room temperature. The scones can be stored in an airtight container or zip-top bag at room temperature for up to 2 days.

bake later

If freezing the scone dough, make the dough and cut it into wedges as directed, then tightly wrap each individual wedge in plastic wrap. Freeze for up to 3 months. When ready to bake, position a rack in the center of the oven and preheat the oven to 375°F. Line a half sheet pan with parchment paper. Unwrap the scones and place them at least 3 inches apart on the prepared sheet pan. Bake for 18 minutes, or until the scones have almost doubled in size and lightly browned. Cool and serve as directed.

variations

supersized

For supersized scones, substitute a 6-inch round cake pan—this will result in scones that are double the height of ones formed in an 8-inch pan. Before sprinkling the dough wedges with sanding sugar, brush the top of each with cream to brown them more in the oven. This variation does not significantly affect Prep, Work, or Bake Time.

lemon poppyseed scones

Make the dough as directed, but add 2 tablespoons of poppyseeds to the dry ingredients and stir the zest of 1 lemon and 1 tablespoon of freshly squeezed lemon juice into the crème fraîche mixture. This variation adds a few minutes of Prep Time to prep the lemon, but does not significantly affect Work Time or Bake Time.

savory cheddar mustard scones

Despite my reputation as a baking and sweets blogger, I must confess: I prefer savory breakfasts. If I had my way, I would take my time and make myself a generous portion of cheesy scrambled eggs, crispy bacon, sliced avocado, and sautéed greens to start the day.

But of course, life gets in the way; I hit the snooze button far too much, and I rarely have time to make my ideal breakfast before the start of my workday. To remedy this, I decided to come up with a savory pastry that I could eat on the go—like these cheddar mustard scones. These scones are so big and hearty that they could be mistaken for their dinner counterpart, biscuits. They're just as tender and buttery, too, because to pack an extra punch, this recipe also uses Kamut, an ancient grain with lots of protein and nutrients and a wonderful nutty flavor that could pass as extra butter.

The best part about this recipe is that it's infinitely customizable: both cheddar and mustard pair well with a lot of pantry staples. I often find myself switching it up on weekday mornings with a dash of hot sauce, a wedge of avocado, or, in the summer, a slice of ripe heirloom tomato. It might not be the full breakfast of my dreams, but it gets pretty darn close.

ACTIVE TIME

20 minutes

prep time: **10 minutes**
work time: **10 minutes**
bake time: **25 minutes**

makes 8 scones

NOTE: Because this recipe uses a lot of ingredients, its Prep Time is a little longer than those of other recipes in this book. To save time, buy pre-grated cheddar cheese; otherwise, grating a block of cheese in your food processor with the grater blade takes just a few seconds.

1½ cups (6.75 ounces) all-purpose flour, plus more for dusting

1½ cups (6.75 ounces) whole-grain Kamut flour

2 teaspoons granulated sugar

2½ teaspoons baking powder

½ teaspoon baking soda

1 teaspoon kosher salt

2 to 4 cranks fresh ground black pepper

¾ cup (6 ounces) **very cold** unsalted butter, cut into 1-inch cubes

¾ cup (6 ounces) **very cold** crème fraîche

1 **very cold** large egg

1½ tablespoons whole-grain Dijon mustard

¾ cup (6 ounces) **very cold** grated sharp white cheddar cheese

1. Position a rack in the center of the oven and preheat the oven to 400°F. Line a half sheet pan with parchment paper. Line an 8-inch round cake pan with plastic wrap and lightly dust with flour.

2. In the bowl of a stand mixer fitted with the paddle attachment, combine the flours, sugar, baking powder, baking soda, salt, and pepper. Beat on low

until just combined, about 15 seconds. Add the butter all at once and beat until the mixture has the texture of coarse meal, with pea-sized pieces of butter throughout, about 3 minutes.

3. In a large liquid measuring cup, whisk together the crème fraîche, egg, and mustard. With the mixer on low, slowly pour the crème fraîche mixture into the dry ingredients. Beat until the dough clumps around the paddle and/or sides of the bowl, about 1 minute. Add the cheese all at once and beat until the cheese is distributed evenly throughout the dough, about 1 minute. Scrape down the bottom and sides of the bowl with a rubber spatula.

4. Dust your hands with flour and knead the dough once or twice into a rough ball. Place the dough in the center of the prepared cake pan. Dust your hands with flour again and, working quickly, lightly pat out the dough so it fills the pan.

5. Use the plastic wrap to carefully lift the dough out of the pan and onto the counter. Flour the edge of a bench scraper and use it to quarter the dough into 4 even wedges. Cut each wedge in half to make 8 wedges total. Place them at least 3 inches apart on the prepared sheet pan.

6. Bake for 25 minutes, or until the scones are doubled in size and golden brown. Cool the scones on the pan on a wire rack for 10 minutes, or until the edges and bottoms of the scones have set and feel firm to the touch. Serve warm or at room temperature. The scones can be stored in an airtight container or zip-top bag at room temperature for up to 2 days.

NOTE: The key to a good scone is to handle the dough as little as possible; this results in that soft-but-not-too-soft crumb. This recipe instructs you to pat the dough in a cake pan, which helps prevent overhandling *and* results in perfectly shaped scones each time. Just be sure to line your pan with plastic wrap to prevent the dough from sticking!

bake later

If freezing the scone dough, make the dough and cut it into wedges as directed, then tightly wrap each individual wedge in plastic wrap. Freeze for up to 3 months. When ready to bake, position a rack in the center of the oven and preheat the oven to 400°F. Line a half sheet pan with parchment paper. Unwrap the scones and place them at least 3 inches apart on the prepared sheet pan. Bake for 28 minutes, or until the scones have almost doubled in size and lightly browned. Cool and serve as directed.

BRUNCH TREATS

After a long week of work, I'm just not one of those people who goes out to a cool bar or hot restaurant on a Friday night. Instead, I rush straight home, change into my pajamas, order takeout, and turn on Netflix for a binge-watching session.

During the weekend, I'm a bit more social: my friends and I will check out the newest brunch spot. Unfortunately, especially in Portland, brunch is a *competitive* sport. We usually wait in line for several hours, fighting off hangovers while eyeing a table. Finally, I decided that I'd had enough. I'm a baker, after all—instead of battling the brunch crowds, why didn't I just make the cinnamon rolls and the yeasted waffles that I loved so much at home?

I knew the answer, of course: *Because yeasted doughs take way too much time.*

Some of my favorite brunch treats are made with doughs that are leavened with yeast as opposed to baking powder and baking soda. When working with yeast, you're usually looking at a four-hour project: most doughs need at least two hours to rise (in a process known as "proofing"), plus an additional two more if you're doing something fancy like shaping it into rolls. And that's not even accounting for the recipe's Prep, Work, and Bake Times.

Over my years of baking, I discovered that there are ways to control and manipulate this proofing time to your advantage. But first, it's important to understand how yeasted doughs work. I've already told you that most dough recipes require two proofing times. This is because in the first proof, the yeast in the mixture will begin feeding on the flour, creating carbon dioxide bubbles that leaven the dough. Punching down or stirring the dough for a second rise refreshes the yeast's environment, breaking up overcrowded yeast clusters to better aerate the loaf during the second proof. Atmospheric temperature affects this process significantly—dry ingredients absorb wet ingredients much faster in warm temperatures.

But when weeknight baking, I actually like to *slow down* this fermentation process by letting the dough proof overnight in the fridge. I noticed that when I proofed dough at room temperature, I found myself trying to "hack" it to rise faster. I watched the clock constantly, I cranked up the thermostat and kept moving the dough around to the warmest spots in my house. But proofing the dough overnight in the fridge allowed me to "set it and forget it." I would simply go to sleep and wake up the next day to a fully-proofed dough waiting for me (since it takes about 8 hours for dough to proof in the refrigerator).

Now, I know it's counterintuitive to recommend you choose the longer route, especially when weeknight baking. But this strategy gives you control over your schedule. You're free to live your life. Which, in my case, means an introverted Netflix-and-chill Friday routine: After my takeout dinner, I take 15 to 20 minutes to mix up the dough and throw it in the refrigerator to forget about it overnight. The next morning, I punch down the dough first thing and prep it for its second rise before heading to the gym and inviting my friends over for brunch. An hour and a half later, we're enjoying fresh baked goods without the hassle of waiting for a table. It's weeknight baking at its finest.

a dutch baby pancake
that lives up to its name

ACTIVE TIME

5 minutes

prep time: **<5 minutes**
work time: **5 minutes**
bake time: **20 minutes**

makes one
10-inch pancake

NOTE: It's especially important that your eggs and milk are warmed to room temperature–your pancake will not rise and puff in the same way if the ingredients are cold. If you're short on time, check out my tips on how to bring your ingredients to room temperature quickly on page 41!

I spent part of my childhood in the Netherlands, a country known for having some of the tallest people and the best pancakes in the world. Naturally, I had to include a recipe for Dutch baby pancakes in this book. But when researching the dish, I discovered something surprising: Dutch baby pancakes aren't actually Dutch! They're German, and "Dutch" is believed to be a mispronunciation of the word *Deutsch*. I guess that explains why I never saw any Dutch baby pancakes when I actually lived in the Netherlands— though real Dutch pancakes are equally delicious, they are thin and flat like French crepes.

Dutch baby pancakes, on the other hand, are tall and puffy, like a giant popover baked in a cast-iron skillet. When topped with fresh cream and berries, a Dutch baby pancake makes a perfect, impressive brunch dish. The best part? The batter comes together in less than 5 minutes, and doesn't require any fancy equipment like a stand mixer or a blender. And because my recipe uses more eggs and flour than most other Dutch baby recipes, the pancake puffs up well beyond the pan, making it extra tall. I mean, it's called a *Dutch* baby, after all.

4 tablespoons (2 ounces) unsalted butter

3 large eggs, **at room temperature**

⅔ cup (5.35 ounces) whole milk, **at room temperature**

⅔ cup (3 ounces) all-purpose flour

1 tablespoon granulated sugar

¼ teaspoon pure vanilla extract

Pinch of kosher salt

Whipped Cream (page 274) or Crème Fraîche Caramel Sauce (page 279), for serving

1. Position a rack in the center of the oven and preheat the oven to 425°F.

2. Place the butter in a 10-inch cast-iron skillet and bake for 5 minutes, or until the butter is completely melted and the skillet is piping hot.

3. Meanwhile, make the batter: In a medium bowl, whisk the eggs until light and foamy, about 30 seconds. Add the milk, flour, sugar, vanilla, and salt and whisk until just combined, about 30 seconds. The batter will look a little lumpy, but that's totally okay, I promise!

4. Remove the skillet from the oven (but keep the oven on!). Swirl the pan to coat with the butter. Pour the batter into the center of the pan and immediately return the pan to the oven.

5. Bake for 20 minutes, or until the pancake is puffed and golden. Cool the pancake in the skillet on a wire rack for 1 minute, then use a metal spatula to turn out the pancake onto the rack to keep its sides from deflating. Serve immediately, with a dollop of whipped cream or a drizzle of caramel.

variation

a dutch baby for dinner

The Dutch baby's crispy and custardy texture pairs well with all sorts of cheeses and fresh herbs, making it the perfect dinner side dish, similar to Yorkshire pudding in England. Preheat the oven and melt the butter as directed. Prepare the batter, but omit the sugar and vanilla. Pour the batter into the hot pan and immediately sprinkle ¾ cup of your favorite grated hard cheese (I recommend an aged Gouda, ya know, to really live up to the Dutch baby name) and ¼ cup of your favorite fresh herbs (chives, rosemary, and thyme would all be delicious), finely chopped. Bake for 20 minutes, or until the pancake is puffed and golden, and eat immediately in all its cheesy glory. This variation adds about 10 minutes of Prep Time for grating the cheese and prepping the herbs.

overnight french toast for a crowd

When I was younger, I used to sleep over at my best friend's house every other weekend. Her household always had a ton of snacks that were contraband in my house—I feasted on all the soda, Pop-Tarts, and candy I wanted. In the mornings, my friend's mom would make me, my friend, and her two little sisters French toast from scratch. We'd wait impatiently as she griddled slices of bread one by one; when she finally handed each of us our plates, we'd yell excitedly and promptly douse our servings with maple syrup.

In an attempt to re-create this fond childhood memory in my adult years, I invited a handful of friends over with the promise of fresh French toast. It was only then that I realized what a chore it was to make French toast for a group. I'd be stuck at the stovetop, griddling individual servings one by one, missing out on all the mimosas and fun conversations at the dining table. I thought to myself that there had to be a better way.

And there is! This recipe allows you to make several servings *all at once* by baking the French toast as a casserole. The result is similar to a bread pudding dessert, but with a breakfasty twist! To impress my friends during our brunches, I like to sprinkle a few tablespoons of coarse sugar over the French toast right before serving, then brûlée the sugar with a chef's torch, giving each serving a crispy, caramelized-sugar topping.

ACTIVE TIME

10 minutes

makes about 8 servings

SPECIAL EQUIPMENT
Chef's torch

NOTE: For this recipe, it's important to use bread that's slightly stale and past its prime, since stale bread will crisp up in the oven better. In a pinch, you can substitute other enriched bread like brioche, panettone, or even croissants sliced crosswise.

1 pound stale challah bread, sliced 1 inch thick (about 8 slices)

2 tablespoons (1 ounce) unsalted butter, melted

6 large eggs

2 cups (16 ounces) whole milk

1 cup (8 ounces) heavy cream

1 teaspoon pure vanilla extract

⅓ cup tightly packed (2.5 ounces) dark brown sugar

1 teaspoon ground cinnamon

½ teaspoon kosher salt

2 tablespoons Demerara, sanding, or other coarse sugar

Whipped Cream (page 274) or Crème Fraîche Caramel Sauce (page 279), for serving

 DAY 1

prep time: **5 minutes**

work time: **5 minutes**

SOAK THE BREAD

1. Lightly spray a 9 x 13-inch cake pan or ceramic casserole dish with cooking spray. Place the bread in the prepared pan, overlapping the slices as necessary but as little as possible. Drizzle the melted butter over the bread.

2. In a large bowl, whisk the eggs until light and foamy. Add the milk, cream, vanilla, brown sugar, cinnamon, and salt and whisk until combined. Pour the mixture over the bread, using the back of a spoon to press gently on the bread to help it absorb the liquid. Cover with plastic wrap and refrigerate overnight.

 DAY 2

work time: **<5 minutes**

bake time: **50 minutes**

BAKE THE FRENCH TOAST

1. Position a rack in the center of the oven and preheat the oven to 350°F.

2. Uncover the bread and discard the plastic wrap. Sprinkle 1 tablespoon of the Demerara sugar evenly over the top. Bake for 50 to 60 minutes, or until puffed and golden on the edges but set in the center. Cool the French toast on a wire rack for 1 minute, then sprinkle the remaining 1 tablespoon of Demerara sugar evenly over the top. Use a chef's torch to brûlée the sugar until melted and golden brown. Serve immediately, with a dollop of whipped cream or caramel.

make in one day

This recipe divides the work over 2 days to allow the bread to fully soak up the egg mixture with little extra Work Time for you. However, you can expedite the recipe to 1 day by shortening the time the bread soaks. Follow the recipe as directed, but soak the bread in the egg mixture for 10 minutes, then use tongs to flip over each slice and soak for 10 minutes more. Bake and serve the French toast as directed.

overnight liège waffles

I graduated from college in 2009, in the middle of one of the worst recessions the world has ever experienced. I took the first job I was offered and found myself living in San Francisco in a cheap-for-the-city-but-still-astronomically-expensive shabby apartment and drawing on my dwindling savings. As a result, I lived off the free weekly newspaper's cheap eats recommendations: $5 bánh mì sandwiches in the heart of the Tenderloin, $3 soup dumplings in the Richmond District, and $6 Liège waffles from a café in the then up-and-coming SOMA neighborhood. Naturally, being a sweets person, I fell in love with the waffles. Liège waffles are made from yeasted brioche dough and studded with pearl sugar. When the waffle dough is baked, the pearl sugar caramelizes like the sugar on top of crème brûlée. My first bite had me obsessed.

When the café went out of business, I was heartbroken, but saw it as the perfect opportunity to learn how to make the waffles at home. They're surprisingly easy—the trickiest part is sourcing the pearl sugar, which is available online on Amazon (see Resources on page 287 for more information). The dough comes together in only 15 minutes and doesn't require a second rise; I like to make these on a Saturday night and proof the dough overnight in the refrigerator, ensuring that the dough is ready to go on Sunday morning. You can easily freeze leftover waffles and toast them throughout the week, just like store-bought toaster waffles.

ACTIVE TIME

13 minutes over 2 days, plus more for Bake Time

makes about 12 waffles, depending on your waffle maker

SPECIAL EQUIPMENT
Waffle iron

2 cups (9 ounces) all-purpose flour, plus more for dusting

1½ tablespoons tightly packed dark brown sugar

1¾ teaspoons instant yeast

¾ teaspoon kosher salt

⅓ cup (2.65 ounces) water, **warmed to between 120° and 130°F**

3 large eggs, **at room temperature**

1 cup (8 ounces) unsalted butter, **melted but still warm**

1 teaspoon pure vanilla extract

1 cup (5.5 ounces) Belgian pearl sugar

MAKE THE DOUGH

1. In the bowl of a stand mixer fitted with the paddle attachment, combine the flour, brown sugar, yeast, and salt. Beat on low until just combined. Slowly pour in the water and beat until a shaggy dough forms, about 1 minute. Add the eggs one at a time, adding the next egg only after the previous one has been fully incorporated, using a rubber spatula to scrape down the bottom and sides of the bowl after each addition. With the mixer on low, slowly pour in the melted butter and vanilla and beat for 1 minute, then increase the mixer to medium and beat for 2 to 3 minutes more, or until no more butter is pooling at the bottom of the bowl. The dough will be sticky, thick, and a little lumpy.

2. Tip the dough out onto a lightly floured counter. Dust your hands with flour and knead the dough once or twice into a rough ball. Scrape down the bottom and sides of the bowl to remove any excess dough. Spray the bowl with cooking spray and place the dough back in the bowl. Cover with plastic wrap. Refrigerate overnight.

DAY 2

Bake Time will vary depending on your waffle iron's capacity per press. I averaged around 4 minutes per press for golden brown waffles.

MAKE THE WAFFLES

1. Preheat the oven to 250°F. Preheat a waffle iron according to the manufacturer's instructions and lightly coat each waffle plate with cooking spray.

2. Uncover the dough and discard the plastic wrap. Use a rubber spatula to fold in the pearl sugar.

3. Divide the dough and cook the waffles according to the manufacturer's instructions until crisp and golden brown, coating the waffle plates with cooking spray between batches as needed. Serve immediately, or place the finished waffles directly on the oven rack to keep them warm and crisp until ready to serve.

make in one day

This recipe divides the work over 2 days to allow the dough to rise overnight in the fridge; to expedite the process and make the recipe in 1 day, make the dough, cover with plastic wrap, and let rise in a warm, dark spot for 2 hours, or until doubled in size, then add the pearl sugar as directed. Cook and serve the waffles as directed.

overnight small-batch cinnamon rolls

When I first started my baking blog, there were a handful of baked goods that I was intimidated to try—like cinnamon rolls. Though I loved *eating* cinnamon rolls, I thought the recipe looked too difficult to master at home. But a friend of mine was famous in our circle for his recipe, and I begged him to teach me his ways. As we baked, I was surprised to find that my anxieties about cinnamon rolls were unfounded; making cinnamon rolls wasn't complicated at all! My friend agreed to write a guest post all about it for *Hummingbird High*. To this day, it's the only cinnamon roll recipe I'll make, since they're the lightest and fluffiest rolls I've ever had.

There was only one problem: in his post, he described setting his alarm clock for "the hour of the wolf" (that is, 5:30 a.m.) so the rolls would be ready at 10:30 a.m. He instructed my blog readers to do the same, and I blanched—five hours was a long time to wait for brunch, and I didn't want anybody getting up that early on a Saturday. Weekends are for sleeping in!

Over time, as I grew more confident in my baking knowledge, I adapted his recipe to be friendlier to us weeknight bakers. Similar to the Overnight Liège Waffles recipe on page 247, this recipe directs you to proof the dough overnight in the refrigerator and breaks up the work over two days (see page 239 for a deeper dive on the how and why). Although you'll still need to let the dough proof a second time, you can make the glaze while you wait. Glazing the rolls straight from the oven while they're still warm will lead to wonderfully gooey and delicious cinnamon rolls.

ACTIVE TIME

37 minutes over 2 days

makes 6 large buns

NOTE: For this recipe, it's important that the egg is warmed to room temperature. You'll be mixing the egg with buttermilk warmed to the perfect temperature to activate instant yeast. A cold egg might lower that temperature significantly and prevent the yeast from activating. If you're short on time, check out page 41 for a quick refresher on how to bring your ingredients to room temperature quickly!

FOR THE DOUGH

3½ cups (15.75 ounces) all-purpose flour, plus more for dusting

3 tablespoons granulated sugar

1½ teaspoons instant yeast

½ teaspoon baking soda

1 teaspoon kosher salt

1 cup (8 ounces) buttermilk, **warmed to between 120° and 130°F**

1 large egg, **at room temperature**

¼ cup (2 ounces) canola oil

FOR THE FILLING

4 tablespoons (2 ounces) unsalted butter

⅓ cup (2.35 ounces) granulated sugar

2 teaspoons ground cinnamon

FOR THE CREAM CHEESE GLAZE

3 tablespoons (1.5 ounces) cream cheese, **at room temperature**

1 tablespoon whole milk

½ teaspoon pure vanilla extract

¾ cup (3 ounces) confectioners' sugar, sifted if lumpy

DAY 1

prep time: **5 minutes**

work time: **12 minutes**

rise time: **overnight**

MAKE THE DOUGH

1. In the bowl of a stand mixer fitted with a dough hook, combine the flour, sugar, yeast, baking soda, and salt. Knead on low to combine, about 30 seconds. Make a well in the center of the dry ingredients.

2. In a large liquid measuring cup, whisk together the buttermilk, egg, and oil. Pour the mixture into the well in the dry ingredients and knead on medium-low for 10 minutes, or until smooth and elastic, using a rubber spatula to scrape down the bottom and sides of the bowl as necessary.

3. Tip the dough out onto a lightly floured counter. Dust your hands with flour and knead the dough once or twice into a rough ball. Scrape down the bottom and sides of the bowl to remove any excess dough. Spray the bowl with cooking spray and place the dough back in the bowl. Cover with plastic wrap. Refrigerate overnight.

DAY 2

prep time: **5 minutes**

work time: **15 minutes**

rise time: **1 to 2 hours**

bake time: **30 minutes**

SHAPE, BAKE, AND GLAZE THE BUNS

1. Uncover the dough and discard the plastic wrap. Tip it onto a lightly floured counter. Line a quarter sheet pan with parchment paper.

2. Make the filling: Melt the butter in the microwave (or in a small, heavy-bottomed saucepan over medium-low heat). In a small bowl, whisk together the sugar and cinnamon.

3. Use a rolling pin to roll the dough into a large rectangle about 12 inches wide and 20 inches long. Press a bench scraper against the sides of the dough to create straight edges. Pour the melted butter into the center of the dough and use an offset spatula to spread it evenly to the edges. Sprinkle the sugar-cinnamon mixture evenly over the butter.

4. Starting from one of the short ends, roll the dough into a tight log. Use a serrated knife to cut the log crosswise into 6 rolls, each about 2 inches wide. Place the rolls cut-side up and at least 3 inches apart on the prepared pan. Cover with plastic wrap and let sit in a warm spot for 1 to 2 hours, or until doubled in size.

5. About 30 minutes into the second rise, position a rack in the center of the oven and preheat the oven to 350°F.

6. Meanwhile, make the glaze: In the bowl of a stand mixer fitted with the paddle attachment, combine the cream cheese, milk, and vanilla and beat on low until just combined. Gradually add the confectioners' sugar and beat until smooth and fluffy.

7. Bake the buns for 30 to 35 minutes, or until the edges are golden brown and a skewer inserted into the center of a roll comes out clean.

8. Immediately use an offset spatula to spread a generous amount of the glaze over the top of each cinnamon roll—the residual heat will help melt and spread the glaze. Serve warm or at room temperature. The cinnamon rolls can be stored at room temperature, under a cake dome or a large bowl turned upside down, for up to 1 day. After that, transfer the cinnamon rolls to an airtight container and refrigerate for up to 2 days more.

make in one day

This recipe divides the work over 2 days to allow the dough to rise overnight in the fridge; to expedite the process and make the recipe in 1 day, make the dough, cover with plastic wrap, and let rise in a warm, dark spot for 2 hours, or until doubled in size, then shape the rolls and proof the dough once more as directed. Bake and serve the rolls as directed.

variation

crème fraîche glaze

For a silkier and tangier glaze, use crème fraîche in the glaze in place of the cream cheese. This variation does not significantly affect Prep, Work, or Bake Time.

ALTERNATIVE DIETS

You've probably guessed that I am neither vegan nor gluten-free. I literally eat everything and anything (except pumpkin seeds, the only thing I am allergic to). But as a frequent weeknight baker, I share whatever I make with my family, friends, coworkers, and neighbors, and they don't always eat as lawlessly as I do. In fact, over the years, more and more of them were asking me to accommodate their vegan and/or gluten-free diets.

While I was happy to make more inclusive desserts, I struggled with most of the vegan and/or gluten-free recipes I attempted. Many used ingredients that were difficult to source, requiring home bakers to buy ingredients in bulk despite only calling for a teeny, tiny bit in the recipe (like xanthan gum—show me a non-gluten-free baker who will use more than a couple teaspoons of that stuff within a year!). Others were too "healthy," and tasted nothing like their traditional counterparts. After many disappointing results, I set about developing my own vegan and/or gluten-free recipes.

My hope is that you'll find these recipes as delicious as those in the rest of the book. The only difference is that every recipe is either vegan, gluten-free, or both. But that doesn't mean they take more time and effort—they're all *still* recipes that come together quickly, with Work Times of 15 minutes or less. Many use ingredients that are already in your pantry; that means absolutely no specialty ingredients like xanthan gum. We're still weeknight baking, after all.

vegan chocolate chip almond cookies

Sometimes, when my team at work was chipping away at a particularly grueling project, I would promise a batch of my famous Chocolate Chip Cookies (page 115) as a reward for meeting certain deadlines and hitting specific milestones. The cookies worked for almost everybody on my team, with one exception—a quiet engineer who followed a vegan diet.

It made me sad that not everybody on my team could enjoy my treats, so I secretly began working on a vegan chocolate chip cookie recipe. As I researched, I was dismayed to find that most recipes call for artificial egg replacer or flaxseed meal, both of which result in dry, crumbly cookies. But a friend tipped me off to an *America's Test Kitchen* recipe that used almond butter instead—the almond butter gave the cookies a classic chocolate chip texture, similar to ones made with eggs and butter. I was convinced it was a winner, and I arrived early at the office the next day to share them with everybody . . . except I didn't tell anybody they were vegan. I watched as my colleagues devoured the cookies, no questions asked. It was only after they were nearly gone that I confessed that my "famous" cookies were actually vegan! Finally, everybody on my team could enjoy my cookies, including my vegan coworker (who, upon discovering he could eat them, promptly inhaled three and declared them to be the best vegan cookies he'd ever had).

Over time, I tweaked the recipe to fit my preferences: I added extra chocolate and roasted almonds for a nuttier flavor. You can also substitute the almond butter with whatever nut butter you have in your pantry, and the cookie dough freezes well for future use.

ACTIVE TIME
20 minutes

prep time: **10 minutes**
work time: **10 minutes**
bake time: **12 minutes**

makes about 22 cookies

NOTE: To make these cookies, you'll need to use coconut oil. You can use traditional coconut oil, which gives these cookies a tropical flavor, or refined coconut oil, which lets the almond and chocolate flavors shine.

10 ounces vegan chocolate (at least 70% cocoa), from a high-quality chocolate bar, hand broken into pieces

½ cup (2.5 ounces) roasted and salted almonds

2 cups (9 ounces) all-purpose flour

1½ teaspoons baking powder

½ teaspoon baking soda

1 teaspoon kosher salt

½ cup (4 ounces) coconut oil, melted

⅓ cup (3.15 ounces) unsweetened creamy natural almond butter

6 tablespoons (3 ounces) water

2 teaspoons pure vanilla extract

1¼ cups tightly packed (9.35 ounces) dark brown sugar

1. Position a rack in the center of the oven and preheat the oven to 350°F. Line two half sheet pans with parchment paper.

2. In a food processor, combine the chocolate and almonds. Pulse for a few seconds at a time until the ingredients are chopped into 1- to 2-inch pieces, 10 to 15 seconds.

3. In a small bowl, whisk together the flour, baking powder, baking soda, and salt.

4. In a large bowl, whisk together the coconut oil, almond butter, water, and vanilla until smooth. Add the sugar and whisk until combined. Add the dry ingredients and mix with a rubber spatula until just combined. Add the chopped chocolate and almonds and mix until evenly distributed throughout.

5. Use a 3-tablespoon cookie dough scoop to portion the cookie dough into balls and place them at least 3 inches apart on the prepared sheet pans. If the cookie dough seems too soft to scoop, refrigerate for 10 minutes. Bake one pan at a time for 12 minutes, until the edges have set but the centers are still gooey. The cookies will look puffed when you pull them out of the oven, but will fall and crack into the perfect cookies as they cool. Cool the cookies on the pan on a wire rack for 20 minutes, or until the edges and bottoms of the cookies feel firm to the touch. Repeat with remaining cookie dough balls (or freeze it to bake later). Serve warm or at room temperature. The cookies can be stored, in an airtight container at room temperature, for up to 3 days.

bake later

Yes, you can freeze this cookie dough, too! Make the dough and form it into balls as directed. Follow the instructions on page 121 to freeze the dough balls. When ready to bake, position a rack in the center of the oven and preheat the oven to 350°F. Line a half sheet pan (or two, depending on how many you're making) with parchment paper. Place the cookie dough balls at least 3 inches apart on the prepared sheet pan(s). Bake one pan at a time for 15 minutes, or until the edges have set but the centers are still gooey. Cool and serve as directed.

~~desert~~ dessert island vegan mocha brownies

While writing this book, I asked my blog readers to help me identify what dessert recipes they wanted to tackle on a weeknight. Frequently, I ran ~~Desert~~ Dessert Island scenarios: Would you rather see a recipe for vegan brownies or vegan pumpkin bread? Vegan brownies or vegan birthday cake? Vegan brownies won by a landslide every time.

Except there was one problem—I didn't *really* want to include a vegan brownie recipe in this book. Maybe it was my mainstream diet snobbery, but I genuinely believed that butter is what makes brownies good. I didn't know where to start when it came to vegan brownies. So I did what I always do when I procrastinate—I baked (Google "procrastibaking"). This time, I baked everything *except* vegan brownies.

One day, while baking a chocolate cake, I noticed that, with the exception of buttermilk and eggs, most of the ingredients in my beloved cake recipe were actually vegan. This gave me an idea: What if instead of trying to adapt my favorite non-vegan brownie recipes (ones that rely so heavily on butter), I tried to adapt my favorite oil-based cake recipe by removing its dairy components and leaveners to give it a dense, fudgy brownie-like texture? It worked! These brownies taste like traditional brownies and look like them, too, complete with a shiny, crinkly sugar top. Oh, except *vegan*. I'd proven myself wrong with this recipe—vegan brownies were plenty tasty, even without butter.

ACTIVE TIME

13 minutes

prep time: **8 minutes**
work time: **5 minutes**
bake time: **35 minutes**

makes 20 brownies

NOTE: To save on Prep Time, boil the water to make the coffee first. You'll have time to prep the rest of the ingredients while the water comes to a boil.

3 ounces vegan chocolate (at least 70% cocoa), from a high-quality chocolate bar, chopped into ½- to 1-inch pieces

¾ cup (2.25 ounces) Dutch-processed cocoa powder, sifted if lumpy

1 cup (8 ounces) **boiling hot** coffee

1¼ cups tightly packed (9.35 ounces) dark brown sugar

1¼ cups (8.75 ounces) granulated sugar

½ cup (4 ounces) canola oil

1 tablespoon pure vanilla extract

2 cups (9 ounces) all-purpose flour

1 tablespoon instant coffee or freshly ground coffee

1 teaspoon kosher salt

1. Position a rack in the center of the oven and preheat the oven to 350°F. Lightly spray a 9 x 13-inch cake pan with cooking spray and line the bottom and sides with parchment paper, leaving a 2-inch overhang on the pan's two long sides. Spray the parchment, too.

2. In a large bowl, combine the chocolate and cocoa powder. Add the hot coffee and let sit for about 1 minute, then whisk vigorously. Add the sugars, oil, and vanilla and whisk to combine. Add the flour, instant coffee, and salt and whisk until just combined. The batter will look a little lumpy, but that's totally okay, I promise!

NOTE: It's better to pull the brownies out of the oven early than leave them in too long—if you overbake the brownies, they'll be tough. They might appear underbaked, but I promise that when they've cooled, they will be perfect.

3. Pour the batter into the prepared pan and use an offset spatula to smooth the top. Bake for 35 minutes, or until a skewer inserted into the center of the brownies comes out with a few crumbs attached. Cool completely on a wire rack before slicing.

4. Run a butter knife or offset spatula along the edges of the pan and use the overhanging parchment as handles to lift the bars out of the pan and onto a cutting board. Slice into 20 rectangles, each about 2¼ inches wide and 2½ inches long, and serve. The brownies can be stored in an airtight container or zip-top bag at room temperature for up to 3 days.

gluten-free meyer lemon cornmeal torte

From time to time, my blog readers will write me to make special requests for recipes. One of those requests was for a more accessible gluten-free cake recipe; a reader was having trouble finding recipes that didn't require specialty ingredients like gluten-free flour blend and cake mixes.

I love a good baking challenge, so I decided to step up and help my reader. The trick to gluten-free baking is to replace all-purpose flour with flavorful, naturally gluten-free alternatives like cornmeal and nut meals. I started by looking through my blog recipes to see if there were any recipes that could easily make the switch, and a recipe for an upside-down blood orange cake caught my eye. I substituted the original recipe's all-purpose flour with cornmeal and almond meal and found that their nutty flavors paired wonderfully with the aromatic blood orange. I sent my reader the new recipe, and received rave reviews.

This is that recipe, but with one more key substitution to make it more weeknight baking–friendly: because blood oranges have a short season and can be hard to find, I replaced the fruit with Meyer lemons, which are more readily available out of season. Meyer lemons are a cross between a regular lemon and a mandarin orange, making them a little sweeter than traditional lemons. Their rind is edible and very fragrant; there's no need to peel them before using in the recipe, saving you even more time in your weeknight baking.

ACTIVE TIME

13 minutes

prep time: **5 minutes**

work time: **8 minutes**

bake time: **50 minutes**

makes one 9-inch cake

NOTE: You can substitute other citrus you have on hand for the Meyer lemons. Regular lemons and orange varieties like blood oranges, clementines, and mandarins work well; just take care to peel the citrus and remove the bitter white pith beforehand (doing so will increase the recipe's Prep Time by 5 minutes).

1 medium-large Meyer lemon, scrubbed

⅔ cup (4.65 ounces) granulated sugar

1⅓ cups (4.65 ounces) almond meal

⅔ cup (3.35 ounces) fine cornmeal

1 teaspoon baking powder

¼ teaspoon baking soda

½ teaspoon kosher salt

½ cup (4 ounces) canola oil

⅓ cup (2.65 ounces) buttermilk

2 large eggs

1 teaspoon lemon extract

Overnight Vegan Whipped Cream (page 276), for serving

NOTE: For this recipe, make sure to spray the cake pan GENEROUSLY; the cake has a tendency to stick to the pan otherwise. To be extra safe, you can even dust the pan with extra almond meal and cornmeal to prevent the cake from sticking.

1. Position a rack in the center of the oven and preheat the oven to 325°F. Generously spray a 9-inch round cake pan with cooking spray.

2. Use a Microplane grater to grate the lemon zest into a large bowl. Add the sugar. Use your fingers to rub the zest into the sugar—this will infuse the sugar with oils from the zest. Add almond meal, cornmeal, baking powder, baking soda, and salt and whisk until no big clumps remain.

3. Slice the lemon crosswise into thin rounds, ⅛ to ¼ inch thick. Arrange the slices over the bottom of the prepared cake pan. (Don't worry if your lemon didn't yield enough slices to completely cover the bottom of the pan—this is a rustic cake! It'll look pretty no matter what.)

4. In a medium bowl, whisk together the oil, buttermilk, eggs, and lemon extract until combined. Pour the wet ingredients into the dry ingredients. Use a rubber spatula to mix until just combined; the batter will be thick and smooth.

5. Pour the batter into the prepared cake pan, covering the lemon slices completely, and use an offset spatula to smooth the top. Bake for 50 to 55 minutes. When done, the top of the cake should bounce back when gently pressed and a skewer inserted into the center of the cake should come out with a few crumbs attached. Cool on a wire rack for 20 minutes, or until the pan is still warm but cool enough to handle.

6. Run an offset spatula or butter knife around the edges of the cake to loosen it from the pan. Invert the cake onto a plate or cake stand. Serve warm or at room temperature, with a dollop of vegan whipped cream. The cake can be stored at room temperature, under a cake dome or a large bowl turned upside down, for up to 1 day. After that, tightly wrap the cake in plastic wrap and refrigerate for up to 2 days more.

erlend's favorite fruit crisp
(vegan and gluten-free)

 ACTIVE TIME

13 minutes

prep time: **8 minutes**
work time: **5 minutes**
bake time: **40 minutes**

makes one 8-inch
square pan

NOTE: Prep Time will vary depending on the type of fruit you choose. Strawberries need to be hulled and sliced, rhubarb needs to be sliced, and stone fruit like cherries, nectarines, and peaches need to be pitted and sliced. Apples and pears will need to be peeled, cored, and sliced. To reduce Prep Time, choose berries like blackberries, blueberries, or raspberries since these fruits don't require any preparation beyond washing.

NOTE: If you're using a fruit that requires extra prep, add 10 to 15 minutes to Prep Time. You can also break up the work over 2 days and prep any fruit the day before making the crisp; if using a fruit that browns when sliced (like apples or pears), toss the prepped fruit with the lemon juice required in the recipe, then refrigerate overnight in an airtight container.

My boyfriend Erlend and I have been together for over ten years; as a result, he's gotten pretty used to eating leftovers from all my baking experiments for *Hummingbird High*. Once, when I was out of town, he panicked—there was no dessert! We'd finished the last stash of frozen cookie dough (see How to Freeze Cookie Dough to Bake Later on page 121), and the fridge and counter were empty.

The next day, when I got home from my trip, Erlend proudly showed me the fruit crisp he'd made. He had improvised his own dessert in my absence. His favorite baked goods have always been fruit-based: pies, tarts, cobblers, and more. But he also didn't have the time to bake a pie from scratch. So instead, he'd taken one of the pie filling recipes from my blog and baked it in a cake pan. Instead of using pie crust, he'd topped it with a streusel crumble I'd made the week before for a raspberry cake. He bragged that the entire recipe had taken him less than 15 minutes to put together. I was impressed! I took a bite—it was delicious.

Over the years, Erlend tweaked the recipe to suit his tastes: olive oil instead of butter, almonds and oats instead of all-purpose flour. His changes not only made the crisp more delicious, they made the recipe both vegan *and* gluten-free.

NOTE: All oats are technically gluten-free, but if you're baking for somebody with a gluten intolerance or celiac disease, make sure that the package specifies "gluten-free." Some oats are processed in facilities that also process ingredients with gluten, which can lead to cross-contamination and trace amounts of gluten in otherwise gluten-free products.

FOR THE FRUIT FILLING

24 ounces (around 4½ cups) fresh fruit, peeled, cored/pitted/hulled, and chopped into 1½- to 2-inch chunks as necessary

¼ cup tightly packed (1.85 ounces) dark brown sugar

¼ cup (1 ounce) cornstarch

1 tablespoon freshly squeezed lemon juice

Pinch of kosher salt

FOR THE OLIVE OIL OAT CRISP TOPPING

1 cup (3.5 ounces) gluten-free old-fashioned rolled oats

½ cup (2.5 ounces) almonds, chopped into ½- to 1-inch pieces

½ cup (1.75 ounces) almond meal

¼ cup tightly packed (1.85 ounces) dark brown sugar

¼ teaspoon kosher salt

½ cup (4 ounces) olive oil

Overnight Vegan Whipped Cream (page 276), for serving

1. Position a rack in the center of the oven and preheat the oven to 375°F. Generously spray an 8-inch square baking pan with cooking spray.

2. Make the fruit filling: In a large bowl, combine the fruit, sugar, cornstarch, lemon juice, and salt and toss to combine. Scoop into the prepared pan and use a rubber spatula to spread it evenly over the pan.

3. Make the topping: In a large bowl, combine the oats, almonds, almond meal, brown sugar, and salt. Add the oil and mix with a rubber spatula until combined. Sprinkle the topping evenly over the filling, using the spatula to spread as necessary.

4. Bake for 40 to 45 minutes, or until the filling is bubbling slowly and the topping is golden brown. Check the crisp 30 minutes into the Bake Time—if the topping is browning too quickly, cover the pan loosely with a sheet of aluminum foil. Cool on a wire rack. Serve warm or at room temperature, with a dollop of vegan whipped cream. The crisp can be stored at room temperature, wrapped tightly in plastic wrap, for up to 1 day. After that, refrigerate for up to 2 days more.

peanut butter pretzel pie
(vegan and gluten-free)

 ACTIVE TIME

30 minutes over 3 days

makes one 9-inch pie

NOTE: It's likely that almost everything you need for this recipe will be in your pantry, with one exception—vegan white chocolate. I like King David white chocolate chips or Pascha rice milk bars, both of which you can buy online (see Resources on page 287).

In my senior year of college, I befriended a group of British exchange students. After a drunken night out at a student union dance party, their favorite thing to do was eat snacks from the 7-Eleven close to campus. I'd tag along as they loaded up on junk food they couldn't find back in England. We'd end the night in somebody's common room, passing around bags of chips, boxes of cookies, and even slices of toaster oven pizza. One of my friends loved to buy a jar of Skippy peanut butter, dunk a pretzel in the jar to scoop out a giant dollop, and shove the whole thing into his mouth. I was skeptical but gave it a try. Immediately, I understood—it was the perfect bite of nutty cream and pretzel crunch.

Fast-forward: I'd initially planned to make a vegan pie crust for this book to substitute for my unapologetically all-butter pie crust. But when I reached out to my vegan food blogger friends and asked them for their input, many warned me that making a good vegan pie crust was a near-impossible task. But I didn't give up—pie crust can be made of many things, including cookies, crackers, and pretzels. As I loaded my cart with ingredients to experiment with, I saw a display of nut butters next to the pretzels and was suddenly reminded of my friend's favorite midnight snack.

From there, this peanut butter pretzel pie was born. I used gluten-free pretzels to make a crunchy pie crust, then topped it with a creamy peanut butter filling made with vegan white chocolate and coconut cream. You can also substitute regular white chocolate and non-gluten-free pretzels for a traditional version of this pie that takes advantage of the ingredients already in your pantry.

NOTE: This recipe divides the work up over 3 days; to expedite the process and make the pie in 2 days, make sure the can of coconut milk has been refrigerated ahead of time (canned coconut milk is shelf-stable, but to ensure that it's ready to go, simply store it in the refrigerator instead of in the pantry when you bring it home from the grocery store). Make and bake the crust as directed. While the crust is in the oven, make the filling. Cool and store both the crust and the filling overnight as directed. On the following day, make the whipped cream, assemble the pie, and serve as directed.

NOTE: To make pretzel crumbs, use a digital scale to weigh out as many pretzels as needed to match the weight listed in the recipe. Use a food processor to pulse the pretzels into fine crumbs.

1 (14-ounce) can full-fat coconut milk

FOR THE PRETZEL CRUST

1½ cups (5.25 ounces) gluten-free vegan pretzel crumbs

6 tablespoons (3 ounces) coconut oil, melted

2 tablespoons tightly packed dark brown sugar

Pinch of kosher salt

FOR THE PEANUT BUTTER FILLING

6 ounces vegan white chocolate, from chips or a high-quality chocolate bar, chopped into ½- to 1-inch pieces

¾ cup (7.15 ounces) unsweetened creamy natural peanut butter

2 tablespoons tightly packed dark brown sugar

FOR THE WHIPPED COCONUT CREAM

½ teaspoon pure vanilla extract

2 tablespoons confectioners' sugar, sifted if lumpy

FOR ASSEMBLY

Toasted coconut flakes

Vegan and gluten-free pretzels

DAY 1

prep time: **5 minutes**

work time: **5 minutes**

bake time: **15 minutes**

PREP THE COCONUT MILK AND MAKE THE CRUST

1. Place the unopened can of coconut milk in the coldest part of the refrigerator and let sit, undisturbed, for at least 24 hours.

2. Position a rack in the center of the oven and preheat the oven to 350°F.

3. In a medium bowl, combine the pretzel crumbs, oil, sugar, and salt and toss with your fingers until the mixture looks like wet sand. Pour the mixture into a 9-inch pie pan and use a tart tamper or your hands to press it evenly over the bottom of the pan, all the way to the edges. (You can use the bottom of a coffee mug or heavy glass to pound the crumbs in place—you want to apply some pressure here so the crust holds its shape.)

4. Bake for 15 minutes, until the crust is set and golden brown. The crust will look underbaked and feel soft to the touch when you remove it from the oven, but will firm up as it cools. If you find that the crust has slumped down the sides of the pan, use the back of a spoon to gently ease it back into place while it's still warm. Cool the crust completely on a wire rack. Store, under a cake dome or a large bowl turned upside down, on the counter overnight.

MAKE THE FILLING

1. Remove the can of coconut milk from the refrigerator, being careful not to jostle or shake the can too much. Open the can—by this point, the coconut milk will have separated from the coconut cream, creating two distinct layers of coconut cream and coconut water. Carefully scoop the layer of thick, white coconut cream into an airtight container with a lid. Continue scooping until the cream starts to look watery—that's when you've hit the layer of coconut water. You should have ½ cup (4 ounces) to ¾ cup (6 ounces) of coconut cream. Seal the container and refrigerate. Tightly wrap the top of the can with plastic wrap to make a seal. Shake the can vigorously for 15 seconds, then pour ½ cup (4 ounces) of the coconut water into a liquid measuring cup. Discard the rest of the coconut water or save it for another use.

2. Place the white chocolate in the bowl of a stand mixer. Fill a medium, heavy-bottomed saucepan with 1 to 2 inches of water and bring it to a simmer over medium heat. Place the mixer bowl over the saucepan (be sure the bottom of the bowl does not touch the water). Cook, using a heatproof rubber spatula to stir the mixture and scrape the sides of the bowl occasionally, until the chocolate has melted, about 10 minutes. Remove the bowl from the pan and add the peanut butter. Affix the bowl to the stand mixer fitted with the whisk attachment and whisk on medium-low until smooth, about 1 minute. Add the brown sugar and whisk until just combined, about 1 minute. Slowly pour in the coconut water. Increase the mixer to medium-high and whisk for 3 minutes, or until the sides of the bowl are cool to the touch and the mixture looks like thick caramel. Pour the filling into the pie crust and use an offset spatula to smooth the top. Cover loosely with plastic wrap and refrigerate overnight.

MAKE THE WHIPPED COCONUT CREAM AND ASSEMBLE THE PIE

1. Place the coconut cream in the bowl of a stand mixer fitted with the whisk attachment. Add the vanilla and whisk on medium-high for 3 minutes, scraping down the bottom and sides of the bowl occasionally with a rubber spatula, until stiff peaks form. Sprinkle the confectioners' sugar over the cream and use a rubber spatula to fold in the sugar—the mixture will resemble traditional whipped cream.

2. Spoon the whipped coconut cream over the filling and garnish with toasted coconut and pretzels. Serve immediately. The peanut butter pie can be stored in the refrigerator, covered loosely with plastic wrap, for up to 3 days. The whipped coconut cream will harden in the fridge, so I suggest using an offset spatula to scrape it off. Store it separately in an airtight container for up to 3 days. Transfer the cream to a stand mixer fitted with the whisk attachment and whisk on medium until light and creamy again, 2 to 3 minutes.

DOLLOPS, DRIZZLES, FILLINGS, AND SPRINKLES

Sometimes, you want to go the extra mile but you can't find even an extra minute. That's where this extra credit comes in. These creams, sauces, and toppings will take your baked goods to the next level, and they won't actually take that much time. Many of them can be stored long-term, ready for use in your favorite dessert recipes.

whipped cream

ACTIVE TIME
5 minutes

prep time: **<5 minutes**
work time: **5 minutes**

makes 1½ cups

Have you ever read the back of a whipped cream can? There's an astonishing number of unpronounceable chemicals in there. One of the advantages of making whipped cream at home is that you know exactly what you're getting: whipped cream, plain, simple, and delicious. In a stand mixer, homemade whipped cream comes together in less than 5 minutes. It's best right after it's made, but you can store it in an airtight container in the fridge overnight.

NOTE: You'll notice that the recipe instructs you to whip the cream to specific textures like "soft peaks" and "firm peaks." The best way to determine the cream's texture is to do a test with a whisk: Dip the tip of a whisk (or the whisk attachment) into the whipped cream, remove it, and quickly turn it upside down. If the cream is too soft, it will slide off the whisk, and you'll need to keep whisking. If the cream has a cloudlike structure, with peaks that lose their shape, you're at the "soft peaks" stage; continue whisking, then test again. If, the next time you turn the whisk upside down, the peaks hold, you're at the "stiff peaks" stage. If you find that the whipped cream starts to clump, you've accidentally made butter. Add a few tablespoons of heavy cream and use a rubber spatula to mix until the cream returns to the "stiff peaks" stage.

CLASSIC WHIPPED CREAM

1 cup (8 ounces) **very cold** heavy cream

1 tablespoon confectioners' sugar, sifted if lumpy

1 tablespoon pure vanilla extract

In the bowl of a stand mixer fitted with the whisk attachment, combine the cream, confectioners' sugar, and vanilla. Whisk on medium-high until soft peaks form, about 3 minutes. If storing overnight, whisk until firm peaks form, an additional minute or so—but be careful not to overwhip or you'll end up with butter!

CHOCOLATE WHIPPED CREAM

1 cup (8 ounces) **very cold** heavy cream

1 tablespoon confectioners' sugar, sifted if lumpy

1 tablespoon natural unsweetened cocoa powder, sifted if lumpy

¼ teaspoon pure vanilla extract

In the bowl of a stand mixer fitted with the whisk attachment, combine the cream, confectioners' sugar, cocoa powder, and vanilla. Whisk on medium-high until soft peaks form, about 3 minutes. If storing overnight, whisk until firm peaks form, an additional minute or so—but be careful not to overwhip or you'll end up with butter!

HONEY WHIPPED CREAM

1 cup (8 ounces) **very cold** heavy cream

1 tablespoon honey

In the bowl of a stand mixer fitted with the whisk attachment, whisk the cream on medium-high until soft peaks form, about 3 minutes. Add the honey and whisk until firm peaks form, an additional minute or so—but be careful not to overwhip or you'll end up with butter!

CRÈME FRAÎCHE WHIPPED CREAM

⅔ cup (5.35 ounces) **very cold** heavy cream

1 tablespoon confectioners' sugar, sifted if lumpy

½ teaspoon pure vanilla extract

½ cup (4 ounces) **very cold** crème fraîche

In the bowl of a stand mixer fitted with the whisk attachment, combine the cream, confectioners' sugar, and vanilla. Whisk on medium-high until soft peaks form, about 3 minutes. If storing overnight, whisk until firm peaks form, an additional minute or so—be careful not to overwhip or you'll end up with butter! Use a rubber spatula to fold in the crème fraîche until just combined.

overnight vegan whipped cream

I like to keep canned coconut milk in my pantry for use in everyday cooking, but canned coconut milk comes in handy for baking recipes, too. Canned coconut milk separates into two distinct layers: coconut cream and coconut water, the former of which can be whipped into a vegan version of dairy whipped cream. Similar to traditional whipped cream, this vegan whipped cream is best right after it's made, but can be stored in an airtight container in the fridge overnight—it may need to be rewhipped before serving, just to make sure it's airy and fluffy.

For this recipe, plan ahead. You'll need to chill the canned coconut milk overnight to encourage the coconut water and coconut cream to separate. The best coconut whipped cream is made from canned coconut milk that consists of only coconut and water; avoid coconut milks with other preservatives and thickeners. My favorite brand is Arroy-D; see Resources (page 287) to find out where to source their coconut milk.

ACTIVE TIME
5 minutes over 2 days

makes 1½ cups

1 (14-ounce) can full-fat coconut milk

½ teaspoon pure vanilla extract

2 tablespoons confectioners' sugar, sifted if lumpy

DAY 1

prep time: **<5 minutes**

PREP THE COCONUT MILK

Place the unopened can of coconut milk in the coldest part of the refrigerator and let sit, undisturbed, for at least 24 hours.

DAY 2

work time: **5 minutes**

MAKE THE VEGAN WHIPPED CREAM

Remove the can of coconut milk from the refrigerator, being careful not to jostle or shake the can too much. Open the can—by this point, the coconut milk will have separated from the coconut cream, creating two distinct layers of coconut cream and coconut water. Carefully scoop the layer of thick, white coconut cream into the bowl of a stand mixer fitted with the whisk attachment. Continue scooping until the cream starts to look watery—that's when you've hit the layer of coconut water. You should have ½ cup (4 ounces) to ¾ cup (6 ounces) of coconut cream. Add the vanilla and whisk on medium-high for 3 minutes, or until stiff peaks form. Sprinkle the confectioners' sugar over the cream and use a rubber spatula to fold in the sugar—the mixture will resemble traditional whipped cream. Serve immediately.

pastry cream

Pastry cream is the all-purpose duct tape of the dessert world. I use it as a creamy filling in between cake layers and to fill The Easiest Brown Butter Tart Shell Ever (page 176) and top with the freshest fruit available. And because it takes only 10 minutes to make, it's an extra credit assignment worth acing.

This is one of the recipes in the book where it's worth sourcing vanilla bean powder (see Resources on page 287); using it in the cream will create a gorgeous, vanilla-speckled custard. In a pinch, use a fresh vanilla bean pod: Slice the pod lengthwise and use the tip of a knife to scrape the beans into the custard as it cooks. Add the pod for extra flavor but discard after straining the custard.

ACTIVE TIME
10 minutes

prep time: **<5 minutes**
work time: **10 minutes**

makes 1½ cups

5 tablespoons (2.15 ounces) granulated sugar

2 tablespoons cornstarch

¼ teaspoon kosher salt

1 cup (8 ounces) whole milk

1 large egg

2 tablespoons (1 ounce) unsalted butter

2 teaspoons pure vanilla extract

1 teaspoon vanilla bean powder (optional)

1. In a medium, heavy-bottomed saucepan, whisk together the sugar, cornstarch, and salt. Add the milk and egg and whisk until combined. The mixture will be a little lumpy, but that's okay, I promise! Bring to a boil over medium heat and cook, whisking continuously, until the mixture thickens enough to coat the back of a spoon, 5 to 8 minutes.

2. Remove from the heat. Immediately add the butter, vanilla extract, and vanilla bean powder and whisk until smooth. Place a fine-mesh sieve over a medium bowl and pour the pastry cream through the sieve to remove any lumps. Set the bowl on a wire rack and let cool completely before using in a recipe or storing for later use. To store, pour the pastry cream into an airtight container and press a sheet of plastic wrap directly against the surface of the pastry cream to prevent a skin from forming. Cover with a lid and refrigerate for up to 1 week.

diplomat cream

Diplomat Cream is a lighter, fluffier version of pastry cream that works especially well in delicate desserts like fruit tarts and cakes. To make diplomat cream, fold 1 cup Classic Whipped Cream (page 274) into the cooled pastry cream. Use immediately—diplomat cream won't keep like traditional pastry cream.

crème fraîche caramel sauce

 ACTIVE TIME

10 minutes

prep time: **<5 minutes**
work time: **10 minutes**

makes about 1½ cups

Although caramel sauce is available in most grocery stores, I've always found the commercial version to be too sweet. This homemade version has some tang thanks to the crème fraîche. Drizzle it as a topping over any of your favorite cakes, tarts, or pies. Swirl it into the dough for Chocolate Chip Cookies (page 115), or the batter for Boxed-Mixed Brownies From Scratch (page 151) and Better-Than-Supernatural Fudge Brownies (page 153) before baking for a gooey version of the recipe.

¼ cup (2 ounces) water

1 cup (7 ounces) granulated sugar

½ teaspoon kosher salt

½ cup (4 ounces) unsalted butter

½ cup (4 ounces) crème fraîche

1 teaspoon pure vanilla extract

NOTE: Avoid stirring the caramel sauce as you add the ingredients; instead, simply pick up the saucepan by the handle and gently swirl to help incorporate the ingredient into the sauce. Using a utensil to stir will cause the sugar to seize, and lead to a grainy, caramelized mess.

1. Pour the water into a medium, heavy-bottomed saucepan, swirling to evenly coat the bottom of the pan. Sprinkle the sugar and salt over the surface of the water. Don't stir—the sugar granules will dissolve with the heat, I promise! Cook over medium-high heat until the mixture starts to boil, about 3 minutes. Add the butter and swirl it into the mixture. Cook until the butter has melted and the edge of the mixture turns a pale gold, then dark amber, 3 to 4 minutes.

2. Once the caramel has darkened, remove the pan from the heat and whisk in the crème fraîche (watch out!—the mixture will bubble and steam violently). Whisk until the crème fraîche is fully incorporated, then whisk in the vanilla. Cool slightly before using or let cool completely before storing; the sauce will thicken as it cools. To store, pour the caramel into a glass jar with an airtight lid, cover, and refrigerate for up to 2 weeks. To reheat the sauce, spoon it into the top of a double boiler or into a heatproof bowl set over a medium, heavy-bottomed saucepan filled with a few inches of simmering water (be sure the bottom of the bowl does not touch the water). Cook over medium-low heat, stirring regularly, until the caramel softens to a pourable consistency. Cool and use as directed.

dark chocolate ganache

NOTE: Throughout this book, I instruct you to chop chocolate into ½- to 1-inch pieces. But for this recipe, you'll need to take it a step further and chop the chocolate into smaller, ¼- to ½-inch pieces. The smaller pieces will melt faster and help prevent your ganache from splitting (see Troubleshooting).

Chocolate ganache is an easy way to class up any dessert. I like to use ganache as a topping for a frosted version of Better-Than-Supernatural Fudge Brownies (page 153) or Cheesecake Bars (page 167). You can also use it as a frosting or filling for any of the recipes in the Cakes chapter. Hardened leftover ganache can be portioned into balls with a 1-tablespoon cookie dough scoop and rolled in powdered sugar or cocoa powder for chocolate truffles.

NOTE: Because this recipe uses so few ingredients, each ingredient must be the very best quality you can find. This is one where it's worth sourcing high-quality chocolate (like Valrhona or Guittard) from bars or fèves, not chocolate chips.

8 ounces dark chocolate (between 60% and 73% cocoa), from whole fèves or a high-quality chocolate bar, chopped into ¼- to ½-inch pieces

1 cup (8 ounces) heavy cream

1. Place the chocolate in a medium heatproof bowl. In a small, heavy-bottomed saucepan, cook the cream over medium-high heat to just under a boil, about 5 minutes. Immediately pour over the chocolate, then place a dinner plate over the bowl to create a makeshift lid. Let sit, undisturbed, for 5 minutes.

2. Remove the plate. Whisk slowly but steadily until the ganache is thick, smooth, and shiny.

3. Use the ganache in the recipe of your choice.

To use the ganache as a topping, set the bowl on a wire rack and cool for 10 minutes, then pour it over the cake or bars of your choice; refrigerate the bars, uncovered, for 1 hour to allow the ganache to set and cool.

To use the ganache as a frosting, cool on a wire rack for 20 to 25 minutes, or until spreadable, with the consistency of frosting.

To save for later, pour the ganache into a glass jar with an airtight lid, cover, and refrigerate for up to 2 weeks. To reheat the ganache, spoon it into the top of a double boiler or a heatproof bowl set over a medium, heavy-bottomed saucepan filled with a few inches of simmering water (be sure the bottom of the bowl does not touch the water). Cook over medium-low heat, stirring regularly, until the ganache is thick, smooth, and shiny. Cool and use as directed.

troubleshooting

Ganache can sometimes "split" or "break," meaning the fat in the chocolate separates to give the ganache an oily, separated appearance. This can happen when the ganache is stirred too vigorously or at too low a temperature. When whisking, aim for a slow, steady motion. If the ganache breaks, set the bowl over a medium, heavy-bottomed saucepan filled with a few inches of simmering water (be sure the bottom of the bowl does not touch the water). Cook over medium-low heat to 92°F, whisking slowly but steadily to re-emulsify the ganache.

overnight homemade sprinkles

I love adding sprinkles to any dessert for extra color and crunch, but let's be honest—grocery store sprinkles don't taste great. The solution? Make your own! Sprinkles are surprisingly easy to make at home, provided you plan ahead so they can dry overnight. Customize this recipe using your own colors, or change their flavor by swapping out the vanilla for other extracts like almond, orange, rose water, and more. If you don't have a piping bag and small piping tip, use zip-top bags instead. Fill them with the tinted paste, snip off a tiny hole in the corner of the bag with kitchen shears, and get piping!

 **ACTIVE TIME**

20 minutes over 2 days

makes about 1½ cups

2 cups (8 ounces) confectioners' sugar, sifted if lumpy

1 large egg white

¾ teaspoon pure vanilla extract

¼ teaspoon kosher salt

Food coloring

DAY 1

prep time: **5 minutes**

work time: **15 minutes**

MAKE THE PASTE AND PIPE THE SPRINKLES

1. Line a sheet pan with parchment paper. In a medium bowl, combine the confectioners' sugar, egg white, vanilla, and salt. Mix with a rubber spatula until combined; the paste will be thick.

2. Divide the paste among three small bowls. Add a few drops of a different-color food coloring to each portion and mix each until combined and tinted to your liking. Immediately pour each paste into its own piping bag fitted with a small tip (or pour into separate zip-top bags and snip off a corner of each).

3. Pipe long, thin lines of paste directly onto the parchment paper, ensuring that the lines do not touch. Repeat the process with the remaining colors. Let set, uncovered, in a dry place overnight.

DAY 2

work time: **<5 minutes**

SLICE THE SPRINKLES

Use a butter knife to break the lines into short, sprinkle-size pieces. Use immediately, or store at room temperature in an airtight container for up to 2 weeks.

HOW TO MAKE ANY RECIPE
A WEEKNIGHT BAKING RECIPE

Congratulations—you made it to the end of the book! By this point, you'll have learned a lot about baking and tried out some recipes, too. You now have insight into which desserts can come together quickly and easily on a weeknight, as well as a basic understanding of which recipes can be broken up into more manageable chunks to fit into your schedule. Although I hope my recipes will be the foundation for much of your baking, the following techniques and methods in this book can be applied to any baking recipe you tackle in the future, too:

1. Ingredient prep can happen far ahead of the recipe, especially if the recipe uses nonperishable or relatively shelf-stable ingredients like chocolate, nuts, and spices. To see this in action, check out the recipe for Choose-Your-Own Pumpkin Spice Bread on page 63; in particular, the recipe for Pumpkin Spice (page 67) can be made up to 3 months in advance of the cake itself!

2. Recipes for desserts made up of different components like crusts, fillings, and toppings can be broken up over a series of a few days. Make one or two components a day and assemble the entire dessert once all the components are ready. I've provided weeknight baking schedules that break up layer cake recipes (page 76) and roll-out cookie recipes (page 134) in this manner. However, these schedules can be applied to other dessert recipes, too!

3. Many drop cookie, muffin, and scone recipes can be refrigerated and/or frozen for baking in smaller batches throughout the week, the month, or even the entire year! Recipes in those chapters have specific notes and instructions providing insight as to how and why.

4. A roll-out cookie or pie dough recipe that requires you to chill and rest its dough for a few hours can and *should* be extended beyond the recipe's recommended time to adapt to your schedule. Doing so will not negatively affect your dough and, in many cases, will actually improve the quality

of your dessert! Read about why cookie dough actually tastes better after being chilled on page 111, or how pie dough gets easier to roll out after resting on page 192. Many of these doughs keep wonderfully in the freezer, allowing you to start and stop a baking project any time you want.

5. Similarly, if you're working with a yeasted dough recipe that instructs you to proof the dough twice (once after mixing, and again after being shaped), you can turn it into an overnight recipe by doing the first proof in the refrigerator overnight. Cold temperatures slow the proofing process considerably—see this in play in my recipe for Overnight Liège Waffles (page 247) and Overnight Small-Batch Cinnamon Rolls (page 249).

6. Finally, know that weeknight baking isn't about rushing through instructions or finding a 10-minute solution for desserts (because that doesn't actually exist beyond the Single Lady Chocolate Chip Cookie on page 113). On the contrary, many of the time-saving tips that I just recapped are about ways to *slow down* a recipe's steps. The magic of baking often lies within its process—it's best to embrace it by taking your time with it. But only within YOUR schedule, of course. Happy weeknight baking, folks!

RESOURCES

ALMOND MEAL
Bob's Red Mill, *bobsredmill.com*

BELGIAN PEARL SUGAR
Lars' Own, *amazon.com*

BLACK SESAME SEEDS
Kalustyan's, *foodsofnations.com*
Kevala, *kevala.net*

CAKE FLOUR
Bob's Red Mill, *bobsredmill.com*
King Arthur Flour, *kingarthurflour.com*
Swans Down, *swansdown.com* (Bleached
   Cake Flour)

CANNED COCONUT MILK
Arroy-D, *amazon.com*

CLEAR ARTIFICIAL VANILLA EXTRACT
McCormick, *mccormick.com*

COCONUT SUGAR
Bob's Red Mill, *bobsredmill.com*

CRÈME FRAÎCHE
Vermont Creamery, *vermontcreamery.com*

CRYSTALLIZED GINGER
Nuts.com, *nuts.com*

DEMERARA SUGAR
India Tree, *indiatree.com*

DUTCH-PROCESSED COCOA POWDER
Guittard Chocolate Company, *guittard.com*
Hershey's, *hersheys.com*
King Arthur Flour, *kingarthurflour.com*
Valrhona, *valrhona.com*

EUROPEAN-STYLE BUTTER
Plugra, *plugra.com*
Vermont Creamery, *vermontcreamery.com*

FÈVES AND CHOCOLATE DISCS
Guittard Chocolate Company, *guittard.com*
King Arthur Flour, *kingarthurflour.com*
Valrhona, *valrhona.com*

**FREEZE-DRIED RASPBERRIES
(AND OTHER FREEZE-DRIED FRUIT)**
Trader Joe's, *traderjoes.com*
Whole Foods Market, *wholefoodsmarket.com*

KAMUT FLOUR
Bob's Red Mill, *bobsredmill.com*

MASCARPONE CHEESE

Vermont Creamery, *vermontcreamery.com*

MATCHA GREEN TEA POWDER

Tea Bar, *teabarpdx.com*
Townshend's Tea Company, *townshendtea.com*

PARCHMENT PAPER SHEETS

King Arthur Flour, *kingarthurflour.com*
   (also on *amazon.com*)

PISTACHIO EXTRACT

LorAnn Oils, *lorannoils.com* (also on
   amazon.com)
The Watkins Co., *watkins1868.com* (also
   on *amazon.com*)

NONPAREIL SPRINKLES

Medley Hills Farm, *amazon.com*
Wilton, *wilton.com*

SANDING SUGAR

Bob's Red Mill, *bobsredmill.com*

SEEDLESS JAM

Stonewall Kitchen, *stonewallkitchen.com*

SPRINKLES

India Tree, *indiatree.com*
Fancy Sprinkles, *fancysprinkles.com*
Sweetapolita Sprinkles + Stuff, *sweetapolita*
   .myshopify.com

SUMAC

Kalustyan's, *foodsofnations.com*

TAHINI

Seed + Mill, *seedandmill.com*

**VANILLA BEAN POWDER AND VANILLA
BEANS**

Beanilla, *beanilla.com*

VEGAN DARK CHOCOLATE

Alter Eco, *alterecofoods.com*
Theo, *theochocolate.com*
Pascha Chocolate, *paschachocolate.com*

VEGAN WHITE CHOCOLATE

King David, *amazon.com*
Pascha Chocolate, *paschachocolate.com*

ACKNOWLEDGMENTS

To Emily Graff, Suet Chong, Lashanda Anakwah, Jessica Chin, Ruth Lee-Mui, Beth Maglione, Ivy McFadden, Emily Simonson, Samantha Hoback, and the rest of the team at Simon and Schuster; *Weeknight Baking* wouldn't have been possible without your enthusiasm, support, and hard work.

To Nicole Tourtelot, my literary agent. Thank you for being one of *Weeknight Baking*'s biggest advocates and helping me navigate the strange world of book publishing. I'll always appreciate your candor. To Lily Diamond, for introducing us and believing that *Hummingbird High* was worth turning into a book long before I did.

To Alana Kysar, for encouraging me to seriously pursue a book in the first place; I likely would not have written one at all had it not been for your infinite enthusiasm and confidence in my ability to do so.

To Michelle Carroll, whose hard work and tireless support made *Weeknight Baking* better in immeasurable ways. Thank you for everything: your photography assistance, your meticulous copyedits, your design feedback, and the way you brought calm and steadiness during the final, frenzied months of *Weeknight Baking*'s production. Thank you for treating my work like it was your own. If this book had a coauthor, it would be you.

To Sze Wa Cheung, for putting up with my annoying Photoshop questions and for acting as *Weeknight Baking*'s unofficial design consultant. Thank you for always being honest, and always telling it like it is (even when you knew I wouldn't like it).

To Jackie Segedin, Anna Fatlowitz, Edie Horstman, and all of the hardworking folks at CookIt Media. You kept the lights on at *Hummingbird High* while I was working on *Weeknight Baking*. Thank you for making my life so much easier, and for always being my brand's fiercest advocates and loyal supporters. No words can begin to describe how grateful I am.

To the many recipe testers of *Weeknight Baking*: Adrianna Adarme, Kristin Canham, Erin Clarkson, Chloe-Rose Crabtree, Erica Gelbard, Tabitha Huizinga, Chelsea Johnston, Alana Kysar, Stephanie Le, Sarah Menanix, Cindy Rahe, Naomi Robinson, Mary Ellen Stefanou, Julie Swoope, Betsy Thompson, and Albina Ziadinova. Thank you for helping make sure that these recipes work in kitchens and ovens beyond my own; your feedback was priceless.

To the generous sponsors and friends who kept me stocked and fully equipped with

ingredients, props, and more throughout the development of *Weeknight Baking*: American Heirloom, Bob's Red Mill, Breville, Crate and Barrel, Guittard Chocolate Company, Staub, Stonewall Kitchen, Valrhona, Vermont Creamery, Williams-Sonoma, and Zwilling. Meredith Bradford, Rachael Calmas, Lauren Condon, Amy Guittard, Greg Harned, Marine Leman, Margaux Maertens, Alex Sacripante, Sarena Shasteen, Amy Stringer-Mowat, and Betsy Thompson—thank you for saving me from many, MANY trips to the grocery store and last-minute Amazon Prime purchases.

To Bonnie Stinson, my assistant for an all-too-short time. Thank you for helping test recipes, running errands, and assisting on *Weeknight Baking*'s photo shoots.

To all the past coworkers who supported *Hummingbird High*, especially Sheena Donohue McCarthy, Tracy Tran, Dan Bufithis-Hurie,* Michelle Carroll, Sze Wa Cheung, and Tammy Kim. Thank you for making the weekdays more bearable, and for never judging me for having a life outside the office.

To the fellow bakers who helped troubleshoot my baking issues and whose recipes have taught me so much over the years: Erin Clarkson, Tessa Huff, Lauren Ko, Sarah Kieffer, Linda Lomelino, Erin McDowell, Stella Parks, Cindy Rahe, Lyndsay Sung, and so many more. Thank you for your hard work. I have learned so much from all of you. You continue to be an inspiration.

To SLAMM: Stephanie Le, Lily Diamond, Alana Kysar, and Molly Yeh. Thank you for always providing the laughter, the lightness, and the fun I desperately needed while writing *Weeknight Baking*.

To Adrianna Adarme, Yossy Arefi, Melissa Coleman, Erica Gelbard, Izy Hossack, Eva Kosmas Flores, Alana Kysar, Betty Liu, Naomi Robinson, and Molly Yeh: Thank you for your invaluable advice and wisdom, and for your candor and honesty about the all-consuming roller coaster ride that is writing a cookbook. Thank you for listening to me vent, rage, and cry (sometimes all at once!) about my book, and having my back throughout my epic *Weeknight Baking* journey.

To Michelle Masterson, Nell Patten, and Cindy Rahe. It's rare for people to understand how much work goes into both blogging and writing a book, and even rarer when they're not directly in the industry or doing so themselves full-time. Thank you for always listening, and more importantly, thank you for never trivializing my work on both *Hummingbird High* and *Weeknight Baking*.

And again to both Michelle Carroll and Sze Wa Cheung, my former coworkers/forever friends. Thank you for always encouraging me to chase The Dream.

To Page Hartwell and John Ellingboe, who provided unconditional enthusiasm and support for *Weeknight Baking* since its beginning. Thank you for all the lovely dinners and for always welcoming me into your home.

To my mom, Bernadette Lopez, for not immediately disowning me when I told her I was leaving my cushy tech job to write a cookbook. Thank you for believing that there are other definitions of success beyond the corporate world.

To the Cat (aka Prince Pennynoodle, Penny, Kitten, Buttface, and Stankbutt), one of the few I love unconditionally. You bring me joy.

---

* who made me move to Denver, what a jerk, but I guess it worked out (no thanks to him).

To Erlend Ellingboe, my partner of many years and the only person who understands how much went into *Weeknight Baking*. Thank you for putting up with the last-minute grocery runs, my all-consuming work hours, and the incredible messes of my baking and photo shoots. But more important, thank you for fully supporting me through all my fears and frustrations while writing this book. You have been there since the beginning of it all, and I look forward to our next chapter together.

And finally, to the readers of *Hummingbird High*. Thank you, thank you, THANK YOU for reading my blog, taking the time to try my recipes, liking and commenting on all my social media posts, and even telling me about your lives. This book wouldn't have been possible without your support, and it's all for you.

INDEX

Page numbers in *italics* refer to photographs.

agave syrup, 25
almond(s):
  berry muffins, 225–26,
    227
  chocolate chip cookies,
    vegan, *256*, 257–58
  coconut cream tart,
    178, 179–80
  Erlend's favorite fruit
    crisp, 265–66, *267*
  nut butter frosting, 106
alternative diets, 255
  dessert island vegan
    mocha brownies,
    259–60, *261*
  Erlend's favorite fruit
    crisp, 265–66, *267*
  gluten-free Meyer
    lemon cornmeal
    torte, *262*, 263–64
  peanut butter pretzel
    pie, *268*, 269–71
  vegan chocolate chip
    almond cookies,
    256, 257–58
aluminum foil, 27

bags, zip-top, 34
baking powder and
    baking soda, 10–11
bamboo skewers, 27
banana(s), 61
  banana chocolate chip
    cake, *90*, 91–92
  bread, 57–60, *59*

cream pie, *212*, 213–15
yogurt muffins, *228*,
    229–30
bars, *see* layer bars
bench scraper, 27
berry(ies):
  almond muffins,
    225–26, *227*
  and cream tart,
    choose-your-LOE,
    185–88, *187*, *189*
birthday cake blondies,
    158
blackberry:
  lime muffins, 226
  lime tart, 184
black sesame
    snickerdoodle
    topping, 129
blender, 27
blondies, 149
  brown butter, *156*,
    157–59
blueberry lemon muffins,
    226
bowls, mixing, 30–32
breads:
  banana, 57–60, *59*
  choose-your-own
    pumpkin spice, *62*,
    63–65
brown butter, *160*, 161
  blondies, *156*, 157–59
  pumpkin bread, 65
  tart shell, 176–77

brownies, 139
  better-than-
    supernatural fudge,
    153–54, *155*
  boxed-mix, from
    scratch, *150*, 151–52
  dessert island vegan
    mocha, 259–60, *261*
brown sugar, 8
  peanut butter cake,
    93–94, *95*
  specialty sugars, 24–25
brunch treats, 239
  cinnamon rolls,
    overnight small-
    batch, 249–52, *251*,
    253
  Dutch baby pancake
    that lives up to its
    name, *240*, 241–42
  French toast for a
    crowd, overnight,
    243–44, *245*
  Liège waffles,
    overnight, *246*,
    247–48
brush, pastry, 32
butter, 9
  bringing to room
    temperature, 41–42
  brown, *see* brown
    butter
  creaming sugar and,
    39
  substituting, 15–16

buttercream frosting:
  chocolate, *102*, 103
  classic American, 99
buttermilk, 10
  bringing to room
    temperature, 42

cake decoration:
  piping bag and piping
    tips for, 33, *108*,
    109
  techniques for, 107–9,
    108
cake flour, 7, 8, 21
  all-purpose flour vs.,
    74–75
cake pans, 28
cakes, 73–74
  baking and freezing,
    76
  banana chocolate chip,
    90, 91–92
  chocolate, 81–82, *83*
  frosting and applying
    crumb coat, 77
  layer, assembling,
    107
  modern red velvet, *84*,
    85–86
  schedule for, 76–77
  white wedding, 87–89,
    88
  yellow, *78*, 79–80
  see also loaf cakes
cake stand, rotating, 33

candy thermometer, 28
caramel crème fraîche
    sauce, *278*, 279
chai pumpkin spice, 67
cheddar mustard scones,
    savory, 235–36, *237*
cheese:
    cheesecake bars, *166*,
        167–69
    choose-your-LOE
        berries and cream
        tart, 185–88, *187*, *189*
    cream cheese frosting,
        100, *101*
    Dutch baby for dinner,
        242
    savory cheddar
        mustard scones,
        235–36, *237*
cheesecake bars, *166*,
    167–69
chef's torch, 28
cherry and pistachio
    oatmeal cookies, 125
chocolate, 12
    banana bread, 58
    better-than-
        supernatural fudge
        brownies, 153–54,
        155
    bittersweet and
        semisweet, 17
    black-and-white
        chocolate chunk
        shortbread cookies,
        144, 145–47
    boxed-mix brownies,
        from scratch, *150*,
        151–52
    buttercream frosting,
        102, 103
    cake, 81–82, *83*
    dark, 16–17, 18
    dark, ganache, 280–81
    dessert island vegan
        mocha brownies,
        259–60, *261*
    fudge frosting, 104,
        105
    ganache cheesecake
        bars, 169
    hazelnut blondies, 149
    milk, 16–17, 18
    substituting, 16–20
    unsweetened, 17
    whipped cream,
        274–75

white, *see* white
    chocolate
chocolate chip(s):
    almond cookies, vegan,
        256, 257–58
    banana cake, *90*, 91–92
    cookie, single lady, *112*,
        113–14
    cookies, 115–19, *116*
    oatmeal cookies, 125
    substituting chopped
        chocolate bars for
        chocolate chips,
        18–20
cinnamon:
    classic snickerdoodle
        topping, 129
    pumpkin spice,
        67–68
    rolls, overnight small-
        batch, 249–52, *251*,
        253
cocoa and cacao, 16–17
cocoa powder, 12, 18
coconut:
    almond cream tart,
        178, 179–80
    toasted, pumpkin
        bread, 64
cookie dough scoop, 28
cookies:
    pie crust, 219
    see also drop cookies;
        roll-out cookies
cooking spray, nonstick,
    32
cornmeal torte, gluten-
    free Meyer lemon,
    262, 263–64
cranberry:
    orange muffins, 226
    white chocolate
        oatmeal cookies, 125
cream, 9–10, 20
    bringing to room
        temperature, 42
    whipped, *see* whipped
        cream
cream cheese frosting,
    100, *101*
cream of tartar, 11
crème fraîche, 10, 20
    bringing to room
        temperature, 42
    caramel sauce, *278*,
        279
    glaze, 252

scones, sweet, 231–34,
    233
whipped cream, 275
crisp, Erlend's favorite
    fruit, 265–66, *267*
cups vs. ounces, 49

dairy products, 9–10
    substituting, 20
digital candy
    thermometer, 28
digital kitchen scale, 28,
    35, 38–39
diplomat cream, 277
double boiler, 28–29
drop cookies, 111
    chocolate chip, 115–19,
        116
    chocolate chip, single
        lady, *112*, 113–14
    chocolate chip, vegan
        almond, *256*, 257–58
    freezing dough for,
        120, 121
    oatmeal, *122*, 123–25
    snickerdoodles, *126*,
        127–29
Dutch baby pancake that
    lives up to its name,
    240, 241–42

eggs, 9
    bringing to room
        temperature, 42
    substituting, 21
equipment, 27–35

fats, 9–10
    substituting, 20
fine-mesh sieve, 29
flavors, 11–13
flours, 7–8
    all-purpose, 7, 21,
        74–75
    bleached and
        unbleached, 22
    bread, 7, 21
    cake, 7, 8, 21, 74–75
    pastry, 7
    sifting, 40
    substituting, 21
    whole wheat, 22
food processor, 29
freezing:
    cakes, 76
    drop cookie dough,
        120, 121

roll-out cookie dough,
    134
French toast:
    cake, 69–70
    overnight, for a crowd,
        243–44, *245*
frosting, 97
    applying, 77
    chilling and thawing,
        97–98
    chocolate buttercream,
        102, 103
    chocolate fudge, 104,
        105
    classic American
        buttercream, 99
    cream cheese, 100, *101*
    dark chocolate
        ganache, 280–81
    decorating techniques,
        107–9, *108*
    nut butter, 106
    offset spatula for, 32,
        107–9, *108*
    piping bag and piping
        tips for, 33, *108*, 109
fruit crisp, Erlend's
    favorite, 265–66,
    267
fruit pie, *204*, 205–7
    underbaked,
        troubleshooting, 208

ganache, 20
ganache, dark chocolate,
    280–81
    cheesecake bars, 169
ginger, crystallized,
    oatmeal cookies, 125
glaze, crème fraîche, 252
gluten-free recipes, 255
    Erlend's favorite fruit
        crisp, 265–66, *267*
    Meyer lemon cornmeal
        torte, *262*, 263–64
    peanut butter pretzel
        pie, *268*, 269–71
grapefruit:
    cheesecake bars, 169
    raspberry tart, 184
grater, 29

halva blondies, 159
hazelnut:
    chocolate blondies, 159
    chocolate chip cookies,
        119

honey, 25
　whipped cream, 275

icing:
　royal, 139
　see also frosting
ingredients, 7–13
　prepping, 38–39, 44,
　　45, 47–48
　temperature of, 41–42,
　　50

jam:
　cheesecake bars, 169
　jammy pie bars, *170,*
　　171–72, *173*

kitchen scale, 28, 35,
　38–39
knives, 29

layer bars, 149
　cheesecake, *166,*
　　167–69
　jammy pie, *170,* 171–72,
　　173
　lime curd, *162,*
　　163–64
　straight edges and
　　smooth sides on, 165
layer cakes, *see* cakes
leaveners, 10–11
　substituting, 22–24
lemon:
　blueberry muffins, 226
　cheesecake bars, 169
　magic dream cream
　　tart, 181–84, *182*
　Meyer, gluten-free
　　cornmeal torte, *262,*
　　263–64
　poppyseed scones, 234
　pound cake, 56
lime:
　blackberry muffins,
　　226
　blackberry tart, 184
　cheesecake bars, 169
　curd bars, *162,* 163–64
　key, pie, 209–10, *211*
liquid sweeteners, 25
loaf cakes, 53
　banana bread, 57–60,
　　59
　choose-your-own
　　pumpkin spice
　　bread, *62,* 63–65

classic pound, *54,*
　55–56
stale, reviving, 69–70,
　71

macadamia, roasted, and
　white chocolate chip
　cookies, 119
maple syrup, 25
margarine, 15
matcha:
　pistachio nut muffins,
　　222, 223–24
　snickerdoodle topping,
　　129
measuring cups, 30, 35,
　39–40
measuring spoons, 30,
　39–40
metal scoops, 30
microplane grater, 29
microwave, 29–30
milk, 9–10, 20
　bringing to room
　　temperature, 42
mixer, stand, 29
mixing bowls, 30–32
mocha brownies, dessert
　island vegan,
　259–60, *261*
muffins, 221
　banana yogurt, *228,*
　　229–30
　berry almond, 225–26,
　　227
　matcha pistachio nut,
　　222, 223–24
　mustard cheddar scones,
　　savory, 235–36, *237*

nonstick cooking spray,
　32
nut butter:
　cheesecake bars, 169
　frosting, 106

oats:
　Erlend's favorite fruit
　　crisp, 265–66, *267*
　oatmeal cookies, *122,*
　　123–25
offset spatula, 32, 107–9,
　108
oils, 9, 20
orange:
　cheesecake bars, 169
　cranberry muffins, 226

ounces:
　cups vs., 49
　fluid ounces vs., 49–50
oven temperature, 32,
　38, 44
oven thermometer, 32

paddle attachment with
　scraper, 29
pancake, Dutch baby
　that lives up to its
　name, *240,* 241–42
pans, 33
　cake, 28
　pie, 32, 191
　sheet, 33–34
　tart, 34
parchment paper, 32
pastry brush, 32
pastry cream, 277
peanut butter:
　brown sugar cake,
　　93–94, *95*
　nut butter frosting, 106
　peanut butter cup
　　banana bread, 60
　pretzel pie, *268,*
　　269–71
pie pans, 32, 191
pies, 175, 191–93
　any kind of fruit, *204,*
　　205–7
　baking, 192, 208
　banana cream, *212,*
　　213–15
　chilling dough for,
　　193
　filling pan for, 191
　forming the bottom
　　crust, *196,* 197–98
　key lime, 209–10,
　　211
　lid designs for,
　　199–203, *199–202*
　peanut butter pretzel,
　　268, 269–71
　pumpkin, the silkiest,
　　216, 217–19
　resting dough for,
　　192
　stand mixer all-butter
　　dough, 194–95
　testing filling of, 208
　underbaked,
　　troubleshooting, 208
　vents in top lid of,
　　208

pie weights, 32–33
piping bag and piping
　tips, 33, *108,* 109
pistachio nut:
　and cherry oatmeal
　　cookies, 125
　matcha muffins, *222,*
　　223–24
plastic wrap, 33
poppyseed lemon scones,
　234
pots, 33
pound cake, classic, *54,*
　55–56
preheating the oven,
　38
prepping ingredients,
　38–39, 44, 45, 47–48
pretzel pie, peanut
　butter, *268,*
　269–71
pumpkin:
　pie, the silkiest, *216,*
　　217–19
　spice, 67–68
　spice bread, choose-
　　your-own, *62,* 63–65

racks, wire, 34
raisin oatmeal cookies,
　classic, 125
raspberry:
　grapefruit tart, 184
　sumac snickerdoodle
　　topping, 129
recipes:
　cups vs. ounces in, 49
　ingredient
　　temperatures in, 50
　making any recipe a
　　weeknight baking
　　recipe, 285–86
　ounces vs. fluid ounces
　　in, 49–50
　prep, work, and bake
　　times in, 45, 47–48
　reading, 37
　shortcuts in, 37–38
　tips for, 47–50
red velvet cake, modern,
　84, 85–86
rolling pin, 33
roll-out cookies, 131–33
　black-and-white
　　chocolate chunk
　　shortbread, *144,*
　　145–47

roll-out cookies (*cont.*)
  chilling dough for,
    131–32
  cutting the cookies,
    132–33
  freezing dough for, 134
  rolling out, 132
  royal icing for, 139
  schedule for, 134
  shortbread, almost-no-
    mess, *140,* 141–43
  sugar, 135–38, *137*
rotating cake stand,
  33
royal icing, 139
rubber spatulas, 33

salt:
  flaky, 25
  kosher, 11–12, 25
  substituting, 25
sauce, crème fraîche
  caramel, *278,* 279
savory:
  cheddar mustard
    scones, 235–36,
    237
  Dutch baby for dinner,
    242
scale, digital, 28, 35,
  38–39
scones, 221
  savory cheddar
    mustard, 235–36,
    237
  sweet crème fraîche,
    231–34, *233*
scoops, 30
scrapers, 27, 29
sesame:
  black, snickerdoodle
    topping, 129
  tahini brown sugar
    cake, 94

sheet pans, 33–34
shortbread cookies:
  almost-no-mess, *140,*
    141–43
  black-and-white
    chocolate chunk,
    144, 145–47
sieve, 29
skewers, 27
snickerdoodles, *126,*
  127–29
sour cream, 10, 20
  bringing to room
    temperature, 42
spice(s):
  grinding your own, 66
  pumpkin, 67–68
spatulas:
  offset, 32, 107–9, *108*
  rubber, 33
sprinkles, 13
  birthday cake blondies,
    158
  carnival topping,
    129
  overnight homemade,
    282, *283*
stand mixer, 29
storage containers, 34
substitutions, 15–25
  butter, 15–16
  chocolate, 16–20
  dairy and other fats,
    20
  eggs, 21
  flours, 21–22
  leaveners, 22–24
  salt, 25
  sugars, 24–25
sugar(s), 8
  brown, 8, 24–25
  confectioners', 8, 24
  creaming butter and,
    39

granulated, 8, 24
  substituting, 24–25
sumac raspberry
  snickerdoodle
    topping, 129
sweeteners, liquid, 25

tahini brown sugar cake,
  94
tart pans, 34
tarts, 175
  choose-your-LOE
    berries and cream,
    185–88, *187, 189*
  coconut almond
    cream, *178,*
    179–80
  easiest brown butter
    tart shell ever,
    176–77
  magic dream lemon
    cream, 181–84,
    182
techniques, 37–45
temperature:
  of ingredients, 41–42,
    50
  oven, 32, 38, 44
  room, 41–42, 50
thermometers:
  candy, 28
  oven, 32
timer, 34
timing, 44
toast, cake, 69
toffee and milk chocolate
  chip cookies, 119
tools, 27–35
torte, gluten-free Meyer
  lemon cornmeal,
  262, 263–64

vanilla, 11
  pumpkin spice, 67

vegan recipes, 255
  chocolate chip almond
    cookies, *256,* 257–58
  dessert island mocha
    brownies, 259–60,
    261
  Erlend's favorite fruit
    crisp, 265–66,
    267
  overnight whipped
    cream, 276
  peanut butter pretzel
    pie, *268,* 269–71
vinegar, 12

waffles, overnight Liège,
  246, 247–48
wedding cake, white,
  87–89, *88*
whipped cream, 20,
  274–75
  overnight vegan, 276
whisks, 34
white chocolate, 18
  black-and-white
    chocolate chunk
    shortbread cookies,
    144, 145–47
  cranberry oatmeal
    cookies, 125
  roasted macadamia
    cookies, 119
wire racks, 34

yeast, 11, 22–24
yellow cake, *78,*
  79–80
yogurt, 20
  banana muffins, *228,*
    229–30
  bringing to room
    temperature, 42

zip-top bags, 34

CONVERSION CHARTS

VOLUME CONVERSION

⅛ teaspoon = .5 mL

¼ teaspoon = 1 mL

½ teaspoon = 2 mL

¾ teaspoon = 4 mL

1 teaspoon = 5 mL

1 tablespoon = 15 mL

¼ cup = 60 mL

⅓ cup = 75 mL

½ cup = 125 mL

¾ cup = 175 mL

1 cup = 250 ml

FAHRENHEIT TO CELSIUS

250° = 120°

275° = 135°

300° = 150°

325° = 165°

350° = 175°

375° = 190°

400° = 200°

425° = 220°

WEIGHT CONVERSION

0.5 ounce = 14 grams

1 ounce = 28 grams

CONVERSIONS OF COMMONLY USED INGREDIENTS

all-purpose flour: 1 cup = 4.5 ounces = 128 grams

cake flour: 1 cup = 4 ounces = 113 grams

cocoa powder (natural and Dutch-processed): 1 cup = 3 ounces = 85 grams

granulated sugar: 1 cup = 7 ounces = 198 grams

brown sugar (light/dark) = 1 cup tightly packed = 7.5 ounces = 213 grams

confectioners' sugar: 1 cup = 4 ounces = 113 grams

butter (unsalted/salted): 1 cup = 2 sticks = 8 ounces = 227 grams